INTRODUCTION TO THE
PSYCHOLOGY
OF MUSIC

Geza Révész

Translated from the German by
G. I. C. de Courcy

DOVER PUBLICATIONS, INC.
Mineola, New York

Bibliographical Note

This Dover edition, first published in 2001, is an unabridged republication of the work originally published in 1954 by The University of Oklahoma Press, Norman, Oklahoma, itself an English translation by G. I. C. de Courcy, with revisions, of *Einführung in die Musikpsychologie* by G. Révész, Amsterdam, 1946.

The present edition converts the two "Tone Tables"–originally inserted as foldout pages–into four turn-pages before the Index, with minor adjustments in the layout of Table II to clarify the presentation of information in this divided format.

Library of Congress Cataloging-in-Publication Data

Révész, Geza, 1878–1955.
   [Einführung in die Musikpsychologie. English]
   Introduction to the psychology of music / Geza Révész ; translated from the German by G. I. C. de Courcy.
       p. cm.
   Reprint. Originally published: Norman : University of Oklahoma Press, 1954.
   Includes bibliographical references.
   ISBN 0-486-41678-X (pbk.)
       1. Music–Psychology. I. Title.

ML3830 .R392 2001
781'.11–dc21

00-065905

Manufactured in the United States of America
Dover Publications, Inc., 31 East 2nd Street, Mineola, N.Y. 11501

To the memory of
BÉLA BARTÓK
in sincere friendship

NOTE

ACKNOWLEDGEMENT is due to Prof. Max Schoen, Department of Psychology, Hamilton College, Clinton, New York and to Mr. H. Lindsay Norden, of Philadelphia, for their kindness in reading certain portions of the translated manuscript and for their valuable suggestions based on their expert knowledge of, and their long experience in, the several specialized fields covered by this book.

PREFACE

THE psychology of sound and music forms a connecting link between musicology, physics, and physiology on the one hand, and psychology and æsthetics on the other. It is not an autonomous science with its distinctive problems and methods, but forms a realm of learning the goals, problems, predominant aspects and methodical principles of which are derived in the main from musical practice and psychology. As a result of this intermediate position it is not easy to delimit the frontiers of this domain in respect to the other sciences. Most of the points at issue cut across one another without thereby sacrificing their own independence. This peculiar position of the psychology of music and the fact that it cannot be dealt with apart from æsthetics and the psychology of sound make it practically impossible to formulate a concrete system in itself.

In writing the present work my purposive goal was primarily a practical one. My aim throughout has been to initiate musicians, musicologists, students, conservatory pupils, and musical amateurs into the most important aspects and issues of the psychology of sound and music. I have therefore laid stress on those topics that presumably only fall incidentally, if at all, within the framework of the theoretical training of the musician but which nevertheless are an integral and fundamental part of musical education.

Part I presents the physical and physiological bases of our sensations of tone. Knowledge of physical acoustics and of the physiology of the auditory apparatus does not, of course, appertain to the psychology of music. But it forms the essential prerequisite to, and at times even the point of departure of, research work in the psychology of sound. The question was whether it should be left to the reader himself to decide how and where he gathered the necessary scientific foundation, or whether one should make a selection for him from the great mass of primary source material. I have chosen the latter course, since physical and physiological acoustics are only of practical value to the musician if they are treated in connexion with psychological and psycho-physiological questions. Such a procedure also seemed expedient, since it affords an opportunity to show the reader how differently sound phenomena are treated by physics and physiology than by psychology, and to point out how easily misapprehensions and ambiguities can arise if one does not know how to keep the two fundamentally divergent points of view sharply differentiated. We see, namely, that what physics presents as a concrete fact is often a " problem " in psychology (e.g. the octave problem) and, obversely, that which in psychology is a phenomenon deductively conclusive in itself is for physics and physiology an object worthy of investigation and theoretical formulation (e.g. sound analysis).

Part II deals with the salient questions of the psychology of sound.   The first two chapters give the results of my own research on the nature of tones and intervals in connexion with the Two-component Theory.   The discussions of pitch discrimination and key characteristics have a direct bearing on this theory.

Part III discusses various elements of the psychology of music. The chapters on musicality, musical talent, the enjoyment of music by deaf mutes, the pathology of musical perceptivity, and the origin of music are based on my own investigations and research.

It is possible, of course, to approach the psychology of music from an entirely different angle; for example, from that of the musical experience and the psychological emotional response to music. Or one can emphasize those problems of musical æsthetics that lend themselves to psychological research. However, I believe that my treatment and choice of themes has the advantage of initiating the reader into most of the important issues of the psychology of music, which to my knowledge has not as yet been done.

I have intentionally avoided the subject of æsthetics as far as possible. In the last chapter only, in discussing the relationship between æsthetics and music psychology, I have touched very briefly on a few of the æsthetic viewpoints of special interest to psychological research.

Those interested in these divers features of the psychology of music can amplify and deepen their knowledge by a study of the works cited in the text and listed in the Bibliography.

G. Révész

PREFACE TO THE TRANSLATION

In presenting the English edition of my "Einführung in die Musikpsychologie" my main objective has been to introduce English-speaking readers to a new science—the psychology of music—and at the same time give a systematic outline of my own research in this domain and that of acoustics. With this end in view, it seemed to me that my theoretical conclusions and the results of my personal experiments and investigations would be most effectively set forth by incorporating them into the pyschology of music and comparing them with the deductions and viewpoints of other psychologists and investigators in this field.

The English edition is not a strict translation of the original work in German, since various revisions have been made in the basic text, including some deletions and the addition of an entirely new chapter: "The Development of Musical Talent in Maturity and Advanced Age". I hope that in this slightly re-edited form the work will prove interesting and informative to readers in England and the United States.

G. Révész

Amsterdam,
January 1952

CONTENTS

xi

PART II
FUNDAMENTAL PROBLEMS OF THE PSYCHOLOGY OF SOUND

PART III
FUNDAMENTAL PROBLEMS OF THE PSYCHOLOGY OF MUSIC

PLATES

PART I
HEARING, SOUND, AND MUSICAL TONE

I

DEPENDENCE OF SOUND PERCEPTION ON PHYSICAL STIMULUS

A. SOUND VIBRATIONS

In the field of physical acoustics, the question that is primarily of interest to the psychology of music is what physical processes must take place in order to produce a sensation of sound.

Sound production can best be demonstrated with the aid of a catgut string. If we pluck a string that is firmly fixed at both ends, we can see with the naked eye that it is set into rapid vibration. This vibration is then communicated to the sounding-board, and through this to the surrounding air particles, which in turn set up vibrations in the tympanic membrane. This motion is propagated in the inner ear to the auditory centre located in the brain, where certain still unknown physiological processes produce the sensation of sound.

It can be easily proved that the air plays a role in producing sound. If the vibrating string is placed in a vacuum under a

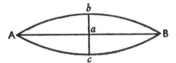

FIG. 1.—Sound Vibration.

bell-jar, no sound can be heard. But if air is pumped into the jar, the sound is distinctly audible at once.

Let us now look at the string itself. If we study the motion very closely we discover a definite periodicity. We find, for instance, that each point of the vibrating string constantly returns to its original position after a definite interval of time. This indicates that the motion of the string is periodic and that it repeats itself exactly within a period. Therefore the string that has been set in motion executes periodic vibrations. Fig. 1 represents such a vibrating string.

The end-points of the string (A and B) that do not alter their position during the vibration are called *nodes*. The points with the maximum displacement (here point *a*) are called *antinodes*.

3

Points *a, c, b* mark the arc of oscillation which attains its maximum elongation at point *a*.

The nature of sound vibrations can best be demonstrated by a tuning-fork. If a tuning-fork is struck with a hammer, or a violin bow drawn across it, it is set into *vibration*. The vibrations can be easily perceived by touching the tuning-fork lightly with the finger. If it is desired to follow the vibration of the tuning-fork more closely, fasten a drawing-point to one end and run a piece of smoked paper under it from right to left with a uniform velocity. The vibrating point will then describe a periodic curve (a *wave line*) on the paper which gives a graphic representation of the vibration. Fig. 2 shows a wave line produced in this way.

By means of a chronographic apparatus the time can be registered on the recording tape in seconds or fractions of seconds.

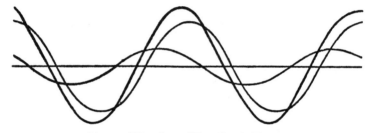

FIG. 4.—Vibrations of Two Simple Tones.

With the aid of this instrument one can ascertain how many waves fall in the segment between two time-marks; that is, how many times the tuning-fork moves to and fro within the space of one second (Fig. 3).

The vibration of a simple tone produces the simple vibration curve shown above. Such a vibration is called a *simple harmonic vibration*, and the vibration curve appertaining thereto a *sine curve*. Sine curves are only obtainable with tuning-forks of very great precision that generate a simple tone without overtone components.

The sound vibrations of musical instruments have a much more complex form. Here every such complex curve must be understood as composed of simple vibrations; that is, of sine curves. Therefore it can be said that every vibration, no matter how complex, is composed of simple vibrations (Fourier's Theorem).

Fig. 4 shows a complex curve resulting from two simple vibra-

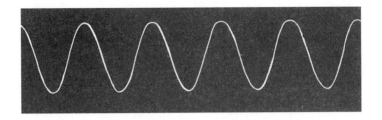

FIG. 2.—Sine Curve of a Vibrating Tuning-fork.

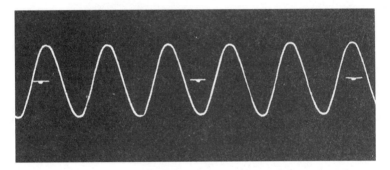

FIG. 3.—Sine Curve of Vibrating Tuning-fork. (The markers indicate 1/100 second.)

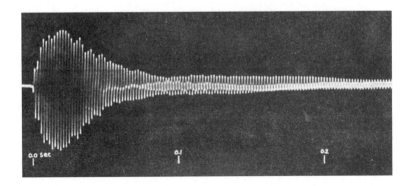

FIG. 7.—Initial Stage of a Vibration.

(Photographs by the late Dayton C. Miller.)

tions. The two thin curves represent the vibrations of the simple tones; the heavy curve, the sound vibration resulting therefrom. The crests of the heavy line are obtained by adding the ordinates of the curves if they are on the same side of the base line, and by subtracting the smaller from the greater if they are on opposite sides.

Fig. 5 is even more complex. Here the curve is composed of four simple vibrations.

In most musical instruments the number of simple tones forming the unitary note, or clang, is still greater, so that the vibration

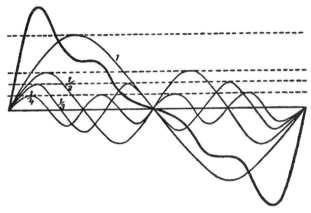

FIG. 5.—Vibrations of Four Tones without Overtone Components.

curve is even more complex. As is well known, the vibrations of all notes produced by musical instruments are periodic. Nonperiodic vibrations only generate noise without musical character.

B. AMPLITUDE OF THE VIBRATIONS

If we look more intently at a vibrating string, it will be seen that every point in the vibration has its own motion backwards and forwards. If the string is drawn aside from its point of rest and let go, point a in the centre of the string moves first in the segment a–b and then in the segment b–c, to return finally to the point of departure a. The total displacement of oscillating point a (segments a–b and b–c) is called a *complete full vibration* of point a. For point a^1 the segments a^1–d–e–a^1 represent the complete vibration. The maximum displacement of each point, when pushed from its position of equilibrium, is called the *amplitude of* *the vibration.* For point *a* the amplitude is the segment a–b (or a–c); the point *a*¹, the segment a¹–d (or a¹–e). When we speak of the amplitude of a vibrating string or reed, we mean by this the maximum elongation of the vibrating body. In the accompanying diagram (Fig. 6) the amplitude of the vibrating string is the segment a–b, because *a* is that point on the string where deviation from the place of equilibrium attains a maximum.*

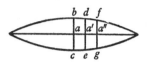

FIG. 6.—Amplitude of the Vibrating Points.

C. Dependence of Sound Perception on the Amplitude of the Vibration

(1) *Amplitude and Intensity.* The intensity of the sound sensation is in direct relation to the amplitude of the vibration. As we know, the sound will be all the louder, the intensity all the greater, the more the string deviates from its point of rest. Thus we have the law: *The intensity of the sound increases with the amplitude of the vibration.*†

(2) *Auditory Response.* Not every periodic sound vibration will be perceived by the human ear as sound. For this it must exceed a certain degree of intensity. The strength of the stimulus necessary to evoke an audible sound varies with the individual. However, there is a fixed mean *threshold of audibility* round which are grouped all the individual variations and below which physical stimulus can evoke *no* sensation.

This threshold of audibility lies very low, which is to say that the ear is extraordinarily sensitive to air vibrations. The following will serve to illustrate the auditory response to physical stimuli. The energy necessary to lift a milligram one centimetre (quarter of an inch) is equal to what is known in physics as one erg. It has been found that the minimum stimulus that is audible to the ear *as sound*, when expressed in units of energy, is not more than a billionth part of this erg. Our ear is so extremely sensitive that

* The loudness of the tone increases directly as the square of the amplitude.
† In music the gradations of tonal strength are indicated by a number of dynamical symbols: ff, f, mf, pp, etc.

there would be no purpose in enhancing auditory sensitivity any further. The threshold of intensity is used to test the acuity of hearing. The acuity of hearing is defined by the *absolute threshold of audibility*. By *absolute* threshold we understand the minimum effective sound that is capable of evoking a just discernible auditory sensation. If the threshold of intensity is low, then the acuity of hearing is great, and vice versa. Consequently we have the law: *The acuity of hearing is inversely proportional to the height of the threshold of intensity*. There are very great individual variations in normal acuity of hearing. These are attributable in part to the function of the auditory apparatus, and again in part to fluctuations in attentive aural observation. The threshold of audibility also depends on the pitch. The maximum auditory sensitivity lies in the four-line octave. For higher as well as lower notes the acuity of hearing is less.

A sound must not only have a definite *intensity* to be perceived, but also a definite *duration*. The duration necessary for sound perception varies between 2 and 20 complete vibrations, according to the pitch and quality of the note. The duration necessary for perception also depends on the progress of the stimulus. Here we have three possibilities: the sound can be constant in intensity from beginning to end; it can be loud at the beginning and die away rapidly (Fig. 7); or it can begin very softly and only gradually attain its full intensity.

The audibility, and to an even greater extent the discriminability, of the note depends on the way it begins and how it dies away. Among musical instruments, the plucked and percussion instruments, in particular, have tones of very brief duration. With the piano, an effort is made to sustain the intensity of the tone as far as possible during its entire duration. This is achieved by the felt cushions on the hammers. In sustaining power, the string and wind instruments are far superior to the piano, in spite of modern hammer mechanism and pedals.* The human voice is the only instrument capable of regulating at will all gradations of crescendo and decrescendo, of controlling constancy and fluctuations of intensity.

* The peculiar mechanism of the organ, of course, enables it to sustain the tone at the same intensity during its entire duration.

Not only the absolute threshold of audibility is important in testing sound perception, but the differential threshold as well. By the latter we mean the minimum discernible difference in intensity that the ear can detect as such. Here we notice a dependence on the intensity of the initial sound. We can detect a much slighter increment in intensity with a soft note than with a loud one.

If we ask in what way the relative threshold of audibility is dependent on the intensity, the *Weber Law* supplies the answer. This fundamental psycho-physical law reads as follows: *Two stimuli of equal intensity can only evoke a just perceptible increase in sensation if they bear a constant ratio to each other.* In other words: if the intensity of the stimulus varies, the relative value of the differential threshold remains unchanged. Let us illustrate this as follows. If a tone of 100 units intensity is only just discernible from one of 120 units, then one of 200 units must be increased proportionately; that is, it must be increased to 240 units to produce a perceptible difference of sensation. A *constant ratio*, and not a *constant increment*, is therefore necessary for a perceptible difference of sensation. In our example the differential threshold is 1/5 or 20% of the initial sound.

Like the absolute threshold of audibility, the differential threshold is also dependent on the tone region. With a^1 as initial note, an intensity difference of about $12\frac{1}{2}\%$ will be necessary; with a, about 20%. According to recent investigations, the percentages are still less.

D. Vibration Frequency

Besides amplitude, the second characteristic of vibration is the time required to perform one full vibration. In our diagram it is the time necessary for the complete oscillation a–b–a–c–a (Fig. 6). This is called the *vibration time*. Since this would lead to infinitesimally small figures, especially in the upper pitches (the time is only a fraction of a second), another unit of measurement has been introduced to designate this—namely, the *vibration number*, or *frequency*; that is, the number of complete vibrations performed in one second of time. There is a relationship between vibration time and vibration frequency that can be expressed mathematically: *the greater the vibration time (the period of vibration), the lower the vibration number (the frequency of the vibration).*

E. DEPENDENCE OF SOUND PERCEPTION ON FREQUENCY

(1) *Frequency and Pitch*. Similar to our inquiry regarding the connexion between amplitude and sound perception, we must now ask what connexion there is between *frequency* and sound perception. This question is easy to answer. The *so-called pitch of the note* depends on the vibration number, or wave-length. *The greater the vibration frequency, the "higher" the note in the pitch scale*. The more we increase the tension of a string, the quicker it will rebound; that is, the greater the number of vibrations in a given unit of time, which raises the pitch of the note.

(2) *The Upper and Lower Limits of Audibility*. The number of physically possible sound vibrations per second is, in principle, infinite. For the ear, however, there is a *lower* and an *upper* limit of audible sound. A string must carry out at least 16–24 complete vibrations per second (about C_2) for the sound to be distinctly audible. Investigations in respect to the upper limits of audibility have produced very divergent results, depending on the instrument employed for the test. With tuning-forks, the upper limit is about f^7 (frequency 22,528 per sec.). I have obtained still higher limits with the aid of the Galton Whistle. For music only notes from C (64 vibr. per sec.) to c^5 (4138 vibr.) come into consideration. Above and below these limits the sounds gradually lose their musical character.

(3) *Pitch Discrimination*. Within the auditory sensation area we can distinguish a very large number of notes one from another, but the ability to discriminate the difference in pitch between two notes depends greatly on the pitch of the notes chosen for the test. In the region of the lower or upper threshold of audibility, differential pitch hearing is conspicuously slight. In these extreme limits of the audible tone series we can discriminate relatively few notes. On the other hand, pitch discriminability within the middle range is very great. For instance, with notes between 130 vibrations (c) and 1046 vibrations per second (c^3) a difference of about 0·5 vibration is still perceptible, while with notes over 3000 vibrations the differential threshold amounts to 10 vibrations. Yet notes in the upper limits of the musical range cannot be discriminated even though the frequencies differ by thousands. Notes with frequencies of 128 and 129

vibrations can be easily discriminated, whereas those with frequencies of 15,000 and 16,000 vibrations per second are no longer discriminable.

F. Dependence of Sound Perception on the Partials

The third characteristic of sound is quality, or tone-colour (timbre), the feature by which the note of one instrument can be distinguished from that of another. Here again we must inquire into the physical reasons. We have already pointed out that the forms of the vibrations of the various musical instruments differ greatly on the same note. We also saw that each vibration, no matter how complex, must be conceived as composed of simple harmonic vibrations. This naturally does not mean that more vibrations actually take place simultaneously. At one and the same time there is only *one* vibration, which comprises all harmonic vibrations. It has been shown that the number and intensity of the harmonic vibrations lend a definite *form* to the total vibration, and it is this that determines the quality.

If we decompose the tone of any musical instrument into its harmonic vibrations (partials) by a definite mathematical method, we encounter a strange fact. The partials are related to each other in the proportion 1 : 2 : 3 : 4 : 5, etc., wherein 1 represents the first (lowest) partial. This lowest note of the series, which is generally the most distinct, is called the fundamental, or generator, and gives the tone its name and its octave designation ; e.g. c in the one-line octave. The second, third partials, etc., are called *harmonic overtones*. From the above series of ratios it follows that the first overtone has a frequency twice as great as that of the generator ; whence the first overtone is the octave of the generator (2 : 1). Accordingly, the second overtone is a fifth above the first overtone, because the ratio of the frequencies is 3 : 2. The third overtone is a fourth above the second (4 : 3), the fourth is a major third above the third (5 : 4), the fifth is a minor third above the fourth (6 : 5), the sixth a subminor or septimal third above the fifth (7 : 6), the seventh a somewhat augmented major second above the sixth (8 : 7), the eighth a major second above the seventh (9 : 8), etc. If we start with the generator c, the upper octave c^1 makes twice as many vibrations per second as the generator c (2 : 1), the fifth (g^1) three times as many (3 : 1), the double octave (c^2) four times as many (4 : 1), the major third of this octave (e^2) five times ($5 : 1$), the fifth (g^2) of this same octave six times ($6 : 1$), the harmonic seventh of the double octave ($b\flat^2$) seven times ($7 : 1$), the third octave (c^3) eight times ($8 : 1$), the major second of the third octave (d^3) nine times ($9 : 1$), and the major third (e^3) ten times ($10 : 1$) as many vibrations per second as the generator c.

Owing to the simplicity of the vibration ratios, the whole series of overtones is called the *series of harmonic overtones* of the given generator. All the overtones are not always actually present in a given instrument. Several in the series may be lacking. The form of the vibration depends on the number of the harmonic overtones and their mutual intensity. And this *form* determines the *quality* of the note that is played.

Up till now sound analysis has been a mathematical procedure based on Fourier's Theorem. In the meantime it has been shown that our ear is also capable of analysing compound sounds up to a certain point. True, this analysis does not coincide exactly with the mathematical, because our ear is only able to hear a limited number of overtones as such, so that we always have a residuum that is incapable of further analysis. But the agreement is sufficiently close to verify the mathematical ratios.

HERMANN VON HELMHOLTZ developed the physical methods by means of which we can hear the simple tones (sine vibrations) that form the constituents of every musical clang (51). If we strike a note in the middle register of the piano, a musically trained observer, with great concentration, will be able to pick out a number of overtones. This is primarily the case if we first ideate the overtone that we intend to perceive, or strike it lightly on the piano beforehand. The analysis of compound sounds is simplified by using the *resonators* constructed by Helmholtz. These are hollow glass or metal spheres with two small apertures. The one aperture is placed directly to the ear. Since a given resonator only reinforces the tone that coincides with its own proper tone, it is not difficult to determine whether a tone appertaining to this resonator is present as an overtone in the compound sound, or not.

Experience shows that the uneven harmonic partials (the even overtones)—for instance, the fifth, third, and seventh—can be heard more distinctly than the even ones; that is, than the octave notes of the prime above all. A trained ear cannot detect more than 7 or 8 overtones in a note without the aid of a resonator. With resonators one can detect as many as 12 or 13.

The first nine overtones of c are given herewith in musical notation (Ex. 1). The symbols are as follows:

(a) The interval formed by the given overtone and the previous note.
(b) Numerical rank in the harmonic upper partial series.
(c) Numerical rank in the overtone series.
(d) Numerical rank in the order of audibility in the prime tone c.

				Maj.	Min.	Aug.	Dim.	Maj.	Maj.
(a) Prime.	Oct.	5th	4th	3rd	3rd	2nd	3rd	2nd	2nd
(b) 1	2	3	4	5	6	7*	8	9	10
(c) Generator 1	2	3	4	5	6	7	8	9
(d) 1	4	2	8	3	7	5	9	6	10

Ex. 1.—Harmonic Overtones of Small c.

As already stated, the *quality* of the different musical instruments depends on the number or relative intensity of the overtones.† Helmholtz, who systematically investigated the upper partials of the leading musical instruments, came to the conclusion that the notes without strong overtones (for example, those of most stopped organ pipes) have a soft and pleasing sound, though they are not very sonorous. Notes with a number of lower overtones (up to about the sixth) are more sonorous, and therefore more useful for music, such as those of the piano, horn, open organ pipes, and the soft notes of the human voice. If only the

* *Christian Huygens*, the great Dutch physicist, was the first (1661) to draw attention to the seventh "natural tone". *Giuseppe Tartini* (1754) laid stress on the seventh "harmonic" in his theory. *Leonhard Euler*, the eminent Swiss mathematician (1739), constructed scales theoretically with this overtone and maintained that *Rameau's* dissonant chord of the seventh was the seventh "natural tone".

† It is perhaps not out of the way to note that there are scarcely any tones that do not yield partials. Tones of this nature can only be produced by complicated electrical devices. Even with the best tuning-forks, a few overtones can still be detected. Rigorous tests have shown that with a tuning-fork with a frequency of 128 the following overtones can be heard, even though faintly.

	Fundamental.	Overtones.			
Frequency	128	793	2340	4480	7820
Interval ratio . . .	1	6·2	18·3	35	61·1

uneven partials are present in an instrument (as in the clarinet and the narrow, stopped organ pipes), the tone is hollow and nasal. If partials above the sixth are distinctly audible, the quality is harsh and penetrating.   But if this is not the case, the notes are really expressive in spite of their incisiveness.   The notes of the bowed instruments, as well as the oboe, bassoon, trumpet, and the higher registers of the human voice, are all of this character. Notes with a great many overtones, some of them inharmonic, have a quality that approximates to noise, and therefore gradually lose their determinate pitch.   This is true of drums, kettle-drums, cymbals, and vibrating plates.*

The following table shows the relation subsisting between the complex note and its constituents according to Helmholtz' findings:

Fundamental alone	soft
Fundamental with first overtone . . .	mellow
Fundamental with many overtones . . .	broad
Fundamental with high overtones . . .	sharp
Fundamental predominating	full
Fundamental with overtones predominating . .	empty
Even overtones predominating	nasal
Dissonant overtones predominating . . .	rough
Dissonant high tones predominating . . .	screeching

The tone quality of musical instruments is influenced not only by the multiplicity of the upper partials, but also by other factors, the most important of which is the ambient noise.   Furthermore, the notes of certain instruments show periodic fluctuations in intensity that also have a more or less important effect on the quality.

Besides the series of overtones, physics and music theory also speak of a series of so-called *undertones*.   Viewed from the prime, this purely constructive series is conceived as an inversion of the overtone series.   The frequency of the harmonic overtones is said to be in inverse ratio of the integers to the prime; that is, $\frac{1}{2}$, $\frac{1}{3}$, $\frac{1}{4}$, etc. (Ex. 2).

An attempt was made to use the series of undertones to explain the major and minor modes, since the minor triad seems to be present in the first six notes of the undertone series, just as the major triad in the first six notes of the overtone series.   Hugo

* See " Handbuch der Instrumentenkunde " (1920), by Curt Sachs, and article by C. V. Raman in " Handbuch der Physik ", Vol. 8, 1927 (Geiger and Scheel), for further information on the tone quality of different musical instruments.

Riemann based his dualistic Theory of Harmony on this physical hypothesis.   Riemann's fundamental idea is that the major scale bears the same relation to the minor as a positive unit to a negative

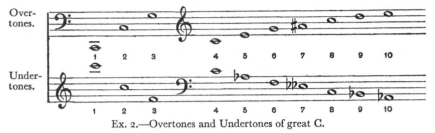

Ex. 2.—Overtones and Undertones of great C.

of the same magnitude.*   In his opinion, the series of undertones is a direct reflection or continuation of the overtone series in the opposite direction.   If we start with the note c and move upwards, we come to the overtones that form the major common chord. Moving downwards, we come to the undertones that form the minor common chord.

C_2	D_2	F_2	Ab_2	C_1	F_1	C	c	c^1	g^1	c^2	e^2	g^2	b^2	c^3
$\frac{1}{8}$	$\frac{1}{7}$	$\frac{1}{6}$	$\frac{1}{5}$	$\frac{1}{4}$	$\frac{1}{3}$	$\frac{1}{2}$	1	2	3	4	5	6	7	8

Minor chord. — Major chord.

Undertones. — Overtones.

Riemann himself was not convinced that the undertones were an objective reality.   He believed them to be merely subjective (123).   It was only recently that B. van der Pol was able to verify experimentally (and make audible) the physical existence of these hitherto only theoretically suppositional undertones through the synchronizing properties (frequency demultiplication) of relaxation oscillations.†

The undertone series is of only theoretical importance. Practically it plays no role in music, since under normal conditions the undertones are inaudible.   I fail to understand how notes that are ordinarily inaudible can play any part in the formation of the minor mode.   From the viewpoint of the

---

* Moritz Hauptmann (50) and A. von Oettingen (91) worked out the fundamental idea of the dualistic theory very thoroughly even before H. Riemann.

† See the British publication *Nature*, 120, 1927, p. 363.   Also *Zeitschrift d. Niederl. Radio-Vereins*, Nos. 3 and 25, 1936.

psychology of music, it is inconceivable that inaudible or barely audible sounds should form the *basis* of a specific genera. The whole question is not yet closed.

It is nevertheless interesting to learn that certain races employ intervals based on the harmonic undertones in their music. The musicologist A. J. Ellis succeeded in establishing such tone relations in a Scottish bagpipe by means of tonometrical calculations (32). The octave was divided into an upper fifth and a lower fourth. The vibration ratios of the scale were as follows:

$$\underbrace{\frac{1}{24} : \frac{1}{27} : \frac{1}{30} : \frac{1}{33}}_{\text{Fifth.}} : \underbrace{\frac{1}{36} : \frac{1}{40} : \frac{1}{44} : \frac{1}{48}}_{\text{Fourth.}}$$

G. Secondary Sound Phenomena

(1) *Beats.* Before leaving the discussion of the psycho-physics of sound perception—i.e. the theory of the relation between physical stimulus and sound perception—I should like to call attention to several phenomena that become audible when two or more notes are sounded simultaneously; namely, beats and combination tones.

If we strike two tuning-forks of equal pitch simultaneously, we hear a quiet, continuous, uniform tone. If we alter the pitch of one a little, or if we strike two consecutive keys on the piano simultaneously and let these two notes die away, we encounter a strange phenomenon; namely, an alternate waxing and waning of the intensity of the sound. These pulsations are called *beats*. The beats are due to the fact that the vibrations of the two notes do not coincide exactly. The air particles are deflected by the two beats, but at one moment these deflexions run in the same direction. They therefore reinforce each other. The next moment they run counter to each other, consequently their intensity is decreased.

This is exemplified in the following diagram (Fig. 8). The two thin lines represent two vibrations (wave-trains) that are slightly out of phase. It can be seen that the one vibrates a little faster than the other. The thick line shows the resulting effect. Maximum intensity (increased intensity) is found at the beginning and the end, minimum intensity (decreased intensity) in the centre of the train.

From this diagram we see that two vibrations (wave-trains) coincide as often in each unit of time as one note makes more oscillations than the other in the same period. The segment between two crests with maximum displacement (as shown in the above diagram) is called a beat. From the diagram it can also be seen that a beat occurs whenever the one note makes one complete oscillation more than the other. Hence we have the law: *the number of beats of two notes in one second is exactly equal to the difference in their frequencies.* If two notes are sounded simultaneously—for example, one with 73 vibr. per sec. (D) and another with 78 (E♭)—we hear 5 beats per second. Since the number of beats depends on the *absolute* difference in frequencies of the two fundamental notes sounded simultaneously, it follows that the number of beats increases with the size of the interval.

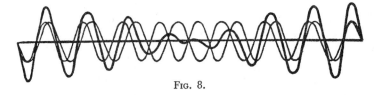

FIG. 8.

They also increase when one and the same interval is transposed to a higher level in the musical range. We will illustrate this by several examples.

The notes C (64.6) and C♯ (68.5) produce 4 beats per second, while c (129.3) and c♯ (137) produce 8, and c^1 (258.7) and c^1♯ (274) 15 beats. In comparison with this, the note pairs b^1–c^2 (minor second), c^1–d^1 (major second), e–g (minor third) c–e (major third), G–c (fourth), and C–G (fifth), though running from a minor second to a fifth, produce approximately the same number of beats per second; namely, 33. It follows from this that with two low notes it takes a much wider interval to produce an equivalent number of beats per second than with two high ones.

The sensation produced by beats depends entirely on the number per second. So long as they are slow, they are not disagreeable. But if they increase in rapidity, the sensation soon becomes very unpleasant, irritating, like the annoying flicker of a film that is run off too slowly. If they continue to increase, they are no longer recognizable as beats. The tone merely sounds rough. If the difference in the frequency of the two notes becomes still greater, then the phenomenon ceases entirely.

The fluctuations in intensity sketched here depend not only on the number of beats per second, but also on the pitch of the vibrating notes. At 100 vibr. per sec. the sensation is most disagreeable at approximately 16 beats per second. At 2800 vibrations it does not become annoying until somewhere round 106 beats per second. It should also be mentioned that beats can arise not only between the fundamentals, but also between the overtones of two complex notes, and between an overtone and one of the fundamentals.

Helmholtz referred to the importance of beats in the phenomena of consonance in his Theory of Consonance. (See Part II, Chapter VI.)

(2) *Combination Tones.* In the phenomenon of beats we have to do solely with periodic fluctuations in intensity. But when two notes are sounded simultaneously, we also hear other tones besides the prime tones; namely, the so-called *differential and summational tones,* known as *combination, or resultant, tones.* The differentials were first discovered by Sorge (1740 or 1745) and Tartini (1754). They were exactly described by Hällström (1832) and Th. Young (1800), while the summational tones were first observed by Helmholtz (1856).

If we take as primaries two notes with the frequencies p and q, it will be found that, under certain conditions, not only are the notes p and q audible, but also notes with the frequency p-minus-q and p-plus-q. The first is called a differential, the second a summational tone. *The vibration number of the differential tone is equal to the difference between those of the generating sounds ; that of the summational tone is equal to the sum of those of the generating sounds.*

If the one primary tone has a frequency of 200 and the other of 300, and both have sufficient intensity, they will produce a differential tone of 100 vibrations—that is, the lower octave of the lower tone—and a summational tone of 500 vibrations per second (or the major sixth of the higher tone).

If we take a definite fundamental as basis of departure and strike the following notes one after the other, under favourable conditions we can produce a whole series of audible differential tones that run parallel with the higher note.

The following diagram shows the differential tones of the principal consonant intervals.

Ex. 3.—Differential Tones of the Intervals in Common Usage.

The differential tones show a much more rapid progression than the upper partials of the intervals. The clang phenomena become more complex when these new tones in turn produce further combination tones. These combination tones of the second order are 2p, 2q, 2p-minus-q, p-minus 2q, etc.

If we calculate the differential tones of the second order of the sustained primary tone c—that is, of the lower note of the interval —on the basis of the above example, we obtain a series of tones running counter to that of the differential tones of the first order.

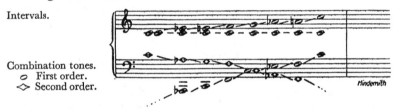

Ex. 4.—Combination Tones of First and Second Order.

Combination tones of the second and higher orders are only observed in exceptional cases. They can prove indirectly annoying, however, if beats occur between the prime tone and a combination tone of higher order very close to it.

Formerly there was great diversity of opinion regarding the nature of the combination tones. Many authorities contrasted beats and combination tones by pointing out that the former were *de facto* entities, while the latter were merely subjective phenomena, therefore without any physical basis in fact. The objective presence of combination tones has recently been successfully established by means of resonators and membranes of varying pitch.*

Differential tones are also of value from a practical point of

* Waetzmann in 1906; Ramann in 1915.

view, since they enable players of stringed instruments to control the true pitch of an interval. A pure interval only needs to be very slightly off pitch to cause a perceptible displacement of the distinctly audible combination tones.

Differential tones are useful, furthermore, in technical science. In every telephone receiver there is a small metal diaphragm that is set into vibration by the voice. This diaphragm only vibrates sympathetically to frequencies between 300 and 2400, so that tones outside these limits are eliminated, or at least have no effect. Since the fundamental range of human speech lies for the most part below 300, only the upper harmonics can set the diaphragm into vibration. The ear of the listener reconstitutes and adds to the audible upper harmonics the differential tone that coincides with the missing first or fundamental harmonic. In this way the original—albeit somewhat altered—voice is transmitted.

The subjective sound of the differential tones has been put to practical application in organ-building for some time. Instead of the very long and expensive labial pipes necessary to produce the deep notes, shorter pipes are used which produce the overtones of the desired note. If two smaller (higher-pitched) pipes are sounded simultaneously, then the differential tone replaces the missing primary.*

Ex. 5.—Audible Combination Tones in a Two-part Melody.

Under favourable conditions, differential tones can be heard very distinctly in a two-part melody. For example, the familiar melody given above (Ex. 5) can be harmonized in such a way that

* We will return to the subject of combination tones later in connexion with the problem of consonance.

the differential tones (which with a few exceptions form the tonic and dominant) are *distinctly audible*.

H. STRUCTURE OF OUR MUSICAL SYSTEM

(1) *The Musical System in General.* I shall now present a theory of scale development which differs from the ordinary concepts, and through which I hope to be able to elucidate the problems and their attempted solutions more cogently, both historically and objectively, than has hitherto been done.

As already mentioned, we have a large number of discriminable notes within the audible musical continuum. There are already more than 1000 discriminable notes in the two-line octave alone; that is, that part of the pitch scale lying between the notes c^2 (525 vibrations) and c^3 (1046 vibrations). Now, the fundamental prerequisite to all music, even the most primitive forms of musical utterance, is that a relatively small number of notes bearing a determinate interval relation to each other be selected from this multiplicity of tones. On the basis of the intervals used in the music of a distinct circle of civilization, the relative pitch of the constituent notes can be determined and arranged in order of pitch. This provides a general view of the *musical-tone material*. From this inventory those tone steps must then be selected that distinctly characterize the musical system in question and that taken together represent the *scale*. By scale we are to understand that series of sequential fixed notes that enter into the composition of all melodies and harmonies in the given music and are confined within the limits of a fundamental and a final note. The totality of scales within the homogeneous music of a people we call the *musical system* of the said people.*

There are two ways open to us by which to construct the scale from the tone material; namely, the theoretical approach and

---

* An extremely fine distinction must be drawn between the terms "musical system", "scale", and "melody". "Musical system" is the sum total of notes available in an instrument in a distinct circle of civilization. Their choice may have been due to various factors; for example, purely musical requirements, mathematical speculations, or cosmological concepts. The scale is merely a selection of notes from the tone system for use in melody. As von Hornbostel points out (*Melodie and Skala* in Peters' "Jahrbuch", 1912, p. 23) the scales are not a norm for the melodies, but the law arising out of the latter through empirical deductions. The so-called "common scale" can be distinguished from the scale proper. The former comprises the principal notes on which a definite composition is built up, arranged in order of pitch. Such a scale (the Pentatonic, for instance) is of interest particularly for musical folklore.

musicological research. There were ancient peoples who noted down their scales in a generally comprehensible manner. We only find exact mathematical data on ancient musical systems among the Greeks, Arabs, and Persians. In studying the musical systems of the Indians, Javanese, Chinese, Japanese, etc., we are dependent on oral traditions and primarily on calculations made on musical instruments. Absolutely trustworthy data can only be obtained from native musicians and singers.

(2) *The Structure of our Musical System Based on Consonant Note Pairs* (*Just Intonation*). In the history of European music we find three principles that have determined the structure of our musical system: the *Principle of Consonance*, the *Principle of Fifths*, and that which I have called the *Pragmatic Principle*. Let us begin with a discussion of the Principle of Consonance.

Comparative musicology has taught us that the musical systems of the most diversified peoples, ancient and modern, civilized and uncivilized, are so far similar in that all the notes of the scale are contained within the compass of one octave, and there is no *specific* interval greater than an octave. (Compound intervals—such as the tenth and twelfth, for example—are not *specific* intervals. They represent intervals expanded an octave.) In other words, the *octave* is the natural interval within which the musical systems arise, partly through acoustical, partly through æsthetic, and partly through technical considerations. This interval furnishes fixed bases for the sub-division of the tonal domain, both upwards and downwards. At the same time it represents the *highest degree of consonance.*

If we compare the other note pairs in our musical system one with another, it will be found that there is a great difference between them as regards euphony and consonance. There are pairs of simultaneous notes that sound very pleasant together; others that are very unpleasant. Those of the first type are called *consonances*; those of the second type, *dissonances*, though a sharp boundary line cannot be drawn between the two. When the physical basis of consonant and dissonant intervals was subjected to rigorous physical investigation (this occurred as far back as classical antiquity), it showed the surprising result that the numerical ratio between the two notes, expressed in string lengths (later in vibrations), was in general much simpler in consonant than in dissonant intervals.

Whether the principle of consonance was the guiding factor in the moulding of our European musical system, it is impossible to say, in view of the lack of incontrovertible historical evidence. But there is no doubt that our musical system is governed by the principle of the simplest ratios. The simplest ratios—which at the same time represent the perfect consonances—provide the melodic and harmonic framework for our music.

From this angle, *the octave*, a perfect consonance, and also the mathematically simplest interval expressible in digits (1 : 2), ostensibly forms the basis of departure. The integration of the musical range in intervals is effected within one octave, and is then simply carried over to the other octaves. If we now construct the simple numerical ratios with all integers from 1 to 16 (with the exception of those containing one of the three primary numbers, 7, 11, and 13), we obtain the following intervals, arranged in order of distance between the pitches; i.e. numerical order:

16 : 15 Diatonic semitone.
10 : 9   Minor tone (minor whole step).
9 : 8   Major tone (major whole step).
6 : 5   Minor third.
5 : 4   Major third.
4 : 3   Perfect fourth.
3 : 2   Perfect fifth.
8 : 5   Minor sixth.
5 : 3   Major sixth.
9 : 5   Minor seventh.
15 : 8   Major seventh.
2 : 1   Octave.

This manner of integrating the octave is called *just or mathematical intonation.** The *heptatonic natural diatonic, or major, scale*

---

* The term " mathematical intonation " is misleading. The intonation does not follow from mathematico-physical speculations—that is, it is not based on any numerical calculation or on physical computations—but proceeds from the *musical ear*, which seems innately inclined to the intonation of pure intervals. That these intervals correspond to simple vibrational ratios is an important cognitive fact, exactly as is the fact that the most consonant intervals (octave, fifth, fourth, and the two thirds) are found in the first five harmonic overtones. But these mathematico-physical considerations have nothing to do either with the structure of the tone system or with the tuning of the instrument. Just intonation did not arise through the ratios or the harmonic overtones. Quite the contrary. It was only through, and consequently after, the calculation of the string lengths (vibration numbers) corresponding to the just intervals that attention was drawn to the simple numerical ratios. Furthermore, it was only later that the agreement between the pure main intervals and the first partials was substantiated.

can be constructed forthwith from the given series. The following ratios subsist between the successive notes of the scale:

$$\begin{array}{ccccccc} c & d & e & f & g & a & b & c \\ \dfrac{9}{8} & \dfrac{10}{9} & \dfrac{16}{15} & \dfrac{9}{8} & \dfrac{10}{9} & \dfrac{9}{8} & \dfrac{16}{15} \end{array}$$

But these intervals are not all equal in size. Wider (9/8 and 10/9) and narrower ones (16/15) alternate. The wider interval we call a whole (minor or major) tone ; the narrower, a semitone.

We obtain a greater variety of notes within an octave when we come to the *twelve-note chromatic scale*. Here we have two possibilities, accordingly two note-series; for instance: c, c♯, d, d♯, e, f, f♯, g, g♯, a, a♯, b and c; and c, d♭, d, e♭, e, f, g♭, g, a♭, a, b♭, b and c. Finally we have the so-called *enharmonic scale* which comprises all components of these two series.*

c	c♯	d♭	d	d♯	e♭	e	f♭	e♯	f	f♯	g♭	g	g♯	a♭	a	a♯	b♭	b	c♭	c¹
1	$\dfrac{25}{24}$	$\dfrac{27}{25}$	$\dfrac{9}{8}$	$\dfrac{75}{64}$	$\dfrac{6}{5}$	$\dfrac{5}{4}$	$\dfrac{32}{25}$	$\dfrac{125}{96}$	$\dfrac{4}{3}$	$\dfrac{25}{18}$	$\dfrac{36}{25}$	$\dfrac{3}{2}$	$\dfrac{25}{16}$	$\dfrac{8}{5}$	$\dfrac{5}{3}$	$\dfrac{125}{72}$	$\dfrac{9}{5}$	$\dfrac{15}{8}$	$\dfrac{48}{25}$	2

The notes of the two twelve-step chromatic scales are obtained mathematically by intercalating a note between all the whole tone intervals. This can be done in two ways: either by multiplying the frequencies of the notes, c, d, f, g, a by 25/24 (which gives us the notes c♯, d♯, f♯, g♯, a♯) or by multiplying the frequencies of the notes d, e, g, a, b by 24/25 (which gives us the notes d♭, e♭, g♭, a♭, b♭ (131)).

Just intonation gives rise to great difficulties in music. This can be seen from the following. If we take as primary any other note than c, and then construct the diatonic scale on such note, we arrive at different intervals. Starting, for instance, with c, the first step of the diatonic scale is c : d = 9 : 8, or a major tone (tonus major). Starting with d, however, the first step is d : e = 10 : 9, or a minor tone (tonus minor). But, trifling as the difference between the two intervals may seem, it causes insurmountable difficulties in the performance of polyphonic music. This is mainly evident when instruments with fixed pitch, primarily the keyboard instruments (piano and organ), are played in combination with stringed instruments and voices which, as we know, use natural intervals, and consequently evoke enharmonic permuta-

---

* The enharmonic genera of the Greek musicians in the classical period progressed in intervals of quarter-tones. The battle between the enharmonic and chromatic genera goes back to about 1000 B.C. Table II in the Appendix lists the tones of the enharmonic scale from C_2 to c^7.

tions.   In these cases it is difficult to assimilate the notes of the instruments with variable and adjustable pitch to the rigid pitch of the piano.   Although the advantages of just intonation were obvious, it was nevertheless proposed to bridge the cleavage by removing all obstacles to polyphony with the least sacrifice of purity of intonation (59).   The various methods of solving the problem will be discussed later.

(3) *The Musical System Based on the Projection of Pure Fifths (Pythagorean Intonation).*   It is a familiar fact that our musical system, particularly the major modes, can be constructed in another manner than by just intonation.   The foundation for this is *one* definite interval, namely, the perfect fifth, which is second to the octave as regards degree of consonance and fusion.   Since we are almost as sensitive to the purity of the fifth as to that of the octave, and since the perfect fifth is an especially characteristic interval, no objections can be raised to its use as a unit of measurement.

If we now descend a fifth from the small octave (c), we come to the note F (c–F).   If we transpose this note to the small octave, we come to the fourth above the note c or to the note f.   If we next add the upper octave of c to these three notes, we have the following four notes : c–f–g–c¹, which represent the three most consonant intervals: octave, fifth, and fourth.   If we do not stop with the upper and lower fifths, but proceed *upwards* in fifths from the fifth above the fundamental, and *downwards* in fifths from the fourth below, and then by transposition integrate these notes within the span of one octave, we obtain the *heptatonic Pythagorean scale.*   It can be seen that the underlying idea of the Pythagorean scale was to obtain scale-notes by the projection of pure fifths and to fill out all the octave segments of the musical range with these notes in the same manner.

The following table shows the notes of the diatonic major scale based upon the projection of a fifth :

c–c¹	octave transposition.
c–g	(c–g–c¹)
c–F (f)	(c–f–g–c¹)
g–d¹ (d)	(c–d–f–g–c¹)
d–a	(c–d–f–g–a–c¹)
a–e¹ (e)	(c–d–e–f–g–a–c¹)
e–b	(c–d–e–f–g–a–b–c¹)

The scale can be most clearly and correctly illustrated by a circle (Fig. 9).

We now find that the notes of the scale obtained by the projection of a fifth do not meet the harmonic requirements of the scale. They do not offer us those degrees of consonance that our harmonic ear apparently demands and that are also realized in the overtone series characterized by just intonation. If we tune our piano according to the Pythagorean principle, it will be apparent that in the heptatonic scale the major third is too sharp, and accordingly sounds out of tune. The reason for this is that

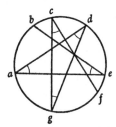

FIG. 9.—Graphic Representation of the Diatonic scale.

the fourth fifth from the fundamental c (e¹) has four vibrations more per second than the fifth partial of C (e¹); that is, 324 vibrations instead of 320.*

This deviation from the natural consonant major third, which is known as a *syntonic comma*, makes the Pythagorean scale unserviceable for polyphonic music since this demands a consonant third (Ex. 6).

* I should like to call attention here to a mathematical construction of the scale, the merit of which seems to be that the major and minor scales are both derived through one and the same principle. This is the Farey " Series " (1816), which was rigorously proved by Cauchy. Farey considered the series of all non-reducible fractions capable of numerical representation as not greater than an arbitrary number " n ". If we collocate these fractions in order of value, we obtain the convergent Farey series F (n). For example, the series F (5) is as follows:

$$\frac{0}{1} \quad \frac{1}{5} \quad \frac{1}{4} \quad \frac{1}{3} \quad \frac{2}{5} \quad \frac{1}{2} \quad \frac{3}{5} \quad \frac{2}{3} \quad \frac{3}{4} \quad \frac{4}{5} \quad \frac{1}{1} \quad \frac{5}{4} \quad \frac{4}{3} \quad \frac{3}{2} \quad \frac{5}{3} \quad \frac{2}{1} \quad \frac{5}{2} \quad \frac{3}{1} \quad \frac{4}{1} \quad \frac{5}{1} \quad \frac{1}{0}$$

$$- \quad A\flat_2 \quad C_1 \quad F_1 \quad A\flat_1 \quad C \quad E\flat \quad F \quad G \quad A\flat \quad c \quad e \quad f \quad g \quad a \quad c^1 \quad e^1 \quad g^1 \quad c^2 \quad e^2 \quad -$$

If, starting from the middle fraction 1/1, we identify this with the note c, then the first five fractions to the right represent the six notes of the scale that combine to form the most consonant intervals. In the same way, reading to the left we obtain the six notes of the scale.

$\frac{1}{1}$	$\frac{5}{4}$	$\frac{4}{3}$	$\frac{3}{2}$	$\frac{5}{3}$	$\frac{2}{1}$		$\frac{1}{1}$	$\frac{4}{5}$	$\frac{3}{4}$	$\frac{2}{3}$	$\frac{3}{5}$	$\frac{1}{2}$
c	e	f	g	a	c¹		c	A♭	G	F	E♭	C
Consonant intervals.							First six notes of the scale.					

This method gives us a pentatonic scale with the major and minor third. The second and seventh are missing.

There is still another difficulty attached to Pythagorean intonation (cycle of fifths). If, for example, we start with sub-contra C (C_2 = 16 vibrations) and progress continually by fifths, we

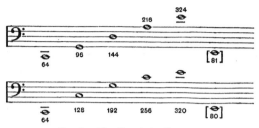

Ex. 6.—The Syntonic Comma.

come (via the notes g, d, a, e, b, f♯, g♯, c♯, d♯, a♯, e♯) to the twelfth fifth (the note b♯♯³ = 2075 vibrations), which does not coincide with the proper higher octave of the fundamental C_2; that is, with c^4 (2048). When we come to the twelfth fifth, therefore, we find a note that is higher than the proper higher octave of the fundamental. This difference is called the *Pythagorean comma*.

	c	d	e	f	g	a	b	c
Tempered:	1	$2^{\frac{2}{12}}$	$2^{\frac{4}{12}}$	$2^{\frac{5}{12}}$	$2^{\frac{7}{12}}$	$2^{\frac{9}{12}}$	$2^{\frac{11}{12}}$	2
Pythagorean:	1	$\frac{3^2}{2^3}$	$\frac{3^4}{2^6}$	$\frac{2^2}{3}$	$\frac{3}{2}$	$\frac{3^3}{2^4}$	$\frac{3^5}{2^7}$	2
Diatonic:	1	$\frac{9}{8}$	$\frac{5}{4}$	$\frac{4}{3}$	$\frac{3}{2}$	$\frac{5}{3}$	$\frac{15}{8}$	2

Fig. 10.—Deviations of the Pythagorean Intervals from the Diatonic.

If we tune our piano to perfect fifths, we accordingly obtain a scale in which the fourth and fifth are strictly pure but the other intervals are not. The disturbing factor is that the octave—the most constant interval (and smoothest consonance)—is out of tune, since it deviates from the perfect natural octave by a Pythagorean comma (74 : 73). The deviation amounts to about one-quarter of a semitone.*

For music history in general, and especially for the understanding of exotic music, there is another interesting system of successive fifths that deviates from the Pythagorean cycle and was

* Stringed instruments are still tuned to perfect fifths. As we know, the four strings of the violin, the viola, and cello are tuned to perfect fifths. When they are used to their full length—that is, are open and not stopped by one of the player's fingers—they produce a succession of four perfect fifths (g; d¹; a¹; e²). The double bass is tuned to fourths (E; A; D; G), the viola d'amore to fifth-fourth-third. With wind instruments perfect fifths are produced automatically by overblowing. For more detailed information on the subject, see the various handbooks on musical instruments.

probably obtained by tonometrical research. According to von Hornbostel, this system is found in Brazilian Pan-pipes, which are tuned to a series of successive fifths. For this reason this system is called the *Cycle of Blown Fifths*. The fifths of this hypothetical progression are somewhat smaller than the perfect and tempered fifths. In comparison with perfect fifths (702 cents),* they show a difference of about 24 cents (678 cents), which almost amounts to a Pythagorean comma. In contrast with the twelve-note system of Pythagoras, the Cycle of Blown Fifths requires 23 successive fifths in order to arrive again at its point of departure. The greatest difference between the Pythagorean system and the Cycle of Blown Fifths is that the former, after 12 successive fifths, arrives at a note that deviates noticeably from the fundamental, which results in impure octaves,† while the Cycle of Blown Fifths, after 23 somewhat smaller fifths, arrives at a note that deviates from the fundamental by scarcely ¼ comma.‡

Computations on ancient and modern instruments have shown that the musical systems of the earlier Hindu-Javanese, Siamese, Burman, and Peruvian races, as well as the still-existent primitive tribes in Melanesia, Polynesia, Brazil, and even a few African tribes, had their origin in a system that corresponds to that of the Cycle of Blown Fifths.

In recent years various objections have been raised to von Hornbostel's hypothesis (18, 132). Even though his theory should be disproved, it is still to his merit that he established physical laws in respect to the structure of the aforesaid exotic tone systems and made plausible the inherent likelihood of their common origin.

(4) *The Musical System Based on the Pragmatic Principle (Tempered Tuning).* The Pythagorean System dominated the music of antiquity and the Middle Ages. There was no reason to break away from the ratio of pure fifths so long as music was preponderantly homophonic. But the introduction of polyphony put an end to the dominance of the Pythagorean System and, with it, of the Pythagorean third, which latter was useful as a

---

* See Section J.

† 12×702 (12 perfect fifths) $= 8424$ cents. 7×1200 (7 octaves) $= 8400$ cents. The difference is 24 cents, or 1 Pythagorean comma.

‡ 23×676 (23 somewhat smaller fifths) $\times 15,594$ cents. 13×1200 (13 octaves) $= 15,600$ cents. The difference is 6 cents, or ¼ Pythagorean comma.

melodic interval. The factor of consonance (harmony) now began to play a certain role. The harmonic structure of music became increasingly important. About 1600 the old ecclesiastical modes also gave way more and more to the major and minor modes.

The Pythagorean scale was consequently unsuitable for the harmonic structure of music. The major third and the excessively sharp Pythagorean third (81 : 64) were incompatible. The latter has to be replaced by the natural third (5 : 4). Meanwhile the introduction of the perfect major third and the notes dependent on it brought difficulties in its train.

The effort to find a solution for these difficulties led to various proposals, inspired by practical considerations. The principal object was to adapt the intervals to the demands of musical practice; that is, to adopt a tuning which guaranteed as far as possible the true intonation of the principal intervals, and yet took into account all the various requirements of harmonic music. In this way one arrived at various compromises: the so-called *musical temperaments*.

Since it was impossible to eliminate the obstructive comma, there was no other recourse than to distribute the difference within the limits of the octave in such manner that the latter would remain absolutely true in intonation, and the other intervals would also be true enough to fulfil their melodic and harmonic functions without difficulty. Fifths and fourths had to remain absolutely true, while a certain distortion was permissible for thirds and sixths, and to an even greater extent for seconds and sevenths.*

The first proposals in this direction were inclined to give preference to the scales in common usage at the expense of the less frequent types. These efforts led to the adoption of divers kinds of *unequal temperament*, or, more correctly speaking, to the *meantone system*.

Of such proposals, the so-called unequal or meantone temperament is the best known. Here the fundamental is a mean between the true major and minor tones. The fundamental tones of the system are obtained by reducing the first four fifths (c–g, g–d, d–a, a–e) by an amount sufficient to produce a true

---

* Walter Odington reintroduced the consonant triad (4 : 5 : 6) about 1300. Here the Pythagorean third was naturally intolerable in an auditory sense (87).

third. In this method of tuning, the major thirds and their inversions, the minor sixths, are tuned true (with a few minor exceptions), while the fifths are a little too flat. Only the fifth g♯–d♯ (the so-called Wolf—a harsh dissonance) is too sharp, its inversion too flat; in consequence, it is intolerable. (Fig. 11.)

The result of this choice of tuning was that only certain scales could be used in musical practice—i.e. those with few accidentals —whereas others had to be avoided. It is interesting and worthy of note that not only the Italian theorist *Gioseffo Zarlino* (1517– 1590), but also the blind organist, *Francisco Salinas* (1513–1590),

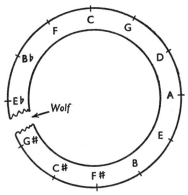

FIG. 11.—Origin of the So-called Wolf.

made valuable contributions to the theory of meantone temperament.*

After long discussions and many proposals, it was finally decided to sacrifice true intonation of all intervals rather than place difficulties in the way of polyphony and complete freedom of modulation. Which led to a compromise. The octave was divided into *12 equal intervals*, which resulted in the *12-interval equal temperament*, or the *so-called standard equal semitone tuning (ETS)*. To Simon Stevin goes the distinction of having divided the octave into 12 equal semitones (145). He calculated the normal semitone tuning while the organ-builder, Andreas Werkmeister (c. 1691), and Arp Schnitger (between 1688 and 1692) employed this method of tuning for their organs. In this system no single interval other than the octave is strictly true; even the fifth is

---

* Arnold Schlick should also be mentioned in connexion with the introduction of meantone temperament (1511).

slightly faulty (about ½ comma). The great merit of this tuning is that all intervals are true to a corresponding degree, regardless of the initial note of the interval.*

The introduction of equal semitones did away with the differences between the enharmonic tones; i.e. between c♯ and d♭, d♯ and e♭. Therefore, in the tempered scale—for example, with c as tonic—we find neither a true c♯ nor a true d♭, but a note lying between the two. For pragmatic—i.e. for purely practical reasons—c♯ and d♭ are assumed to be identical, though it is possible for our ear to distinguish these two notes one from the other. The c♯ (the raised prime) bears a ratio of 25 : 24 to c, while d♭ (the diminished second) bears a ratio to it of 27 : 25.

Since the days of *Johann Sebastian Bach* and *J. Ph. Rameau*, we have grown so accustomed to equal temperament that we now scarcely notice the mistuning of the intervals. For this we have to thank the elasticity of our sense of hearing. Owing to our aural adaptability, intervals that are approximately alike sound alike to us, and we are not disturbed by comma differences in harmonic combinations. Although tempered tuning was unanimously adopted because of the advantages it offered, opinions of musical scholars differed as to its practicability. Among other things, attention was drawn to the noticeable dissonances that arise in polyphonic music as a result of equal temperament. These are caused by differential tones, especially by those in the immediate proximity of the ground bass. They stand out most distinctly on the harmonium and violin.†

But the introduction of the equal temperament scale did not do away altogether with the pure natural intervals. Certain instruments, primarily the stringed instruments and the human voice, still use untempered intonation (just intervals) if they are not

---

* Table I in the Appendix lists all the tones in tempered tuning with their frequencies and ratios with reference to the fundamental C_2 (131).

† Since in the 12 semitone system the thirds are about 2/3 of a comma, or approximately 1/8 semitone too sharp, different suggestions were made to introduce equal temperaments with more intervals. Among these were the 53-tone temperament of Nicholas Mercator (1675) and the 31-tone temperament of Christian Huygens (1629–1695). The 31-interval tone system offers certain advantages, but the fifths are not so good as in the 12-tone division. The 53-tone equal temperament that Bosanquet developed practically later on for the harmonium (1875) has one merit over the 12-tone division in that the deviation of the third from the mathematically just intonation is about ten times less. In addition, the fifths are also almost perfect. P. v. Janko's 41-tone division produces even better fifths and thirds. However, all so-called just intonation systems with more than 12 tones have proved inexpedient in actual practice.

required to adapt themselves to keyboard instruments (piano, organ, etc.). In these cases one is not bound exclusively to the tempered tone system. If the musical effect of pure orchestral music, chamber music, and a-cappella singing is compared with that of the keyboard instruments tuned to equal temperament, the great æsthetic loss resulting from equal temperament is immediately apparent (7, 90).

I. Absolute Tuning and Standard Pitch

The tuning discussed in Section H is a *relative tuning*. But in order to establish the musical scale absolutely and definitely, it is still necessary to fix *one* note once for all in *absolute pitch*; i.e. according to its vibration number. This note is called the *standard or chamber pitch*, or *diapason*, and its tuning *absolute tuning*.

Formerly there was no standard pitch in this sense. In the 17th and 18th centuries the *Kammerton* (normal standard of pitch) was generally very high, about a major third higher than now. The standard pitch a^1 varied between 375 and 500 c.p.s. Between 1700 and 1859 the Grand Opera in Paris raised standard pitch from 404 to 441 c.p.s. Later the latitude was a little less; namely, between 432 and 466 c.p.s. Arbitrary action in determining the Kammerton, which bred such great confusion in musical practice, and particularly in the musical instrument industry, was definitely eliminated in 1885, when the international pitch conference in Vienna fixed an a^1 of 435 c.p.s. as the official standard pitch. Subsequently the International Federation of Standardizing Associations officially based standard concert pitch on $a^1 = 440$ c.p.s., which was adopted by the Union International de Radio Diffusion.*

In order to standardize this pitch on a^1, standard tuning-forks were constructed that give the standard note exactly at a temperature of 15° C. Official tuning-forks are ordinarily stamped with the figure 880 (instead of 440); that is, with the number of half vibrations. This is at variance, of course, with the mathematico-physical concept of the period.

In spite of international pitch there is still the tendency, especially with many orchestras and chamber-music ensembles, to

---

* A standard pitch is also occasionally used in extra-European music. For instance, Chinese music has its own standard pitch, the so-called Huang-tchong at 366 c.p.s.; that is, about $f\sharp^1$.

raise the pitch of the standard tone a^1 to about 445 c.p.s. This excessive rise of standard pitch is due mainly to the strings, which consider that it enhances the brilliance. Singers and a-cappella choirs remain true to the lower pitch for obvious reasons.

J. Measuring System in Terms of Cents

In physics, as in music, intervals are expressed by the ratio of the smaller to the larger vibrational numbers. However, the scales of all the different peoples can be compared only approximately by means of the ratios. In addition, the ratios give the intervals as theoretically established, and not those that are actually sung or played, which latter often deviate very greatly from the mathematico-physical tuning. Alexander John Ellis (1814–1890), the founder of comparative musicology, who made searching and exhaustive inquiries concerning the theoretical determination of extra-European musical scales was moved by these considerations to introduce a numerical device which would

TABLE I *

Scales expressed in Cents

The tempered C major scale in cents: $a^1 = 440$, $C_2 = 16\cdot35$

Tones	C	D	E	F	G	A	B	C
Frequency .	65·4	73·4	82·4	87·3	98·0	110·0	123·4	130·8
Cents	I 200	II 200	III 100	IV 200	V 200	VI 200	VII 100	I¹
Sum . .	0	200	400	500	700	900	1100	1200

The pure C major scale in cents: $a^1 = 400$, $C_2 = 16\cdot5$

Tones	C	D	E	F	G	A	B	C
Frequency .	66	74·2	82·5	88	99	110	123·7	132
Cents	I 204	II 182	III 112	IV 204	V 182	VI 204	VII 112	I¹
Sum . .	0	204	386	498	702	884	1088	1200

Scale of a Javanese Gambang in cents (71)

Tones	f♯¹ (366)	g¹ (396)	a¹ (440)	b¹ (475)	c♯² (550)	d² (594)	e♭² (675)	f♯² (733)
Frequency .	360	397	432·5	481	542	589	674	720
Cents	I 170	II 148	III 184	IV 207	V 144	VI 233	VII 114	I¹
Sum . .	0	170	318	502	709	853	1086	1200

* The Roman numerals indicate the steps of the seven-step scale; I is the fundamental, I¹ its octave. The figures alongside give the cent values of these intervals. The bottom row gives the cent values of the intervals.

provide a more accurate means of comparing the size of the intervals than is possible by ratios. Ellis proposed that the tempered semitone be divided into 100 equal parts, into 100 small ideal intervals (31). Accordingly, octaves were divided into 1200, fifths into 700, and fourths into 500 parts. These small intervals are called cents. For example, if we express the intervals of the tempered c major scale in cents we arrive at the above values (Table 1).

The following table lists the most important intervals expressed in ratios and cents according to Ellis's tabulation.

TABLE 2

Interval	Ratio	Cents
Pythagorean comma . . .	524 : 531	24
Quarter tone	239 : 246	50
Chromatic semitone . . .	24 : 25	70
Tempered semitone . . .	84 : 89	100
Diatonic hemitone (Limma) . .	15 : 16	112
Minor tone	9 : 10	182
Tempered whole tone . . .	400 : 449	200
Major tone (second) . . .	8 : 9	204
Tempered minor third . . .	37 : 44	300
Pure minor third	5 : 6	316
Pure major third	4 : 5	386
Tempered major third . . .	50 : 63	400
Pythagorean major third (ditone) .	64 : 81	408
Perfect fourth	3 : 4	498
Tempered fourth	227 : 303	500
Pure augmented fourth . .	32 : 45	590
Tempered augmented fourth .	99 : 140	600
Tempered fifth	289 : 433	700
Perfect fifth	2 : 3	702
Tempered minor sixth . . .	63 : 100	800
Pure minor sixth . . .	5 : 8	814
Pure major sixth	3 : 5	884
Tempered major sixth . . .	22 : 37	900
Pure minor seventh . . .	5 : 9	1018
Tempered minor seventh . .	55 : 98	1000
Pure major seventh . . .	8 : 15	1088
Tempered major seventh . .	89 : 168	1100
Octave	1 : 2	1200

II

PHYSIOLOGICAL ACOUSTICS

A. Function of the Auditory Apparatus

THE organ of hearing is usually divided into the outer, the middle, and the inner ear. The *outer ear* consists of the external part (or pinna) and the *ear canal* (the auditory meatus), which is closed off from the middle ear by the membrana tympani, or ear-drum. The outer ear plays hardly any role in hearing. It cannot even be said that the sound is regularly reflected by the outer ear. When the latter was completely masked and an ear-trumpet inserted into the auditory canal, no appreciable decrease in auditory acuity was noted.

The *middle ear* is formed by the tympanic cavity, which is provided with four separate apertures. Three of these—the ear-drum, the oval and the round windows—connect with a delicate elastic membrane of skin, while the fourth aperture debouches into the Eustachian Tube, which in turn opens directly into the throat. The chain of ossicles (hammer, anvil, and stirrup) extends across the tube, the hammer being directly attached to the drumskin. Sound is propagated by the inner ear. The ear-drum, as resonating membrane, vibrates sympathetically with the sound and conveys the vibrations to the ossicles (especially to the stirrup or stapes), which in turn transmit them to the inner ear.

The *inner ear or labyrinth* consists of three parts—namely, the vestibule, in which the stapes articulates with the membrane-covered window known as the oval window; the three semi-circular canals, and finally the cochlea. Only the cochlea serves for hearing, while the semi-circular canals form the reflex mechanism of equilibrium of the head, and therefore of the entire body. The cochlea consists of two parts—the upper and the lower gallery—which are separated from each other by the basilar membrane. Fastened to this *membrana basilaris* are the neural terminals of the cochlea—the Cortis Organ—so that the vibrations of the basilar membrane are transmitted directly to the end of the auditory nerve (nervus acusticus), and set up action in the corresponding brain centres. The ossicles enable the ear-drum

34

to transmit air vibrations—that is, tones—to the labyrinth, which is entirely filled with fluid (lymph). Every sound thrusts this fluid against the walls of the labyrinth, where it impinges on the round window with its flexible elastic membrane and sets this in motion according to the intensity and pitch of the tone. The sound vibrations are transmitted to the ear—the organ of hearing —by atmospheric vibrations. There they excite the auditory nerve and the nerve terminals in the brain. We can view the physiological process taking place in the brain as the direct cause of the sensations of tone.

The inner connexion between the physiological process (stimulus in general) and the psychical process (sound sensation)

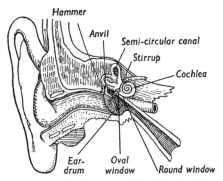

FIG. 12.—Cross-section of the Human Ear.

is unknown to us. There are various theories that attempt to explain this psycho-physical connexion. They are known as the Theory of Reciprocal Action and the Theory of Psycho-physical Parallelism. We will not go into these theories here. That would take us too far afield. The statement must suffice that there is a causative relation between material and psychical reality, that the psychical states and processes depend on cerebral processes, and the latter in turn on the physical stimuli. At the same time we should never overlook the fact that the sensory perceptions evoked by material stimuli represent something *entirely new* and in their phenomenological form are not to be compared with the physiological processes causatively associated with them. A physical tone, a sound vibration, should therefore not be identified with sound perception. The existence of a sound vibration does not depend on whether a person perceives it aurally or not. It belongs to the material world independent of the psyche, and is only perceived, only evokes a sound sensation, when the necessary physical and psychical conditions are fulfilled.

B. Theories of Auditory Perception

A theory of hearing is only satisfactory if it is able to bring the physical and anatomical-physiological conditions of hearing into causative connexion with the *acoustical phenomena*. There is no such theory as yet. Present theories of hearing have to do exclusively with the investigation of the *physical processes* in the inner ear induced by sound vibrations. They therefore pin their attention on the peripheral parts of the auditory apparatus, and try to explain the physiological processes taking place in the inner ear, by or through the transmission of acoustical vibratory processes, on the basis of our present physical knowledge.

The *theories of physical auditory perception* can be divided into two groups; namely, the *resonance* and the *sound-pattern theories*. The theory of resonance was promulgated by Hermann von Helmholtz; the sound-pattern theory by J. R. Ewald. All other theories of auditory perception, no matter how greatly they may differ in detail from these original theories, can only be considered modifications of them.

(1) *The Helmholtz Resonance Theory*. In formulating his theory of hearing, the so-called *Resonance Hypothesis* (Harp Theory), Hermann von Helmholtz proceeded from our anatomical-physiological knowledge of the sense of hearing (51). On the basis of the histological structure of the basilar membrane, he assumed that it represented a system of strings, each one of which responds to a determinate tone and is set into sympathetic vibration as soon as the sound strikes the ear. According to Helmholtz (1868), the basilar membrane is so constituted that it does not have the same tension in all directions, there being little tension in the direction of its length, while there is great tension in the direction of its breadth.

> But (said Helmholtz) if the tension in the direction of its length is infinitesimally small in comparison with the tension in the direction of its breadth, then the radial fibres of the membrana basilaris may be approximately regarded as forming a system of stretched strings and the membranous

connexion as only serving to give a fulcrum to the pressure of the fluid against these strings. In that case the laws of their motion would be the same as if every individual string moved independently of all the others and obeyed by itself the influence of the periodically alternating pressure of the fluid of the labyrinth contained in the vestibule gallery. Consequently any exciting tone would set that part of the membrane into sympathetic vibration for which the proper tone of one of its radial fibres that are stretched and loaded with the various appendages corresponds most nearly with the exciting tone; and thence the vibrations will extend with rapidly diminishing strength on to the adjacent parts of the membrane.

According to Helmholtz, the cochlean nerves (Cortis Organ) of the basilar membrane act as resonators and strings tuned to particular tones. Only one vibrates to a single pure tone, according as larger or smaller groups of aural resonators are damped out. However, several vibrate to a complex note, or clang, dependent on the number of partials. In form, the basilar membrane resembles the string-plate of a piano. At the oval window it is relatively narrow, and gradually widens towards the vertex of the cochlea. From their beginning to the vertex of the cochlea the transverse fibres (the physiological resonators) widen to 12 times their original size; namely, from 41 to 495 micro-millimetres ($1\mu = 0.001$ mm.).

According to the Helmholtz Theory, tones of the highest pitch are sensed near the stapes, those of the lowest pitch at the apex of the cochlea. Experiments also supported this assumption. For instance, if the apex of the cochlea is removed in dogs, they become deaf to sounds of low pitch, while the removal of the base of the cochlea makes them deaf to sounds of high pitch (Munk). It has been further observed that the base of the membrane of the Cortis Organ will be destroyed if the ear of an animal is continually subjected to tones of very high pitch (Wittmack and Joshii). The fact that an ear fatigued by a tone of 300 vibrations per second does not lose its sensitivity to an adjacent tone (one of 310 vibr. per sec., for example) also supports the theoretical contention that the organic sensation is limited to a very small spot in the membrane.

The sensation process in the ear can be demonstrated by the resonance of the piano. If we raise the dampers and sing a musical note against the strings, then only those strings resonate that are components of the sung note. According to the Helmholtz hypothesis, therefore, in the Cortis Organ only those transverse fibres vibrate that respond to the fundamental and its upper partials. This, in the opinion of Helmholtz, explains why we can analyze musical sounds. The clangs decompose into their partials purely physiologically, without any action on our part, by causing the fibres to vibrate when in resonance with the tone proper to the fibre.

As to the number of transverse fibres in the basilar membrane, it is sufficiently large to view the fibres as resonators for the great mass of audible tones. The number is variously estimated; at all events it is not less than about 14,000 (data varies between 14,000 and 24,000); that is, a number that far exceeds the number of aurally discriminable tones.

The resonance hypothesis can also easily explain a number of pathological phenomena of abnormal hearing; for example, the so-called tone gaps or tone islands. It sometimes happens that patients are deaf to many tones. For the most part a fairly sharply defined region of the tone domain is affected. The resonance theory explains this by the assumption that a determinate part of the basilar membrane has lost its function through an affection of the Cortis Organ. The strange pathological phenomenon whereby smaller or larger sections of the tone domain are heard higher or lower than they actually are is explainable as result of a local swelling (morbid growth) on fibres tuned to particular tones.*

Though admittedly impressive, the Helmholtz theory nevertheless confronts us with great difficulties. It can scarcely be assumed that fibres merely a fraction of a millimetre in length can vibrate sympathetically to tones requiring very stout strings, and sometimes strings of even very great volume. It is physically inconceivable, for example, that a horn, the fortissimo of which makes our whole body tingle, only affects an infinitesimal portion of the delicate basilar membrane. An attempt has been made to eliminate these difficulties by pointing out that in a string the tone depends not only on the length, but also on the volume. Since the fibres of the basilar membrane are not loose, like the strings

---

* It should also be mentioned that the assumptions of Helmholtz have been substantiated quite recently by two English scientists, Hartridge and Banister (49).

of the piano or the violin, but are embedded in the membrane, the vibrating mass of the " resonating " fibres is increased. But in my opinion not even this explanation can surmount the aforesaid difficulty.

The objections regarding the hearing of beats and combination tones, the sharpness of the resonance and the damping, and in particular the phenomenon of trills are of special importance. As early as the close of the last century, a very heated controversy arose over all these questions, which led to modifications of the original Helmholtz concepts * but did not contribute much towards a real clarification of the physiological problems of hearing. One modification derives from H. E. Roaf † and Fletcher.‡ These authors attribute resonance to the motion of the fluid in the cochlea while the basilar membrane is supposed to vibrate in its entirety, one distinct point of maximum resonance vibrating more intensely than the rest (83).

M. Meyer's theory deals mainly with the origin of the differential tones whereby he abandons the resonance theory and explains these phenomena through a new hypothesis (84). The theory of Th. Wrightson (163) is limited to the summational and differential tones which he tries to trace to mechanical causes. The sound-pattern theory of J. R. Ewald with its comprehensive perspective (35) aroused the greatest interest of all.

(2) *Ewald's Sound Pattern Theory.* In the opinion of Ewald (1899) the entire basilar membrane is set into sympathetic vibration by the sound stimulus and decomposed into a system of stationary waves. This stationary wave system in its totality generates a *special sound pattern* for *every tone*. The simple tones are differentiated according to the wave-lengths of the vertical vibrations. Complex tones and chords give sound patterns that result from the superposition of the sound-waves, without, however, altering the length of the wave, so that no sound pattern is lost. The analysis of complex tones and chords is explained in this way (35).

Ewald describes the process of sound perception as follows: In the ear, the impulses generated by the sound create a sound pattern on the basic membrane of the cochlea, the special form

* Wundt, Stumpf, Hermann, Ebbinghaus, Wien.
† *Philosophical Magazine*, 43, 1922.   ‡ *Journal of the Franklin Institute*, 1923.

of which enables the membrane to effect a physiological connexion between sound stimulus and sound perception. The specific form of the sound pattern is characteristic of the corresponding sound sensation, and determines it unequivocally.

Ewald's theory met with approval on account of its correct physical premises. The fact that he succeeded in demonstrating the presence of the presumptive sound patterns of the basilar membrane on an extremely thin, small, artificial membrane contributed to its success. If a membrane of approximately the same size as the basilar membrane is subjected to sound stimuli, then we actually obtain sound patterns, clang-forms, in keeping with Ewald's assumptions.

The sound patterns can be made visible by giving the artificial membrane a glossy finish so that the images reflected on it are perceptible. If we hold a tuning-fork to such a membrane, a sound pattern covering the entire surface of the membrane is clearly visible. If the membrane is set in motion by means of two tuning-forks of different pitch, one after the other, it can be seen distinctly that the fork of higher pitch generates shorter waves with correspondingly smaller distances between them than the fork of lower pitch.

The distances between the standing waves are inversely proportional to the frequency of the vibrations. With a tuning-fork of 1800 vibrations per second, the total distance between four standing waves is 11 mm.; with one of 900 vibrations, it is 22 mm.

It should also be pointed out that the Ewald Theory was verified experimentally through partial or complete operations on the cochlea of animals.

The merit of the Ewald Theory over that of Helmholtz is obvious, since Ewald was able to verify his contention on an artificial membrane similar to the basilar membrane. The proponents of the resonance hypothesis were unable to offer a similar demonstration. Tone islands and tone gaps are also convincingly explained by Ewald's Theory, since he told of membranes that proved insensible to certain tones as a result of small irregularities in construction. On the other hand, this theory finds some difficulty in explaining clang analysis.

The theories of C. H. Hulst (1895), E. Bonnier (1901), E. ten Kuile (1900), M. Meyer (1896), and G. von Békésy (1928) represent modifications of the sound-pattern theory. All these theories

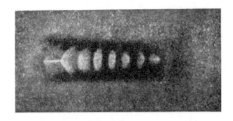

(a) Sound Pattern of the Note a¹ (435 vibr. per sec.)
The membrane is 0.7 mm. wide and 8·0 mm. long.

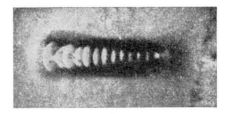

(b) Sound Pattern of the Note e² (625·5 vibr. per sec.)
The same membrane as shown in the above photograph.

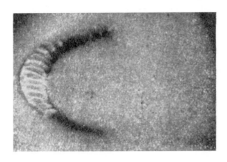

(c) Sound Pattern on a Semi-circular Membrane 0·7 mm. in width.

FIG. 13.—Sound patterns of a¹ and e².

(F. Auerbach : AKUSTIK, 1909.)

focus attention exclusively on the form of the movement of the basilar membrane and the fluid of the cochlea. Among all these sound-pattern theories, the most interesting and best substantiated by experiment is that of von Békésy. He disputes Ewald's contention that (as explained above) a sine-shaped motion of the stapes in the direction of the length of the membrane generates a series of standing waves, the length of which depends on the frequency of the tone vibrations. Instead of standing waves, he assumes a progressive wave-train which he demonstrated on a model ear and also on the human membrane of a dead body. He lays special weight on the genesis of two small vortices which excite the auditory nerves through pressure effect (also mechanical).*

Although the sound-pattern theories undoubtedly have certain merits over the resonance theories, we must nevertheless admit that the modified resonance theories do greater justice to most of the phenomena of physical acoustics, especially the phenomena of clang analysis, resonance, and consonance. True, they are unable to explain all acoustic phenomena. They also do not seem to be altogether satisfactory in the physical sense; but on the score of universality alone, none of the newer theories of hearing can surpass them, or even approach them. If the principles of Helmholtz and Ewald could be combined, it would then be possible to arrive at a satisfactory theory of hearing. Békésy attempts such a combination when he advances the auxiliary hypothesis that the membrane decomposes into single diagonal bands, which then function as detached aural resonators. In this way his theory can explain subjective clang analysis without further postulations.

* See Watt (157) for detailed information on other less important theories of hearing.

III

THE HUMAN VOICE

A. The Function of the Vocal Organ

THE vocal organ in the broadest sense consists of the lungs, the windpipe, the larynx, the mouth, and the nose. It is customary to compare the human vocal organ to a membranous reed-pipe. A more recent tendency is to liken it to a soft or double-reed pipe. The lungs are supposed to play the role of the wind-chest, the windpipe that of the conduct pipe, the larynx that of the reed, and the nose and cavity of the mouth that of the resonator.

In order to produce a vocal sound (spoken or sung), an air current must pass through the closed glottis, which requires pressure from the abdominal and thoracic muscles. The whole process—i.e. the breathing in and the breathing out, the control of the breath in exhaling, the voluntary and involuntary control of the breathing—is extremely important not only in the teaching of singing, but for correct speaking as well. This will be clear if we consider that not only the intensity but also the pitch of the sung note change with increasing breath pressure. It is the singer's task to regulate this rise in pitch automatically. Correct intonation and delicate tonal shading also depend on the breathing technique.

The entire slit of the larynx (the glottis) serves for the passage of the air current. The front part of the larynx, the glottis, and the vocal chords (the real generators of the voice), are the principal factors in voice production. Physiological text-books, particularly the work of H. Gutzmann, " Physiology of the Voice and Speech ", explain the function of the larynx, and the mechanism of speaking and singing.

B. Compass and Registers of the Voice

The human voice comprises the musical range lying between great C and three-line c. Its compass extends from tones of about 65 to 1044 vibrations per second. A bass voice seldom extends beyond contra E. Soprano voices that extend beyond three-line c are by no means rare. The individual voice does not usually have a range of more than two of the four octaves in question, though there are cases where the range is two and a half octaves. The locus of these octaves in the tonal continuum differs with the sexes. Disregarding the intermediate voices, there are two compasses for each sex; namely, one for the soprano and alto, and another for tenor and bass. Mezzo soprano and baritone are intermediate voices.

Fig. 14 gives a clear idea of the compass and general pitch of the human voice. The range of each type of voice is indicated by the musical notes.

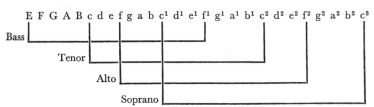

FIG. 14.—Compass and General Pitch of the Human Voice (151).*

Experience teaches that the compass of the voice develops during childhood to reach its maximum at the age of 12 or 13. An investigation of 300 school children ranging from 6 to 15 years, which was supplemented later by a test of children up to 6 years, showed that up to this age the vocal compass increased downwards; from the sixth year on in both directions. Ex. 7 shows the results of this investigation (which was confined to boys' voices) in musical notation. The compass of girls' voices coincides in general with that of boys, except that girls have one whole tone more at the top.

Age: Infant 1–2 3–5 6 7 8 9 10 11 12 13 14 15
Ex. 7.—Compass of Boys' Voices at Different Ages.

Voices differ not only in general pitch but also in their *specific timbre,* which is partly due to the vocal organ and partly to the composition of the individual tone. The compass of the voice

* Waetzmann (155) gives the following compasses for male and female voices: bass from F to e^1 (about 85–320 Hertz); tenor from c to a^1 (128–435 Hertz); alto from f to e^2 (170–640 Hertz); and soprano from c^1 to a^2 (260–853 Hertz). (1 Hertz ≡ 1 c.p.s.)

should not be confused with the *register*. In voices, register has exactly the same meaning as in the organ; that is, it is the quality of the tones or sounds in the same general pitch. The registers are determined by various mechanical principles. Every person can produce sounds in different registers. The registers, the tone quality, can be changed according to the character of the vocal chords and the adjustment of the resonance chamber. All speech-sounds belonging to one register are similar in character, independent of any modifications they may undergo in respect of the character of the clang or the intensity. The registers overlap in a part of the vocal range, so that we can produce the same tones in different registers.

The human voice is generally divided into two principal registers—namely, the *chest voice* (the most important and natural

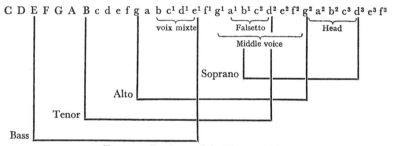

FIG. 15.—Registers of the Human Voice.

register) and the *head voice* (the falsetto or false treble)—between which lies a middle register : the so-called middle voice or voix mixte.

These terms give rise to misapprehensions. In my opinion they were chosen because one distinctly feels the chest resonance in the chest register, and in the head register that of the head. The chest register is characterized by a full round tone, the head or falsetto register, on the other hand, by a tense, sharper, and brighter tone colour. Singing teachers make further distinctions in register, but these are nothing more than the middle register lying between the chest and head registers. As a whole, the chest register is lower than the head register, but the two overlap. Yodelling is a sudden change from one to the other.

A special question that is of greater pedagogical than psychological interest is the accuracy with which the voice can emit a definite note. Tests in this connexion have shown that the difference between the vibration numbers of the heard and the sung note is very small with musical persons, provided they have absolute control of the vocal muscles. It has been shown furthermore that accuracy of production is almost the same at high or low pitch; but that no singer is able to maintain a given pitch for a long time.

C. Analysis of Human Speech-sounds

The nature of the human voice and phonology aroused the interest of physicists, physiologists, and musicians at a very early period. RAMEAU (1688–1764), the celebrated composer and real founder of the theory of harmony, and also D'ALEMBERT (1717–1783), the encyclopædist and eminent physicist, made and communicated the results of investigations on the composition of the human voice.

It is principally the *physical prerequisites to speech-sounds* that are the subject of experimental investigations. It is the analysis of the vowels—that is, their disintegration into partial tones—that primarily interests the investigators. Various methods are used for this. The simplest and most common is the *subjective method*. In this the speech-sound is observed with the ear alone and analyzed. Since the analysis of speech-sounds with the ear alone is rarely successful and, in addition, is very deficient and inexact, one has had to have recourse to resonators for this purpose. Tuning-forks of various pitch, or the familiar conical resonators, can be used for this. The following exemplifies the procedure: Tuning-forks tuned to different notes are passed across the ear one after the other to ascertain which of them vibrates sympathetically with definite spoken or sung vowels (or consonants). The stronger the tone of the tuning-fork, the more exactly it corresponds to one of the partials of the vocable. For instance, if a resonator tuned to $b\flat^1$ is held to the ear and a bass voice is required to sing the vowels in turn on one of the harmonic undertones of $b\flat^1$—that is, on $b\flat$, $e\flat$, or $B\flat$—it will be found that on a full round O the $b\flat$ sounds loudly in the ear; with an intermediate vowel lying between A and O much less so; and practically not at all with U and I. The partial tones of the vowels can be ascertained in this way.

In this connexion, mention should be made of the influence of the cavity of the mouth as a resonator of the vowel-sounds. This funnel-shaped cavity acts as an adjustable resonance chamber, the resonance of which depends on the various positions of the cavity. The notes to which the air mass of this cavity is tuned are ascertained by the aforesaid method. The mouth is brought into the position of the several vowel-sounds and then, by means of a series of resonators, we ascertain for each vowel the note that produces the strongest resonance. These are the *proper tones of the cavity of the mouth* at a definite position.

The *objective method* of vowel analysis does not ask how the vowels are perceived by the auditory apparatus. It investigates instead the effect of the vowels on a special *mechanical apparatus*. The first to determine the vowel-sounds by the objective method was the great Dutch physiologist F. C. DONDERS, who carried out his analysis with the aid of the so-called phono-autograph. This was soon replaced by the Edison phonograph, which enabled a graphic analysis of the vowel-sounds in a simple manner (27).

An optical method introduced by the physiologist L. HERMANN was widely used, which was far superior to all others in precision and elegance. In this procedure a membrane fitted with a small mirror and set into vibration by the speech-sound transmits its vibrations to a photographic plate moved at a uniform speed (54, 55). The newer and more complicated graphic methods of SCRIPTURE, HENSEN, ZWAARDEMAKER, SAMOILOFF, and STRUYCKEN are based either on the phonographic or the photographic method.

In order to give an idea of the vowel-curves, some of the curves communicated by KAISER and STRUYCKEN are shown in Figs. 16 and 17.

In the investigation of the nature of the vocables, two methods have generally been employed: the *analytical* and the *synthetic*. These bear on two questions that are conditioned by the methods themselves. The object of the analytical method is to *decompose the vocables* into their ultimate acoustical constituents; that is, to analyze sung or spoken vowels, voiceless speech-sounds (such as whispered vowels), and finally consonants. The synthetic method aims at a *synthetic artificial* construction of *voiced vowels* from *partials*. The empirical and theoretical controversies, which in spite of numerous model investigations have not yet been settled, turn mainly on these questions.

The controversial aspects became apparent during the first

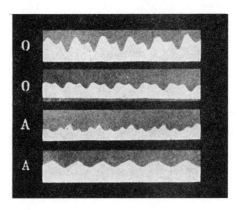

Fig. 16.—Vowel-curves.

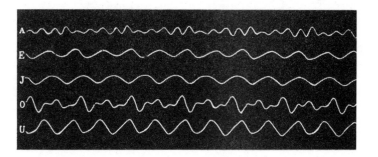

Fig. 17.—Oscillographic Vowel-curves.

stadium of the rigorous scientific investigations. The most important of the opposing concepts derived from HELMHOLTZ and HERMANN (51, 55). Both investigators proceeded from the general assumption that the *vocal colour* of a sound or tone is determined by the presence and predominance of one of the partials of a *certain determinate pitch*. According to this, certain *constant* partials correspond to the fundamental vowels U, O, A, E, I, independent of the fundamental tone on which the vowel is sung or spoken. HERMANN called this characteristic tone a *formant*. The views of Helmholtz and Hermann were in agreement in respect to the general character of vowel formation. Both were firm in their contention that the formant of every vocable is limited to a certain region of resonance in the note series. The views of the two investigators also did not differ greatly regarding the fixed absolute locus of the formants. The table below gives the Helmholtz–Hermann data on the vowel-forms, supplemented by the findings of other scholars.

TABLE 3
Formants of the Vowels
Pitch of formant according to the findings of

Vowel	Helm-holtz	Her-mann	Don-ders	König	Gutz-mann	Bocke	Samoi-loff	Révész
U	f^1	d^1	f^1	$b\flat$	d^1	d^2	f^1	c^1
O	b^1	g^1	d^1	b^1	a^1	c^2	c^2	a^1
A	b^2	g^2	b^1	b^2	a^2	c^3	$g\sharp^2$	a^2-b^2
E	b^3	a^3	$c\sharp^3$	b^3	b^3	f^4	c^4	b^3
I	d^4	e^4	f^3	b^4	d^4	d^4	e^4	e^4

The disagreement in the characteristic notes of one and the same vowel is due on the one hand to the methods employed, and on the other to the fact that the formant alters its position according to whether the vowel is located at the beginning, in the middle, or at the end of the spoken or sung syllable.

The principal difference between the HELMHOLTZ and HERMANN theories is that according to Helmholtz the formant is a harmonic constituent of the vocable; that is, the vibrational number is a round multiple of the vibrational number of the speech sound (Overtone theory). According to Hermann, on the other hand, the formant is not necessarily a harmonic overtone. It can equally well be inharmonic; that is, not a partial of the speech sound (formant theory).

Hermann verified his theory of the importance of the fixed tone —the so-called formant—by an elegant test on the phonograph. If we record vowel-sounds on the phonograph and then, in playing back the record, let the instrument run slower or faster than during the recording, this alters the pitch of the formant by an interval corresponding to the ratio between the two speeds. As soon as we get beyond the pitch and intensity that is characteristic of the vocable in question, the vowel-sound ceases. As a matter of fact, this is true of all vocables, especially when the phonograph is set at slow speed. It will be perceived that the character of the vowel-sound sung into the phonograph changes as the speed is increased or decreased. *I* changes in the direction of *O*, *O* in the direction of *A* or *E*, etc. Many vowels lose their essential character altogether.

More recent research apparently settled the fundamental difference between Helmholtz and Hermann (the controversy over whether the vowels are *harmonic* or *inharmonic* overtones of the speech-sound) by asserting that there is a grain of truth in both concepts (41). According to Gartner, the vocables are rich in harmonic overtones. This would confirm Helmholtz' contention. On the other hand, the cavities of the mouth and pharynx are said to generate inharmonic vibrations that contribute to the vocal character of the speech-sound. These would be the inharmonic formants of Hermann.

This compromise was not especially edifying; but it was tranquillizing, at all events. Then STUMPF came along with his new investigations, put an end to the compromise again, and expressed himself as more in favour of Helmholtz (51). By means of the Interference Method (whereby the partials of every sound can be weakened or entirely eliminated), Stumpf established the following: First of all, the so-called formant is, generally speaking, not one single tone, but a *certain region of resonance* that contributes in large part to the special character of the vowel. In the vowels this formant region has a maximum intensity. According to Stumpf, the only exception to the rule whereby the formant shall consist of a number of component tones is when the second partial (the octave of the fundamental) lies in the formant region, for then—and then only—is this single partial sufficient to form a distinct vowel. Thus if the octave c^2 is added to the speech-sound c^1 in sufficient intensity, we obtain the vowel O.

Stumpf also succeeded in establishing the fact that the formants mount slowly with the pitch of the speech-sound. This means that the locus of the formant is dependent to a certain degree on the locus of the speech-sound. Helmholtz' assumption that the formant has a *salient pitch* is therefore incorrect. The variations are indicated in the following table.

TABLE 4

Formant Region of the Vowel O

Note	Formant region	Variation tendency	
		Note	Formant
C	e^1–g^1	C	e^1
G♭	$g♭^1$–$d♭^2$	↓	↓
c	g^1–c^2		
g♭	$g♭^1$–$d♭^2$	c^1	c^2
c^1	c^2	↓	↓
$g♭^1$	$g♭^2$		
c^2	c^3	c^2	c^3

This table shows not only the gradual rise in pitch of the formants, but something else besides, and this is the third fact we owe to Stumpf. It shows, namely, that the lower formant limit is always the *first harmonic overtone* within the formant region. With the fundamental C it is e^1, not f^1 nor $e♭^1$. With c it is g^1, and not $g♭^1$ nor $a♭^1$. This undoubtedly points to the fact that harmonic overtones contribute to the character of the tone. This gives strong support to Helmholtz' theory. On the other hand, this is no proof that there are no inharmonic overtones in the natural vowels. Stumpf tried to prove this by his *synthetic* test. In artificially produced vowels (especially A and O, the very vowels that were the leading bones of contention in the Hermann Theory) he found no inharmonic constituents—at least, not among the lower partials.

It is therefore an established fact that the formant of a vowel is not one note but a unique sound structure composed of a number of notes having a definite locus in the tone domain; furthermore, that the formant shifts its locus with the changing speech-sound; and finally, that the formants are composed largely of harmonic overtones of the sung or spoken fundamental.

The locus of the formants in the musical continuum may be seen from the following table.

TABLE 5

Formants of the Vowels within the Tone-region from C to c^5

Note	Frequency	Formant	
$f\sharp^7$	23410		Upper limit of audibility
c^6	8277		Upper limit of consonants and whispered vowels
c^5	4138	} I	Upper limit of music
$f\sharp^4$	2926	} E	
c^4	2069		
$f\sharp^3$	1463	} Ä, Ö, Ü	Upper limit of the human voice
c^3	1035	} A	
$f\sharp^2$	732		
c^2	517	} O	
$f\sharp^1$	366		
c^1	259	} U	
$f\sharp$	183		
c	129		Lower limit of consonants
C	65		Lower limit of human voice
C_1	32		Lower limit of music
$F\sharp_3$	11		Lower limit of audibility

Stumpf's conclusions shattered the *octave theory of the vowels*, which was first promulgated by the French investigator R. KOENIG (66) and later by W. KOEHLER (65). Both scholars claimed that certain characteristic tones—the so-called formants of the principal vowels U O A E I—bear an octave relation one to another. It was even Koehler's opinion that pure c tones (free of upper partials) could be heard distinctly as vowels, an opinion that I was unable to substantiate, in spite of employing the same method.

The extensity of the formant region, as established by Stumpf's findings, clearly shows the untenability of the octave theory for each vowel (see Table 6).

The octave theory is therefore inconsistent with recent experimental findings. I have also failed to substantiate Koenig's and Koehler's claims, in spite of repeated tests with a number of experimental musical subjects. Furthermore, none of the older research scholars were able to verify an octave relation, and even less a predominance of the c tones.

There is only one valid point in Koehler's vowel theory, and that is that vowel colours seem to have belonged originally to several simple tones without overtones, and that these consequently could be viewed as inherent properties of these tones. The assertion, however, that the vowel colours of the simple tones represent the primary vowels and that the empirical vowel character of the sounds could be traced to them is altogether untenable.

We will not go into the question of the artificial production of the vowel, since it is of purely theoretical importance. As is known, the problem of the mechanical production of the vowels aroused interest long before the problem of scientific vowel formation. Mention should be made of the artificial speech machines of the elder KEMPELEN which caused a great sensation in their day; in addition, the little mechanisms inside talking dolls.

TABLE 6

Formant Region According to Stumpf

Vowels	Formants		Formant region	
			Total compass of the formants for the fundamentals C–g♭¹	Central region of the formants G♭–g♭ common to the fundamentals
	Koenig	Koehler		
U*	b	c¹	—	—
O	b¹	c²	e¹–g♭²	g¹–c²
A	b²	c³	c²–g♭³	g♭²–d³
OE			f³–e⁴	b♭³–d⁴
AE			b♭³–a♭⁴	d♭⁴–e♭⁴
UE			g♭³–a♭⁴	d♭⁴–e♭⁴
E	b³	c⁴	g♭³–a♭⁴	d⁴–f⁴
I	b⁴	c⁵	c⁴–a♭⁴	e⁴–g⁴

* The alleged formant for E (c¹) has not been verified; that for O (c²) and for A (c³) has been verified but those for E (c⁴) and for I (c⁵) were not found as stated. According to the above table, the " octave theory " would only be valid for O and A (g♭²–g♭³).

The fact that it has been possible to reproduce certain vowels with the aid of the formants is no longer surprising. The artificial reproduction of AO and U has been especially successful. Even with an ordinary penny whistle (squawker) which operates by blowing up a rubber balloon, we can produce vowels very distinctly by giving the cavity of the mouth the position of the desired vowel.

In connexion with the question of artificial vocables, Helmholtz told of a pretty experiment made on a piano. If the dampers are raised by pressing down the forte pedal and a vowel is spoken against the strings, it will re-echo from the inside. " It sounded to me (said Donders) as though a choir of voices singing the given vowel rose mysteriously from the depths."

PART II

FUNDAMENTAL PROBLEMS OF THE PSYCHOLOGY OF SOUND

IV

BASIC ELEMENTS OF MUSICAL TONE

A. The Three Fundamental Characteristics

In the discussion of musical acoustics, we have already drawn attention to three characteristics of musical sounds; namely, *pitch, quality, and intensity*. Of the three, pitch is the most important physically and musically. Intensity is not to be considered a specific characteristic of musical sounds, since variations in intensity are found in all domains of sensory perception. They are encountered in visual, tactile, gustatory, and olfactory sensations as well as in tone sensations. As for quality, this is, of course, a property that is found *only* in tone sensations. But it is not a distinguishing attribute in the sense of characterizing the tones within the musical continuum as units of the tone system. It lends the musical sounds a peculiar character (colour), but it has nothing to do with their reciprocal relations.

Therefore the only specific tone characteristic of elementary formative importance is *pitch*. The continuous alteration of the notes within the tone-realm as an ascending sequence from the lowest to the highest level of pitch, and the diversity of keys, intervals, and chords, are essentially traceable to this one-tone characteristic (one-component theory). This concept is also taught in most theoretical works on music, in psychological handbooks and text-books on music and æsthetics. This same view is likewise held by acousticians for the simple reason that the multiplicity of notes in the tone domain is producible through one physical variable—i.e. through the alteration of the vibratory ratios—which, in turn, corresponds with the alteration in pitch. This explains why tonal diversity is graphically represented by a *straight line*, the terminals of which denote the upper and lower thresholds of audibility, while the other notes are ranged between the terminal points according to pitch. This straight line expresses the continuity of the tone series; i.e. the tone series comprising all perceptible notes or the notes between 16 and 16,000 vibr. per sec.—in other words, the musical tone or note series.

Now comes the question: can we exhaustively set forth and

describe the character of the notes within the musical tone system through the aforesaid one tonal characteristic?

B. PITCH AND TONE QUALITY

If we visualize the tone series ascending or descending, we perceive first of all the phenomenon of " rising " or " falling "—a phenomenon to be regarded as the alteration of the pitch characteristic in a constant direction.

The phenomenon of rising and falling is all the more striking, the more rapidly the individual notes succeed one another. It is especially noticeable in a rapid scale passage, and even more so in a rapid succession of notes flowing constantly one into the other (glissando). The phenomenon has claimed more attention than any other, and therefore is the only phenomenon of tonal diversity that has been treated theoretically to date.

In general, it was felt that the most salient property of the tone series had been exactly and completely characterized through this reference to the phenomenon of rising and falling (which parallels the increase or decrease in the vibration rate). Accordingly, one proceeded from the point of view that every step of the tone series—e.g. every individual note therein—was determinable through one single quantity; namely, through the physical pitch. The conviction that the tone series can be unequivocally characterized by a continuous straight-line progression of a single property formed the basis of departure for physical and musical acoustics.

Plausible as this point of view may be, it is—as I attempted to demonstrate—thoroughly *inadequate from the phenomenological as well as from the musical angle*. If we start out from a given note—from c, let us say—and then gradually increase the vibration number, we find that the consecutive tone sensations (c, c♯, d, d♯, e, etc.) differ more and more from the prime tone c, till we come —imperceptibly, as it were—to a note that bears a unique resemblance to the prime tone. This note is called the *octave*. The octave note c^1 therefore bears a *double relation* to the prime tone c. In one respect, of all the notes within the span of the octave, it is the one most dissimilar to the prime tone, since it is the farthest from it in point of *distance*. In another respect, however, it is the note most *similar* to the prime tone, since of all the notes through which we passed, it is the one most similar to it in *quality*. If we continue in the same manner, after passing dissimilar notes we again come to a c (c^2), which, like c^1, bears a striking resemblance to the prime tone c. This note is the *double octave*. In this way we come successively to the various c notes; namely, to c^3, c^4, etc., ascending, and to C, C_1, and C_2 descending. These notes differ more and more in pitch and distance from the prime tone c, but they are similar to it pheno- menologically; that is, in " quality ". In playing the tone series, we find not only a progressive *rise* in pitch, but at the same time a certain *periodicity*, in that similar sensations recur in the octave notes. This phenomenon is apprehended with special clarity if we play a series of major thirds, minor thirds, whole, or semitones throughout several octaves. It is advisable here to introduce a new terminology for later use. We will call two notes that differ from one another by the span of one or more octaves *equivalent notes*.

The similarity of the octave notes has been recognized from the earliest times, as attested by the fact that they all bear the same names. This is shown by mediæval musical nomenclature. In Byzantine musical notation the octave designated A was followed by the note B. The same was true in the tenth century, when the Greek alphabet was replaced by Latin letters. The seven notes of the diatonic scale were designated by the first seven letters of the alphabet. After A, B, C, D, E, F, and G, one arrived again at A.* We find the same with the Chinese and ancient Indians. The old Indian notation agreed in principle with our modern notation. Here the periodically recurring tone qualities were also given the same names and symbols, for instance, not only the upper octave of d♭, but also the lower octave was called SA,

---

* " Notae autem in monochordo hae sunt. In primis ponatur Γ graecum a moder- nis adiunctum. Sequuntur septem alphabeti litterae graves, ideoque maioribus litteris insignitae hoc modo. A B C D E F G. Post has hae eaedem septem litterae acutae repetuntur, sed minoribus litteris describuntur, in quibus tamen inter a. & ♮ aliam b. ponimus, quam rotundam facimus; alteram vero quadravimus. Ita a. b. ♮. c. d. e. f. g. Addimus his eisdem litteris, sed variis figuris tetrachordum a b ♮ c d superacutarum, in quo b. similiter duplicamus, ita a b ♮ c d. Hae litterae a multis dicuntur superfluae; nos autem maluimus abundare, quam deficere. Fiunt itaque a b ♮ c d simul omnes XXI. hoc modo Γ A B C D E F G. a b ♮. c d e f g. a b ♮ c d. Quarum dispositio cum a doctoribus aut fiuisset tacita, aut nimia obscuritate perplexa, adest nunc etiam pueris breviter ac plenissime explicata." GUIDO VON AREZZO, *Micrologus* (c. 1000). M. Gerbert's *Scriptores ecclesiastici de musica sacra potissimum*, St. Blasien 1784.

while the upper pitches were differentiated by various distinguishing symbols (H̊ H̥).

In the phenomenological analysis of the tone series we have
found that the latter can be conceived in two ways: first, as a
linear series of sensations, the course of which is adequately
characterized by the phenomenon " ascending—descending ",
and second, as a series repeating itself, the course of which is
characterized by a definite periodicity, a cyclical repetition. If
anyone proceeds to analyze the tone sensations without bias, he
cannot fail to perceive this *basic phenomenon of the series of tone
sensations* (106).

The analysis of the phenomenological structure of the tone
series leads us, therefore, to the indisputable fact that here we have
to do with two fundamentally distinguishable characteristics,
from the combination of which the musical tone series originates,
as it were. One characteristic is that which changes with the
vibration number, apprehensible phenomenologically through
the rising or falling. This fundamental characteristic we call
the *musical pitch*. The second characteristic recurs from octave
to octave—in other words, with the doubling of the vibration
number—and this we call the *musical quality* of the tone sensation.
Consequently that in which the octave notes differ one from
another is the pitch. That in which they are similar is the
quality of the tone sensation.

The *tone qualities* of the chromatic and other scales form a
recurrent series, all the components of which are contained within
a single octave. The pitch, however, represents a linear series in
a one-way direction, which, though theoretically infinite, does
not actually extend beyond the region of the seven-line octave.
According to this concept, c^1 and c^2, for example, are equivalent
notes, similar in quality but dissimilar in pitch; while c^1 and g^1
represent different notes, different not only in pitch but likewise
in quality. As a result of the two fundamental characteristics,
two notes always bear a double relation to each other: the one
rests on a *similarity in quality*—equivalence—and the other on a
quantitative tonal distance. In the qualitative respect, therefore,
the tenth c^1–e^2 is similar to the third c^1–e^1, while it is dissimilar
to the twelfth c^1–g^2, or the fourth extended an octave c^1–f^2.

In accordance with the aforesaid exposition, every note in the
musical tone system can be unequivocally defined psychologically

through two components: through its quality (c, d, e, etc.) and through its general pitch (one-line octave, small octave, etc.).* Consequently the designation " a " embraces all " a " notes of the tone system, while " a^1 " or " a^2 " indicates the general pitch (locus) of the " a " tone in the tone system.

C. The Two-component Theory

An analysis of the note series induced us to replace the *One-component Theory* (which traces the diversity of our sound perceptions to the alteration of a single constantly changing property— the pitch) with the *Two-component Theory*, which ascribes *two fundamental musical properties* to our sound perceptions.

The *fact of the octave* forms the core of the Two-component Theory, and this theory alone can explain it in an altogether satisfactory manner. Before the promulgation of my Two-component Theory (1912) there were two diametrically opposite concepts of the octave notes, since the double relation of the notes was ignored. There were some theorists who found similarities in the octave notes (Rameau, Brentano), and there were others again who spoke of dissimilarities (Herbart, Sully, Stumpf).

Helmholtz was the first to make a thorough investigation of octave notes and seek an adequate ground for their similarity. According to him, the similarity of the octaves to the prime is attributable to the fact that the octave contains no overtones that are not present in the generator. For example, there are actually no overtones to speak of in the note " c " which are not already found in its lower octave C.

The partials of the notes " C " and " c " are as follows:

$$C \quad c \quad g \quad c^1 \quad e^1 \quad g^1 \quad b\flat^1 \quad c^2 \quad d^2 \quad e^2 \quad f\sharp^2 \quad g^2 \quad a\flat^2 \quad b\flat^2 \quad b^2 \quad c^3$$
$$c \quad\quad\quad c^1 \quad\quad g^1 \quad\quad\quad c^2 \quad\quad e^2 \quad\quad g^2 \quad\quad b\flat^2 \quad\quad c^3$$

According to Helmholtz, it is therefore quite natural that there should be a great resemblance between C and c. The Helmholtz explanation for the similarity of the octaves was accepted without further discussion, and formed one of the basic pillars of musical acoustics (51). But if we examine the logical conclusions of the Helmholtz concept, its untenability is apparent.

---

* Here pitch signifies the rising characteristic (upward trend) in contra-distinction to absolute pitch, which has reference to the vibration frequency. See the comments of H. J. Watt (157) who translated my terms as " pitch-quality " and " octave quality ".

1. If Helmholtz were correct in his deductions, then one should expect to find *no similarity whatever* between widely dispersed octaves (as C and c^3, for example), since these two notes do not have one single partial in common. The octave note c^3 itself is the 16th upper partial of C—that is, an inaudible overtone— and yet, *in spite of all this*, there is the same similarity between C and c^3 as between C and c.

2. Furthermore, the twelfth g should show a greater similarity

Frequency   64 128 192 256 320 384 448 512 576 640 704 768 832 896 960 1024(c^3)

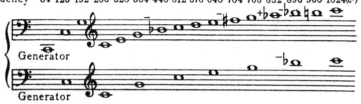

Ex. 8.—Partial Tones of C (64 vibr. per sec.) and c (128 vibr. per sec.).

to the fundamental C than a remote octave, since the twelfth has more partials in common with the fundamental than, for instance, the three-line c.

Partial tones of the fundamental C: C c g c^1 e^1 g^1 bb^1 c^2 d^2 ($f\sharp^2$) g^2 (ab^2) bb^2 b^2 c^3
Partial tones of the twelfth g: g g^1 d^2 g^2 b^2
Partial tones of the octave c^3: c^3 c^4

3. Finally, if the Helmholtz contention were correct, the octave notes C and c should exhibit no similarity if all the overtones were eliminated from these sounds by a reliable physical method. For in this case c would not appear as an overtone in C, since the latter has no overtones whatever. My acoustical investigations have shown, however, that *even under these conditions the similarity between the octave notes is as marked as ever* (106).

It follows from these observations that the similarity of the octave notes is not rooted in the common overtones, but is a primary property of the octave phenomena itself. The octave theory therefore is: *the essential similarity of the octave notes rests on the similarity of their qualities.* Through the differentiation of the two components, through the musical pitch and the tone quality, the phenomenon of the octave is strictly and conclusively circumscribed.

Carl Stumpf's attempt to trace the similarity between the

octaves and the primary tone, or fundamental, to the high degree of fusion appertaining to coincident tones an octave apart must be viewed as a failure (151). The fusion phenomena (the tendency of two notes to blend into one) are only found in two notes sounded simultaneously—that is, in chords of two or more notes—whereas we can only actually speak of octave similarity in notes sounded successively. The octave similarity does not rest on *fusion* but, on the contrary, the fusion of the octave notes rests on their *phenomenological similarity*.

The Two-component Theory gains very greatly in persuasive power through its having been possible to deduce proof that the two fundamental characteristics not only perform different acoustical-musical functions, but in certain circumstances are even *separable in fact*. The truth of the matter is that we not only find similar tone qualities combined with different pitches (as is the case, for example, with the octave notes c^1, c^2, c^3), but pitches are also occasionally combined with different tone qualities. In a few pathological cases we established the fact that within a definite sector of the note series one and the same tone quality could occur at different pitches (see pp. 72 and 216). Furthermore, notes of fairly salient pitch, but without any quality, could be apprehended. This is the case, for example, with many drum notes, in which we clearly perceive a difference in pitch without, however, being able to establish any quality. Notes in the upper part of the audible tone domain also manifest differences in pitch without the factor of quality (for example, the notes of high organ pipes).

The phenomenon of the octave—that is, the recurrence of the primary tone at another pitch level—is the *Alpha and Omega of the musical system and the musical ear*. The octave experience represents the fundamental fact of musical acoustics, and is of basic importance for every acoustical-musical theory. The octave holds an exceptional position among all the tone relations. It proves that in the phenomenological note series a change can be observed that obeys another law than musical pitch. This fact cannot be gainsaid either through terminological arguments or through the attempt to trace the octave to simple vibratory ratios. Octave similarity also cannot be explained by the common overtones or by the especially full fusion of the octave notes. Even Stumpf, who attempted the latter, abandoned it later (influenced by my arguments) in favour of the Two-component Theory.

The similarity of the octave notes is a *fundamental acoustical-musical phenomenon* that strikes us forcibly both in complex sounds and in simple tones. This direct impression of octave similarity is unique in its category. Of course we hear at times of a similarity in the fifths also, since these notes are easier to confuse with octave notes than the notes of other intervals. A certain tone relation is undoubtedly at the roots of this alleged similarity. We do not yet know the nature of it. But at all events it differs from that of octave notes.

It is true that the repetitive impression produced by a musical figure played on the octave provides no conclusive proof of the qualitative similarity of the octaves. This repetitive impression

Ex. 9.—Repetitive Impression with Transposed Octave and Fifth.

is due chiefly to the *constancy of the melody*. The melody will also give a repetitive impression if the passage begins on the fifth or the sixth.

But the decisive fact is that among all transpositions there is only one that gives the impression of a *perfect image* of the original melody so that we are often not even conscious of the octave transposition. These impressions of recurrences of likeness connected with octave transposition find their natural explanation in the quality common to all notes in octave relationship.

Therefore the importance of the Two-component Theory for the octave problem lies not only in the recognition, but also in the interpretation, of the similarity of octaves.

But the importance of the Two-component Theory is not limited to the analysis of the tone sensations and the musical note series. It has proved to be an *explanatory principle* of undreamed-of scope. On it is based a *new theory of intervals* with the concepts of " distance " and " interval " (p. 70), the discovery of a hitherto unknown type of *absolute pitch* (p. 100), and in addition the explanation of several phenomenological forms of *amusia* and abnormal hearing (p. 213). The fact that the Two-component Theory led to the discovery of new and hitherto unknown phenomena that are of especial significance for the system of sensory perception also speaks for its scientific value. Among other things it has been possible by means of this theory to prove the occurrence of a mixture of tonal qualities (sound mixture) similar to the mixture of visual qualities (colour mixture), which removed what was formerly one of the greatest fundamental variances between the domains of optics and acoustics and gave one uniform interpretation to the phenomenon of mixture.

The division of pitch into two properties, i.e. into a complexity-multiplicity (height) characterized by a one-way direction (rising aspect); and a cyclical series (musical quality)—a factual apprehension which led to my formulation of the Two-component Theory—is now generally considered a *fundamental phenomenon* of the psychology of sound. This is fully attested by psychological text-books (Fröbes, Höfler), and special works by Watt (156, 157), Ogden (92), Wellek (158), Nadel (87), Feuchtwanger (49), Bachem (4), Straub, etc. This interpretation, which represents a radical break with the concept of pitch that was current for hundreds of years, was adopted after some hesitation by the most eminent musical theorists and psychologists. I will here cite only two of these: H. Riemann and Carl Stumpf. In the beginning, Riemann took a negatory attitude towards my views (126). Later on, however, he retracted his attacks (127) and came out openly in support of my theory. Stumpf also abandoned his previous point of view in favour of mine (148).

The same attitude was manifested by numerous other musico-logists and theorists who not only adopted my views but also arrived at new conceptual apprehensions through their agency. The fertility of my theory has therefore been established beyond a doubt. Furthermore, the fact has been proved by the recent investigations of Maecklenburg (82), Nef (88), and Bachem (4), and above all by the evidence of a binaural qualitative mixture which I could not have discovered without my Two-component Theory (106).

In view of all this, I was surprised to see the well-known musical historian, JACQUES HANDSCHIN, adopting in his recent work *Toncharakter* (1948)—after a preliminary discussion of my views

—the old, wholly outmoded standpoint of the one-dimensional multiplicity of the tonal series, without noting that in so doing he threatened to nullify all the progress that has hitherto been so arduously achieved in the psychology of sound. Since he still could not disregard recent research altogether, he felt that he had found the right solution by substituting another conceptual term for " tonal quality ". He thus arrived at the concept " tonal character ". On closer investigation it is found that this " tonal character " is nothing else than a new term for the Gestalt modalities of the different pitch relations; in other words, for the interval experience. Albersheim, who in a detailed study on the subject of tone and clang properties subjects existing theories (especially the Two-component Theory) to a critical review (3), also substitutes " tonal character " for " tonal quality "; that is, pitch relation for tone property.

Handschin maintains that notes have no quality in themselves. They only have inter-relational characteristics with other notes. Notes, in his opinion, are just as dissimilar in character as the pitch they occupy in an ascending or descending series of fifths. (His whole theory is based on our European scale system, without regard to the numerous other systems.) For instance, if we start with the note c (as centre of tonal gravity) and proceed upward in a series of perfect fifths, we come to g. According to Handschin the note g is most similar to the note c *in character*; i.e. it manifests less character differences than other notes. The next greatest difference in character is manifested by the major second d (the second fifth above c), while the third fifth above c—that is, a—manifests a still greater difference, and so on. In other words, the order of occurrence in the cycle of fifths determines the tonal similarity or relationship, an assertion that cannot be verified in fact. But what is the situation, then, in other musical systems where the notes of the scales are not based on a progression of fifths? That Handschin's " tonal character " has nothing to do with the properties of our sensations of tone is obvious. Tonal character is a matter of successive intervals; i.e. of intervallic, not tonal quality. The theory of tonal character, as far as I can see, has led to no new knowledge. Here it is merely a question of the introduction of a new terminology (the word itself has often been employed) to designate the variety of the interval experience. It is apparent on the face of it that Handschin's

" tonal character " is unable to explain any of the phenomena (octave similarity, types of absolute ear, pure pitch series, etc.), as is possible with the Two-component Theory. His criticism of the investigations of pathological cases, whereby I was able to verify the actual separableness of quality and pitch, is erroneous. Anyone who has never worked experimentally, and therefore can have no correct conception of the circumstances that form the basis for testing and interpreting pathological phenomena, must take his exceptions with great reserve and corresponding qualifications. When it comes to a clinical investigation of aural sensations affected by pathological processes, a musical historian is no more competent than a literary historian in respect to aphasic research.

D. Some Historical Data on the Octave

The octave problem in itself is as old as the theory of music. More than 2000 years ago, in fact, eminent Greek thinkers tried to solve it. So long as it was impossible to emancipate oneself from the physical ratios on which the octave was based (length of string, vibration number, etc.); so long as one went back to given physical conditions as basis of departure and ascribed only secondary importance to the purely psychological (phenomenological) approach, the way to the solution of the problem was blocked. The Pythagoreans and the Platonists, through their mathematical speculations, injected the mathematico-physical standpoint into music theory, a point of view that has not yet been wholly abandoned even in our time. The phenomenon of the octave, which forces us to a dualistic conception, presented no difficulty for the mathematical theorists, since they thought they had adequately explained this strange phenomenon through reference to the simplest numerical ratio of the octave to the primary (2 : 1). Although Aristotle and his pupil, Aristoxenus of Tarentum, in particular, emphasized the qualitative, as opposed to the quantitative, point of view of the Platonists, the mathematico-physical tendency of the " canons " still dominated the entire music theory of antiquity and the Middle Ages. It did not lose its great authority even later on. Since Plato had become an absolute scientific authority in the theory of music, and since the physical sciences naturally embraced the " quantitative conception of the world ", it became practically impossible to continue to work along Aristotelian lines (40). The first to find himself back again on the right road was Franz Brentano, who in his lectures, as was shown later, laid the germ of a two-component theory. Brentano's idea failed to carry conviction because neither he nor others had tested its validity owing to a lack of empirical foundation. Brentano's hypothesis was only verified when I succeeded in drawing up the Two-component Theory through an entirely different approach, and applying it to various acoustical problems.

It should also be mentioned that every theorist who supported the assumption of the identity of the octave notes was still far from championing the dualistic theory. By " identity " they meant nothing more than the especially great and striking similarity of the octave notes. Meanwhile their assertion that the octave notes were identical was absolutely wrong, because the octave notes are by no means identical notes. They are only identical *in one direction*, and the whole problem tapers down to the question in *what* direction they are identical. Therefore M. Hauptmann (50), Th. Lipps, and H. Riemann cannot be viewed as precursors of the dualistic theory, though they more or less distinctly affirmed the similarity, identity, uniformity, of the octave notes. Riemann, through the very fact of his polemics against me, showed how far removed he was from the dualistic concept to which he became converted later, on the strength of my discussions (126).

In order to describe exhaustively the nature of the octave notes, I should like to add that the octave differs from all other intervals not only in being similar to the prime in respect to quality, but also because—of all musical intervals—it exhibits the highest grade of consonance. The consonance of the octave is of a special nature, unique in music. In the theory of consonance it is customary to rank the octave with the fifth as the highest degree of fusion, and this with more or less justice. Nevertheless, if we compare without prejudice the ordinary intervals in our music, and in so doing do not allow ourselves to be influenced by the physical ratios, we will find that the consonance of the octaves is of an entirely different character from that of the other consonant two note clangs.*

* E. Kurth (73) also considers that the octave phenomenon is the cardinal point of the theory of consonance, and of the greatest importance for harmony. In the octave sensation (he says) dualism takes a peculiar form because *qua* dualism it manifests the maximum consonance and yet approximates so closely to the prime that

E. Graphic Representation of the Two-component Theory

If the note series is characterized not by one but by the synthesis of two characteristics, one of which progresses continuously and in a one-way direction (pitch) and the other continuously and periodically (quality), then we must choose a three-dimensional scheme to give a graphic representation of the tone series. The latter can best be plotted by means of a spiral line, the axis of which is conceived as vertical (Fig. 18). The continuity of direction of the pitch series is expressed by a continuous line from the starting point; the periodicity of the quality series by the dots corresponding to notes of similar designation (e.g. octaves) which lie on the spiral line vertically one above the other.

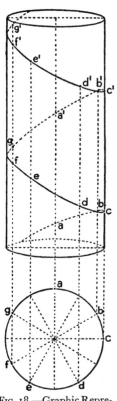

If we distribute the notes on the spiral line in such manner that each revolution of this line represents an octave, then all c's (C_2, C_1, C, c, c^1, c^2, c^3, etc.) lie one above the other on a vertical line, as do also all the d's, e's, etc. In one distinct respect the octave, compared with all intermediate notes, is farthest removed from the prime (distance prime-octave measured on the spiral line). In another respect, however, it is closest to the prime (distance prime-octave measured on the vertical connecting line).*

Fig. 18.—Graphic Representation of the Two-component Theory.

---

it can just as well be characterized as unison. He points out further that the octave, which corresponds physically to the simplest numerical ratio, is " psychologically one of the greatest puzzles ". This puzzle has been solved by my Two-component Theory, a fact that Kurth admits without reservations.

* G. Albersheim (3) discussed and expanded the Two-component Theory in detail. In his account of the genesis and development of the Theory, this author—unjustly and with malice aforethought—attributed it to Hornbostel, who ten years after the publication of my work, and inspired and influenced by my ideas and personal discussions, formulated my concept virtually unchanged (3, 110).

F. THE ALLEGED EXTENSITY OF SOUND PERCEPTIONS

At this point I should like to call attention to a psychological question that is very closely related to the term " pitch ".

There are psychologists who understand the term " pitch " as implying the *extensity* of our sound perceptions. The fact that we are accustomed to localize low notes *at the bottom* and high notes *at the top*, and that furthermore the various tongues use the same erroneous spatial concepts to characterize differences in pitch, seems to speak for the original spatial nature of the impressions of height and depth in the musical continuum. However, if we compare the tone sensations with the actual spatial impressions (optical and tactual), we soon find that there is not the slightest phenomenological similarity between the spatial and the acoustical concepts of " height " and " distance ", let alone ideational identity. The fact that the various tongues use spatial expressions (high and low) for the rising and falling aspects may well be interesting from a linguistic-psychological point of view. But one cannot deduce from this the extensity of the tone sensations.* There is no doubt that here one has to do, not with spatial relations, but simply with analogies, exactly as with the concepts tone " colour " and colour " tone ". Tone colour has as little to do with colour as tone " height " (Tonhöhe, i.e. pitch) has to do with height in its actual sense.

But now the question arises : what impelled man to describe and designate an ascending scale or glissando as an upward movement? One might infer from this that the origin of the expressions " high " and " low " had something to do with the dependence of the position of the larynx on the pitch of the sound. Times out of number experience has shown us that the larynx is lowered in the lower speech-sounds while it rises in the higher ones. However, whether the movement of the larynx had anything to do with the choice of the terms, and if so, to what extent, cannot be determined. But it seems to me that one might offer a more convincing explanation for the choice of designation.

If we sing a low note, we feel a distinct vibration in the region of the chest (chest resonance) ; that is, comparatively *low down*. However, if we sing a high note, we localize it *high up*, in the head (head resonance) as a result of the vibrations in the body. The

* See G. Révész, " Gibt es einen Hörraum ? " *Acta Psychologica*, III, 1937.

same phenomenon can be apprehended in hearing notes. The vibrational sensations engendered by the bass viols and the deeper notes of the cellos (if one is in the proximity of these instruments) are usually felt in the middle part of the chest. If the bass viols make a sudden entrance in a string orchestra, it is as though the chain of vibrations immediately dropped lower in the body. The notes of the drum, trombone, and bassoon, as well as the bass voice and the deeper registers of the alto voice, are also located in the chest. High drum-notes are located higher, while the notes of the violin and flute and the upper notes of the human voice generate vibrations in the head.

This might lead us to trace the impressions " high " and " low " to the localized vibrational sensations in the body. If we concede this hypothesis some measure of plausibility, then high and low would refer to spatial conditions; not to the extensity of the notes but to certain regions of the body. However, if we adopt the view that in the choice of the terms high and low the vibrational sensations played no role, we must consider them purely analogous. Hornbostel and Koehler were of the opinion that the tone attribute associated with the rising sensation referred to tone brightness instead of height. Any discussion as to which term is the more apt is futile in my opinion, since in point of fact notes are neither high nor low, bright nor dark.

Since the concept " pitch " is now definitely established and has to do with a characteristic physical experience, it is preferable to " brightness ", quite apart from the fact that " bright " and " dark " already serve to describe the tone colour (quality). I myself have only one objection to make to the word " pitch ", and that is that it is also a physical concept relating to the note as a whole. If we designate the latter as *absolute pitch* and differentiate therefrom the *musical pitch* as a distinct characteristic of the tone sensation, any misunderstanding should be obviated.

In addition, I would only state here that other spatial terms which are also employed in musical acoustics, æsthetics, style, and form to indicate the progression of parts (such as interval, general pitch, distance, melodic line, contrary as well as parallel and lateral motion) can also only serve as analogies to the spatial perceptions.*

* With respect to the kinetic character of the tone content (volume, pressure, force, tension, etc.) which forms a bridge between the sensory perceptions and the æsthetic effects, see the expositions of E. Kurth (73), who, moreover, shares my point of view regarding the analogous significance of the aforesaid musical terms.

V

THEORY OF INTERVALS

In the chapter on physical acoustics we pointed out that the striving for unrestricted freedom of modulation led musical practice to abandon the Pythagorean musical system for that based on equal temperament. The twelve notes of the equal-temperament chromatic scale within the limits of an octave (with reference to a starting note) yield all the intervals used in our music. The intervals that extend *beyond* an octave are to be considered equivalent intervals (i.e. intervals expanded one or more octaves and apprehended as such).

We find intervals in two forms; namely, as a *successive* (melodic) and a *simultaneous* (harmonic) impression of two sources of sound. By *intervals* in the narrow sense of the word we will understand those tone patterns formed by two notes sounded *in succession* (known in music as broken, or melodic, intervals). The tone pattern resulting from the *simultaneous occurrence* of two notes we will call a *two-note clang* (bichord or harmonic interval), and that of more than two notes, a chord.*

For the acoustic theories such as those of Helmholtz, Ewald, and Stumpf, the interval presents *no* new problems. If, for instance, we view the note series as the alteration of *one* variant, as that of pitch (and here the older concepts were all in complete agreement), then the various intervals can be clearly defined simply by the size of the tone step, by the so-called *tonal distance*. In this point of view, the difference between a third and a fourth consists merely in the fact that the third involves a smaller distance (or pitch interval) than the fourth. The type or specific character of the interval impression is due to the differences in tonal distances.

This explanation, at first sight, seems convincing. But it fails to take into account the phenomenon of the *equivalence of the notes*.

---

* A successive interval and a clang (two-note clang, chord) must be strictly differentiated one from the other, since they represent phenomenally different tone patterns. For example, the fact that the major third and its reflex, the minor sixth, can be easily confused as two-note clangs shows that there is a difference between the impression of a third sounded successively and one sounded simultaneously. For this is not true of a broken third and minor sixth. Furthermore, clangs manifest the phenomena of consonance and fusion, which are wholly lacking in broken intervals.

The equivalence of the notes results in a corresponding equivalence of intervals. From the equivalence of the notes c–c¹ and d–d¹ there results an equivalence of the *intervals* c–d and c–d¹ (i.e. of the major second and the ninth). Similarly, the octave or double octave and the prime are equivalent. As a result, *every type of interval* is represented within the span of a single octave, and we designate them by the customary terms: prime, second, third, fourth, etc. The variety of these intervals is due to the diversity of their *intervallic quality*. It follows from this that the intervallic qualities, like the tone qualities, are all present within the span of an octave. We find them again in the expanded intervals. Thus ninths and tenths coincide in intervallic quality with seconds and thirds; but they differ from the latter in tonal distance. The importance of equivalence for the interval impression lies in the fact that the musical person finds less difference between equivalent intervals or two-note clangs. Thus the interval c–e seems to differ far less from the interval c–e¹ than from the interval c–g. Harmonically it is in fact the same, though in the first the tonal distance is far greater than in the second. If the size of the distance between two notes were the sole determining factor, then it would be impossible to understand how all intervallic qualities can be found within the limits of *one octave* and why in greater distances (e.g. over an octave) we find no new intervallic qualities, either melodically or harmonically. If only the tonal distance played a constructive role in the formation of intervals, then the interval impressions would not recur from octave to octave.

These very evident difficulties can, in my opinion, be easily solved by the Two-component Theory.

According to the Two-component Theory, the concrete note series, as we already saw, has two aspects, which we represented graphically on page 67 through a spiral line. The first aspect is the *pitch* which characterizes the notes with reference to their ordinal arrangement in the pitch scale. In the diagram this property is represented by the geometric height of the corresponding point on the spiral line. In the concrete note series, it is true, we do not find a series of pure pitches, since there pitch and tone quality are inseparably fused. However, we can get an idea of a fairly pure pitch scale in a glissando and also in very high notes where it is impossible for us to say what the interval ratio is between the given notes. But so much we can still distinctly hear, and that is that one note sounds higher and the other lower. The pure pitch scale has a one-directional character, and can therefore be graphically represented by a straight line. In the diagram it can be represented by a vertical line, e.g. by the axis of the cylinder (Fig. 19).

For a fictitious observer who only perceives pitch, the note series would be without tone quality, just as for the colour-blind the colour spectrum merely shows differences in brightness without differences in colour.

This hypothetical case was realized to some extent in a very

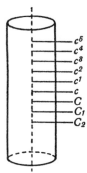

FIG. 19.—Graphic Representation of the Pure Pitch Series.

musical person who suffered from acute paracusis (abnormal hearing).* It was found that there was one sector of the note series in which the pitches were normal, but the notes lost their quality—i.e. were reduced to a single quality, namely to g♯. An analogous case would be that of a colour-blind person for whom a sector of the colour spectrum—e.g. that part with the intermediate hues of yellow and green—would seem like one solid colour; yellow, for example. Our patient stated that he did not hear the notes between g♯² and d³ qualitatively as a, b♭, b, c, c♯ and d, but that he heard them all as g♯.

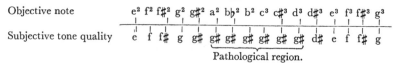

Here the differences of pitch remained *normal*, which is to say

* P. V. Liebermann, M.D.

that the pseudo g♯ notes occurred at different pitches. Accordingly, the patient heard g♯ notes at the pitches $g\sharp^2$, a^2, $b\flat^2$, b^2, c^3, $c\sharp^3$, d. For the patient, therefore, all notes between $g\sharp^2$ and d^3 were equivalent notes. For him they were like the various octave notes to one with normal hearing, only at a very much reduced distance. On the diagram we have therefore not represented the pathological region of the note series of this patient by a spiral line. In his case a vertical line should be substituted for this part of the spiral line between $g\sharp^2$ and d^3 (124).*

The second aspect is the *tone quality*. It is graphically represented by projecting the spiral line on a cross-section of the cylinder. This projection will be a circle, and appertains *exclusively* to the apprehension of the second characteristic, altogether isolated from the first, from the pitch.

A fictitious test subject who apprehends tone quality *only* but not differences in pitch, or who apprehends all tone qualities at one and the same pitch, would detect absolutely no difference between equivalent notes (coincident tones an octave apart). For such an observer there would be only one c, one d, one e.

Instead of such an imaginary test subject (who is a little difficult to conceive), we can also take a real observer if we offer the musical notes not as isolated tones, but as a whole system of equivalent notes. For example, instead of striking a single c or c^1, let us strike the whole clang: C_4–C_3–C_2–C_1–C–c–c^1–c^2–c^3—all notes of the clang equally loud. Point c on the circle, which represents the projection of *all c notes* on the spiral line (lying on a vertical line one above the other), corresponds exactly to this clang. This will also explain why the quality series is an *absolute whole, or unity, in itself.* If, for instance, we repeat the experiment with the clang of all d's, all e's, all f's, etc., we arrive finally at exactly the same clang of all the c's with which we started, provided the system of equivalent notes is conceived each time as infinite in both directions.

Let us now investigate how the interval phenomena appear in the light of the Two-component Theory. If we observe pitch alone, then the interval gives an impression of tonal distance together with a mounting (rising) impression, or tension. The

---

* In point of fact it should be represented by a splotchy defusion and distortion of the spiral line since the linear character is more or less lost.

tonal distance is represented by a projection on the vertical axis of the spiral line.   As a result we can speak of distances of a third, a sixth, an octave, a tenth, double octave, and triple octave. Thus c–e and c^1–e^1 represent distances that correspond to the third, while c–c^1 corresponds to the sixth.

From the standpoint of distance, there is a greater difference between c–e and c–e^1 than between c–e and c–g♯.   In point of fact the tonal distance c–e is less in comparison with the distance c–g♯, and the latter, in turn, less in comparison with c–e^1.   If we only consider the pitch properties of the notes, and in so doing pay attention exclusively to the degree of the ascent in the pitch scale, disregarding meanwhile the differences in quality, the tonal

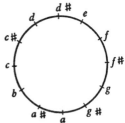

FIG. 20.—Graphic Representation of the Pure Tone-quality Series.

distances are isolated as it were and can be judged according to their size.

As regards the tonal distance—the steps in the pitch scale— this, too, presents no difficulties for the Two-component Theory. However, there is no doubt that the interval impression is not due to the tonal distance alone.   This is attested first by the aforesaid fact that the interval qualities such as second, third, etc., are all complete within an octave and that all intervals, the fundamental and upper note of which have the same tone quality (such, for instance, as c–g, c–g^1, c–g^2), evoke the impression of equivalent intervals melodically as well as harmonically; and finally by the fact that notes manifesting only difference in pitch (like the very high notes outside the musical range) are not able to generate *interval impressions*, but merely *impressions of distance*.   This was shown in the case of abnormal hearing just described, where the patient judged any note pair in the pathologically affected region —that is, between g♯^{2} and d^3—as prime in the sense of the pseudo note g♯, whereby the fact did not escape him that these g♯ notes differed in pitch. All these facts prove that the interval impression depends not only on the pitch but also to a large extent on the tone quality, or, more strictly speaking, on the distance in the tone-quality series.

In the relation between intervallic quality, distance, and interval, we find the same relation again as subsists between tone quality, pitch, and tone sensation. Interval is a combination of intervallic quality and distance, and between successive notes forms the real musical relation, just as the combination of quality and pitch represents the real *musical element*, the *tone sensation*. Intervallic quality, like tonal quality, is a characteristic thrown into relief by a psychological analysis; they are not isolated factors, because their existence is bound up with the *musical* note

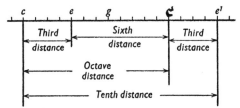

FIG. 21.—Tone Distances within the Compass of a tenth.

series. True, distance and pitch are also such factors abstracted from the actual note series as a whole, but in certain circumstances—e.g. with notes without quality—they can be apprehended in isolation.

As we have seen, the impossibility of apprehending tone qualities in isolation can be compensated by the apprehension of complete systems of equivalent notes. This can also explain the concept of intervallic quality.

Let us now illustrate the pure qualities by clangs of equivalent notes. It is clear that the successive clangs of all c's and all g's can be taken for a fifth just as easily as a fourth (or twelfth or eleventh, etc.). We should really find a new designation for this intervallic quality; for example, fourth–fifth, or fifth–fourth.

In the same way the thirds or the sixths, in a purely qualitative sense, should be replaced by one common quality, the third–sixth or the sixth–third. The same is true of the second–seventh and the prime–octave. But here it should be noted that the two third–sixths, for instance, that are formed from a major or minor

third should not be designated " major " or " minor " third–
sixths (" large " and " small " third–sixths in German terminology), because the concepts " major " and " minor " refer
to distance, and not to quality. The major third corresponds
with the minor sixth, and vice versa. The qualitative equivalence
of the intervals and their inversions will be especially clear if a
broken interval (not too large— c–f, for instance) is played in the
lowest part of the pitch scale. In this case one time we hear an
ascending fourth C–F and another time a descending fifth C–F$_1$,
all according to attitude.

However, since fifths and fourths, for example, do not differ in
quality but blend into the common intervallic quality of the
fourth–fifth, the actual difference that one hears between a fourth

Wagner, Fliegender Holländer

Ex. 10.

and a fifth is due solely to the difference in tonal distance. This
is most clearly evident when a fourth–fifth (c–g, for instance)
occurs in turn as ascending fifth and as descending fourth in a
theme. Qualitatively and in ordinal succession the two notes
forming the concrete intervals are identical, but this is not the
case as regards their distances and directions (Ex. 10).

Although tonal qualities determine the intervallic qualities, it
is impossible to produce an interval impression (simultaneous or
successive) without the contributing factor of tonal distance. In
the musical note series both characteristics are always found in
conjunction, and combine to form the musical interval. Neither
pitch differences nor qualitative differences alone can produce an
interval impression. Phenomenally there is only the *interval of
the third*, which is formed by a definite spacing in pitch *and* by a
note pair of definite quality.

Through the introduction of the concept " intervallic quality ",
and through a new and more precise formulation of the concept
" tonal distance " (which we owe to the Two-component Theory),
we are able to overcome difficulties in the Theory of Intervals
that the earlier theories could not surmount.

VI

THE CONSONANCE PROBLEM

A. Consonance and Dissonance

It has already been pointed out that the musical continuum comprises a very large number of notes, only a very small percentage of which are used in music. The notes used in music form the *musical note series*. The vibration numbers of the notes of this series bear a *fixed, constant* relation to each other. The constancy of the tonal relations, the fixation of the intervals, is an important—perhaps the most important—prerequisite in music. Where there are no fixed intervals, there are no modes, no motives, no musical form, and also no harmony.

Now the question arises as to the principle on which the notes for the musical tone series were chosen from the entire tonal material. Musical folklore and comparative musicology teach that the choice was made by the different ethnological groups in various ways. In spite of the diversity, certain general tendencies can be noted in the musical systems of the different races, which limited arbitrary action and reduced the musical systems to a relatively small number (33). To these belong the division of intervals within an octave, the preference for pentatonic and heptatonic scales, the fixation of intervals through the length of strings and flutes and, above all, through the use of definite euphonious intervals such as the octave, fifth, and fourth. Since only a definite musical system permits the formation of perfect consonances, it is therefore assumed that in the development of the scales such notes (or, more correctly speaking, such tonal relations) were chosen as made it possible to form and use these consonant intervals.

In point of fact, in our musical system intervals can be formed on every note which, when sounded simultaneously, produce the most euphonious sounds and blend best with one another. It cannot be denied that this fact seems a plausible explanation for the choice of the scale notes. We must only find requisite historical proof of it. It seems by no means out of the question that our knowledge of Greek music and Greek musical instruments could furnish evidence for this assumption.

77

It is to be assumed that in Western music consonance played a role in the construction of the scale, for otherwise it would be difficult to understand why the most consonant tonal relations, such as the octave, fifth, third, and fourth (which together form the components of the major triad), form the groundwork of the diatonic scale.

The phenomenon of consonance aroused the interest of the music theorists not because of its presumable function in the formation of scales, but because of its *harmonic significance*. The consonance problem was for a long time in the forefront of scientific research. That is the reason why we go into the theories of consonance, and all the more so because in so doing we learn the various points of view that, sometimes consciously, sometimes unconsciously, determined the line of psychological research.

Before we turn to a critical discussion of the most important theories of consonance, let us briefly describe consonance and its counterpole: dissonance.

If we proceed from the notes of our twelve-step scale, then we find on the one hand that through the combination of these notes, intervals can be formed that, when played simultaneously, blend closely together. On the other hand, we also find others that are more or less discordant. Two-note clangs of the first category are called *consonances*, the others *dissonances*. This distinction is psychologically tenable, though the contrast between the two types of intervals is not so sharp that a line can be drawn between them.

It would be possible and thoroughly justifiable to speak in general of different kinds of consonances, some of which are designated as consonances on account of their homogeneity *qua* consonances, others as dissonances on account of their harshness. In this sense, consonance can be defined as a lesser degree, dissonance as a higher degree, of tension between two notes. The musician of today will consider this point of view more correct than the classification into consonances and dissonances.

B. Mathematical Theories of Consonance

The phenomenon of consonance and dissonance was very exhaustively investigated as far back as the ancient Greek music theorists. From them derives the distinction between symphonic (consonant) and diaphonic (dissonant) chords. In Greek music theory two trends were operative. One was represented by Democritus, Archytas, and the so-called Pythagoreans. This trend proceeded from living music, and its object was to verify the already known mathematical laws of intervals by experience. The other, represented by Plato and his school, proceeded from the phenomenal factuality that the first four figures of the ordinal numbers (the relative rates of vibration of unison, octave, double octave, fifth, and fourth are $1 : 1$, $2 : 1$, $4 : 1$, $3 : 2$, $4 : 3$) are found in the ratios of the perfect consonances. Following this, Platonism held the view that the nature or essence of the consonance is concealed, as it were, in these numbers, and that these suffice to construct the scale *a priori*, i.e. mathematically without regard to experience and musical practice. In his work " The Republic " (97, 40), Plato expressly states that

> " they (the Pythagoreans) are just like the astronomers—intent upon the numerical properties embodied in these audible consonances; they do not rise to the level of formulating problems and inquiring which numbers are inherently consonant and which are not, and for what reasons." *

Plato's object was to formulate a mathematical theory of harmony based on arithmetical postulates—a theory that has nothing to do with the scales or intervals of actual Greek music. His aim was to grasp the ideal figures in their purity, and he placed reasoning above hearing. The striking coincidence of the consonance and dissonance with the simple and less simple numerical ratios led the Platonists, in keeping with their philosophical views, to metaphysical hypotheses that no longer had any relationship with living music.

In contrast thereto, it was the object of Pythagoras, Democritus, and Aristoxenus to bring harmony into agreement with the acoustic musical phenomena.†

The theory of the importance of the simple mathematical ratios for the comprehension of consonance and harmony dominated music theory up to the end of the 18th century. Although still under the influence of the Greek conception of the simple ratios,

---

* Translation of Francis Macdonald Cornford.

† It should be mentioned that in music theory Aristoxenus depended much more on the ear than did the Pythagoreans. In the realm of music theory he may be considered the precursor of the Renaissance, which laid weight on the " senso ", on the " udito ". Compared with Pythagoras, Aristoxenus was more akin to modern music, since he considered thirds consonant intervals, whereas with Pythagoras it followed from his cycle of fifths that thirds were dissonant.

the great philosopher Leibniz (1646–1716) was the first to take an important step forward when he sought a psychological explanation for consonance. He tried to trace the connexion between consonance and the first six numbers to a kind of " unconscious " counting.* In one of his letters he wrote that

> " music is a hidden arithmetical exercise for the soul in which the soul counts without being aware of it. They err who think that nothing can take place in the soul of which they themselves are unconscious. Although the soul is not aware that it is counting, it nevertheless feels the effect of this unconscious counting, that is, consonances produce a pleasant sensation, dissonances an unpleasant one, as the natural consequence." †

The celebrated mathematician Leonhard Euler (1707–1783), leaning on the authority of Leibniz, also assigned as reason for the consonance experience the soul's " unconscious arithmetical exercise ". He believed that one counts the *ratios* of the vibrations unconsciously, as it were, and that the less one has to count, the greater the consonance; i.e. the more agreeable the musical sound. According to this, consonance would rest in general on the pleasure of counting, and in particular on having to count as little as possible (34).

The following objections can be raised to the admissibility of the Euler concept. His interval theory is inconsistent with musical experience. In principle, degrees of consonance can be calculated indefinitely by means of mathematical formulæ, but fixed limits are set to our acoustic-musical impressions, which are furthermore bound to definite acoustical configurations. For instance, from a musical aspect there is absolutely no justification for according the minor seventh the same degree of consonance as the major and minor triads. It is even less defensible when Euler, on the basis of mathematical speculations, accords the same degree of consonance to the major second as to the six-four chord.

---

* All primary consonances, for instance, can be expressed by the integers 1 to 6. Prime 1, octave 2 : 1, fifth 3 : 2, fourth 4 : 3, major third 5 : 4, minor third 6 : 5, major sixth 5 : 3, even the minor sixth 8 : 5 can be viewed as inversion of the major third 5 : 4.

† Epist. ad divers. I, p. 154. "Musica est exercitum arithmeticae occultum nescientis se numerare animi. Errant qui nihil in anima fieri putant et eius ipsa non sit conscia. Anima igitur, et si se numerare non sentiat, sentit tamen eius numerationis insensibilis effectum, se voluptatem in consonantis, molestiam in dissonantis inde resultatem."

Today Euler's concept requires no further discussion. Like other mathematically oriented music theorists of early days, his sole object was to establish a connexion between numerical ratios and intervals, whereby they omitted to verify if their ideas coincided with musical phenomena or not.

Without doubt it is very stimulating to study the connexion between arithmetic (i.e. the theory of numbers) and interval formation. But in each case we must test empirically if the result agrees with the musical concept or not. Furthermore, we should not overlook the fact that here it is a question solely of *European* music, therefore of only a small part of the consonance problems of the different races.

C. Physical Theories of Consonance

For centuries science was content to elucidate the consonance problem by reference to the volumic and numerical ratios of tonal material, which were being increasingly apprehended and recognized. Nowadays nobody even thinks of them. The physical angle of approach was the next step towards the solution of the consonance problem. Rameau (1721), d'Alembert (1762), and Tartini (1754) gave the impulse to an empirical–physical attitude towards this problem. The first two used the overtones to explain the harmonies, Tartini the combination tones. These theories led directly to the physical theory of Helmholtz, who supported the contention of d'Alembert and Rameau.

In his " Sensations of Tone ", Helmholtz gives two definitions of consonance. His principle definition reads: " Consonance is a continuous, dissonance an intermittent, sensation of tone ". This definition rests on the phenomenon of *beats* (the primary tones and their upper partials) which do not occur in consonances but are very prominent in dissonances and have a great deal to do with the total impression. Therefore, according to Helmholtz, it is the measure of the pulses of tone and the roughness that determine the degree of consonance or dissonance. Notes bearing the relation of octaves, fifths, or fourths to each other form the purest consonances because they evoke no beats, or practically none. The more audible the beating, the less the degree of consonance, according to Helmholtz. This agrees with the fact that the strongly consonant thirds and sixths evoke scarcely perceptible beats, while the major seconds and sevenths evoke more distinct ones, and the very pronounced dissonances (such as semitones, diminished and augmented intervals) *very* great ones.

Proceeding from his theory of beats, Helmholtz undertook a classification of the consonances. He distinguished absolute consonances (octave and double octave), perfect consonances (fifth and fourth), medial consonances (major third and major sixth), imperfect consonances (minor and minor sixth), and dissonances (second, seventh, augmented fourth).

In the main, the following arguments can be adduced against this.

According to Helmholtz' investigations, beats are most noticeable when they occur at a rate of about 33 per second. When they occur at the rate of 132 per second they cease to be sensible. Consequently the *same* intervals that sound dissonant in the great or small octaves as a result of their low beating would lose their dissonant character in the two- or three-line octave and almost take on the character of consonances.

Let us exemplify this by the augmented fourth c–f$\sharp$. In the contra-octave this interval is determined by a frequency difference of 13; in the great octave of 27·5, in the small octave of 55, in the one-line octave of 110, in the two-line octave of 220, in the three-line octave of 440, and in the four-line octave of 880. If the theory of beats were correct, then the augmented fourth would alter its degree of consonance as the general pitch of the interval increased. At very low pitches it would sound consonant, in the one-line octave strongly dissonant, in the three-line octave more dissonant still. But this is by no means the case. The degree of consonance of the augmented fourth is independent of pitch.

Stumpf adduced further arguments against the Helmholtz theory (151). First, that there are *beats without dissonances*—namely, *consonant* intervals in the low reaches of pitch; the fifth in the contra-octave C_1–G_1 (32 and 48 vibr.), or even the octave C_1–C (32 and 64 vibr.) evoke, of course, distinctly audible beats—in the latter case, in fact, the most distinctly perceptible beats (32 in number)—and still the interval remains consonant. On the other hand, there are *beatless dissonances*; namely, *dissonant intervals* in the *upper pitches*. The minor second or the seventh in the four-line octave evoke no perceptible beats, and, for all that, do not lose their dissonant character. Beatless dissonances can also be produced in the middle octaves. If we take two tuning-forks with a difference of pitch of a second (e.g. tones of 800 and 900 vibr. per sec.) and hold one before each ear, we hear a second very distinctly, without any trace of beats. The following example gives several chords without perceptible beats. In the first pentad every note discords with all the rest; but there are no beats.

These facts therefore prove that it is incorrect to attribute dissonance to perceptible beats.

Helmholtz gives still another definition of consonance. This has reference to the phenomenon of the coincidence of the *overtones* of both primary tones. According to this definition the consonance is due to the " similarity " of two notes traceable to

Ex. 11.—Beatless Dissonant Chords.

the presence of common partials, consequently to the so-called *clang relationship* (an undisturbed kinship between the notes), while dissonance is due to a lack of such concurrence. This theory breaks down as soon as we choose notes that either have no overtones whatsoever or none that coincide. If, for example, we sound two-note clangs that have practically no overtones (like the notes of tuning-forks or perfectly pure tones generated by means of the interference method), then according to the Helm-holtz theory we should expect the two notes to sound equally dissonant, since they have no overtones. That this is not the case is no longer open to argument.

The factors deduced by Helmholtz to explain consonance (beats and coincident partials) play a certain role in two-note clangs, in that beats *further* the sensation of intermittence and roughness in the dissonances, while sensuous compatibility (clang relationship) promotes the sensation of unitariness and balance of proportions in the consonances. But they cannot come into question as a *fundamental explanation* of the consonance phenomenon. That the Helmholtz hypothesis, in spite of its shortcomings, still ranks as the foremost in this field is due, in my opinion, to the fact that nothing better has yet been found.

Let us now turn to the consonance theories that hold the *differential tones* responsible for all diversities in consonance.

The first person to assume a connexion between differential tones and consonance and dissonance was again Helmholtz. But the first theory to pay extensive consideration to the relations of the differential tones as an explanation of consonance derives from W. Preyer. Later on F. Krueger propounded his theory of differential tones in line with Preyer's deductions. According to him the degree of consonance depends on the number of differentials. The octave has no differentials, the fifth one, the fourth two, etc. An immediate and justifiable objection was raised to Krueger's concept on the ground that there are two-note clangs in which the differentials have no effect and yet the clangs are nevertheless very dissonant. Krueger's theory of the origin of consonance and dissonance lacks all empirical foundation (69).

But criticism of the difference-tone theory of consonance cannot neutralize the importance of combination tones in the formation of intervals. Even though these concomitant phenomena are insufficient in themselves to explain consonance and dissonance, they still play a role in the total sensation of two-note clangs—that is, as regards clarity and harmonic distinctness—that should not be under-estimated. It is manifest that a constant relation subsists between intervals and combination tones, a fact to which Hindemith has also drawn attention (57). The intervals can be so arranged that if one starts with the octave and proceeds over the consonant intervals to the dissonances, each succeeding simultaneous interval loses from step to step more of its harmonic clarity. The differential tone of the octave only doubles the fundamental. At the next step (the fifth) we hear combination tones of the first and second order as an octave reduplication of the lower note. The next step (the fourth) also shows an octave reduplication of one of its notes; i.e. the upper note. But the two combination tones no longer coincide, as they did in the fifth. Instead, they themselves form a lower octave. In the major third and the minor sixth we also find repetitions of one of the notes. But in addition there is a new tone that is not present in the interval. The minor third and the major sixth produce two new combination tones, etc. We see that the interval pairs manifest the same arrangement as regards their combination tones and their degrees of consonance. It is therefore apparent that the impression of tension, the degree of consonance, increases with the increasing number of the simultaneously perceptible components.

In line with the Helmholtz range of ideas, mention should be made of the consonance hypothesis of Ernst Mach (81). He expressed the idea that there were physical resonators (for which he would substitute physiological resonators) in the organ of

Ex. 12.—Relation between Intervals and Combination Tones.

□ Combination tone of the first order.   ◇ Combination tone of the second order.

hearing. He tried to explain the phenomena of consonance by "subjective overtones". Both assumptions lack all empirical foundation.

As with the theories of beats, overtones, and differential tones, it can be said that none of the other consonance theories which attempt to explain the harmonic sensation of two notes through certain physical factors or relations can be taken as a basis for a theory of consonance, because of their numerous contradictions.

D. Theory of Fusion

Since the attempt to formulate a theory of consonance by tracing consonance and dissonance to overtones and differentials, or even beats, proved unsuccessful, it was natural that one should try to base the phenomena in question on a psychological principle.

In his psychology of sound, Stumpf propounded a purely psychological theory of consonance (147, 151). He was of the opinion that the difference between consonant and dissonant two-note clangs did not lie in the concomitant tone phenomena but in the two primary sounds themselves; i.e. in their *degree of fusion*. According to Stumpf, fusion is an ultimate psychological fact which is incapable of further deductions and is to be viewed as the only basis of consonance.

The fusion idea is not new in music theory. Euclid, in fact, defined the consonance of two notes as their fusibility, and dissonance as their lack of fusibility. Furthermore, Külpe, Meinong, Titchener, and chiefly Theodor Lipps also accorded fusion a major importance in the theory of consonance.

By fusion Stumpf understands the approximation of a two-note clang towards *unison*. The clang of two notes evokes the sensation of a single note, sometimes more so, sometimes less. The more consonant a two-note clang, the more the primary tones fuse, the more they will approximate towards the sensation of unison. The octave, the highest degree of consonance, evokes the sensation of unison even when its components (with attentive aural observation) stand out prominently in the clang. To a lesser extent we find this same tendency towards unitariness of mass effect, towards fusion, in the fifth, third, and sixth. In the other intervals there is no longer any fusion, or only to a very slight degree.

Stumpf tried to verify his consonance theory empirically. He offered two-note clangs of different grades of consonance to a large number of unmusical persons who were required to state whether they experienced the two-note clang as *one* note or as two. His findings are summarized in Table 7. Five different simultaneous intervals (two-note clangs) were sounded in the small, one-, two-, and three-line octaves and the number of correct judgments (two components) ascertained.

TABLE 7

Correct Judgments in Small, One-, Two-, and Three-line Octaves regarding the Presence in the Clang of Two Notes

Total for each clang	Aug. fourth	Major third	Minor third	Fourth	Fifth
864	657	631	608	557	428

This shows that the number of correct judgments (two notes) decreased as the grade of consonance of two-note clangs increased. On the basis of the quantitative results, no sharp dividing line can be drawn objectively between consonances and dissonances. We can only speak of greater or less fusion and arrange the intervals according to their grade of fusion.

Besides the theory in general, Stumpf also propounded a few special rules for fusion. According to these, " the grade of fusion is first of all independent of the tone region " (i.e. of the pitch region). In my opinion, this rule is valid at most for the middle and upper regions of the tonal series. According to my experience, which is also substantiated by other observers, the fusion of consonant two-note clangs in the great and contra octaves is far less distinct than in the upper reaches of pitch. That seems quite reasonable when we consider that in all two-note clangs, even in the consonant chords, there are beats between the primary tones and differentials in the lower reaches of pitch that interfere with fusion.

Stumpf asserted, furthermore, that the degree of fusion is also independent of the *stretching of the intervals*, that an expansion of one or more octaves cannot affect the fusion of the notes. Consequently there would be no difference between the third and the tenth as regards the grade of fusion. This law of fusion is also incorrect. The fusion decreases with the stretching of the interval (the octave excepted). Stumpf himself became aware of these difficulties, and tried to overcome them by attributing the difference between major third and major tenth, or between octave and double octave, not to the degree of fusion but to the distance between the two notes. Stumpf failed to answer the question whether (or to what extent) distance affected the fusion.

The theory of fusion attracted especial interest and attention in the field of music psychology, where it was viewed as an advance over the Helmholtz theory. I can by no means agree with this point of view, all the more since the two theories cannot be compared in any way.

That of Helmholtz is a causative-genetic theory of consonance that endeavours to determine the objective-physical basis of the consonance phenomena. Stumpf's theory of fusion, on the other hand, represents a descriptive-phenomenological concept that strives to trace the consonance phenomena to an ultimate psychological fact—to fusion.

If we investigate the *theoretical basis* of the theory of fusion and Stumpf's contributions to the support of his contentions, we come to the conclusion that this theory, too, impressive as it may seem, is not consistent with facts.

Stumpf lays the greatest weight on the phenomenon of fusion.

He believes he has discovered in this the primary cause of consonance; that is, that special feature that basically constitutes two-note clangs in the musical sense. In the term " fusion " Stumpf had two things in mind: first of all, the difficulty of analysis, which he erroneously cites as argument for his theory (instead of symptom). And then something else quite different, something that is presumably consonance: harmony itself. The difficulty of analysis can neither be a characteristic nor a gauge of consonance or fusion, because first of all there are dissonant bitonal chords the notes of which can only be separated with difficulty and yet the two-note clangs still maintain their dissonant character. Secondly, because there are consonances the components of which can be easily separated, and yet they are still not dissonances by any means. A dissonant two-note clang with constituent notes of different intensity can serve as an example of the first. As example of the second there are the compound (expanded) consonant intervals which are indeed analysable, and more easily so than most of the dissonant bitonal chords within the span of an octave, without their degree of consonance being in any way affected thereby.

In my opinion the contradictions and the erroneous data regarding fusion arise from the fact that Stumpf identifies, as it were, fusion and consonance. This concept not only led him to a false interpretation of the facts, but also to incorrect psychological deductions. The flaws in his argument and in those of the theory of fusion in general can best be demonstrated on the phenomenon of the compound intervals.

Stumpf flatly asserts that the simultaneous intervals (two-note clangs) and their expansions (such, for example, as third and tenth, fifth and twelfth) are identical in degree of fusion. That this assertion does not rest on unbiased observation is apparent on the face of it. No one who compares the degree of fusion of the fifth and twelfth can maintain that both fuse to the same extent, approximate to the impression of unity (one sensation) in the same way.

That which Stumpf observed and studied was not fusion, but *consonance*. He overlooked the fact that in judging bitonal chords, two attitudes are possible which sometimes lead to the same, sometimes to different, results. If we concentrate attention on the sensory phenomenon, then fusion plays the main role; if, on the other hand, attention is directed primarily upon the harmonious character of the apprehended two-note clang, then the phenomenon of consonance takes first place. Within the span of an octave, fusion and consonance are well-nigh approximate. This explains why in investigating the acoustic fusion phenomena we preferably limit ourselves to *one* octave and find no conspicuous deviations between the grades of consonance and fusion. Only when we exceed an octave does it become clear to us that here we have to do not with *one* phenomenon, but with *two*, which are closely associated but by no means identical.

The identification of fusion and consonance—in other words, the claim that consonance is physically dependent on fusion, this keystone of the theory of fusion—cannot be sustained in the light of the above facts. In my opinion the fundamental difference between fusion and consonance lies in the fact that fusion is a *purely sensory phenomenon* linked directly with the existence of the clang and apprehended by everyone in the same way, irrespective of musical education and taste, and of the musical system indigenous to the specific culture of the observer; while consonance and dissonance are *phenomena of æsthetic perception*, of *æsthetic valuation*. In the course of time, taste has changed as regards the sensory agreeableness of two-note clangs; but this is not true as regards their degree of fusion. There was a time when the third was considered just as dissonant as the seventh, though even then one had to concede a much higher degree of fusion to the third than to the seventh.*

If we wish to determine the role and significance of the theory of fusion for musical acoustics and the psychology of music, we

---

* In antiquity and the Middle Ages, under the dominance of the Pythagorean diatonic note series, the third was regarded as dissonant. It is very probable, however, that the natural third 5 : 4, as introduced by Aristoxenus and again in 1300 by Walter Odington (*De speculatione musices*), was regarded as a consonance right from the start. Besides his mathematical speculations in virtue of which he considered the fifth equal to two-thirds of the sum of the major and minor thirds ($4/5 \times 5/6 = 2/3$), Odington was also supported by English musical practice of that period in which the Gymel (Latin " twin song ", a two-part song consisting of a succession of parallel thirds) played a role. Odington wrote as follows (E. Coussemaker, *Scriptorum de Musica Medii Aevi*, Milan, 1931, p. 199a):

" Verum tamen quia vicine sunt sesquiquarte (major third) et sesquiquinte (minor third) habitudinibus quarum unitas facit differentiam, idcirco plurimi existimant consonos esse. Et si in numeris non reperiantur consone, voces tamen hominum subtilitate ipsos ducunt in mixturam suavem, et penitus inconsonum quadam dulcedine nota fit suave et consonum. . . . "

The change in our attitude towards the third as consonance or dissonance is surely due to an objective change in the third.

arrive at the following conclusion: the theory of fusion contributed nothing new to the theory of consonance. It stressed a special feature; namely, that of fusion, which Greek music theorists had already defined as the most important characteristic of harmony. Fusion is one of the factors that determine the total consonant or dissonant impression of two-note clangs, but it is not the causative factor of consonance or dissonance in respect to their specific capacities. True, the attempt of the psychologists to arrive at the ultimate causative explanation of consonance by means of the phenomenon of fusion was unsuccessful. However, the efforts and work of the investigators were by no means in vain. They discovered a goodly number of factors that are responsible for the distinctness and abundance of the consonance phenomena.

An attempt has recently been made to give a new turn to the consonance problem (87, 154). The Gestalt psychological and phenomenological investigations of the consonance and dissonance phenomena have drawn our attention to features to which little regard was previously paid. It was found, namely, that consonance has the following special features: independence, unitariness, definiteness, and balance of proportions. In contrast thereto, dissonance manifests dependence, need of resolution, instability, and dynamic tendency. It is also interesting from the point of view of music theory that dissonances gradually lose their original unpleasant character—a change that seems to come about in an extremely short time. True, these and similar analyses of the consonance and dissonance experience enrich our knowledge in respect to the psychological and æsthetic properties of bitonal chords, but they furnish no basis for a causative explanation of the consonance phenomena.

E. Consonance and Concordance

Our music is a dualistic system based on the major and minor principle. In these two systems the triads on the tonic, dominant, and subdominant hold a central position. In chords of three and more notes we encounter consonance and fusion phenomena similar to those in two-note clangs, which, however, we should not translate as consonance and dissonance. These concepts have reference to two simultaneous notes, and can therefore not be used offhand where it is a question of clangs of more than two components. They were replaced in the chordal system by another pair of concepts; namely, concordance and discordance.

Chords fall into two classes: *concords* and *discords*. Stumpf characterizes as *concords* all primary and secondary major and minor triads, together with their inversions and expansions. A *conditio sine qua non* for every concord is that it contain a fifth or its inversion, a fourth; and a third, or its inversion, a sixth. All the others can be designated as *discords*; i.e. such as result from the addition to triads of definite rationally justified notes, or through certain permutations of the triads themselves (147).

The following facts point to the essential difference between consonance and concordance.

1. A two-note clang in itself can be either consonant or dissonant. However, it can only be concordant with reference to the further components of a chord. Thus, for instance, the notes e–g♯ are consonant, as a clang in itself. Meanwhile the same two-note clang, as component part of the E major triad, will be considered concordant, but as component part of the augmented triad c–e–g♯ it will be regarded as discordant, since in the latter case it is a constituent part of a chord that contains no perfect fifth.

2. The consonance of notes is not affected by the addition of a new note. However, such an addition can change its concordance to discordance. The triad e–g♯–b is a concord when e is taken as tonic. But it becomes a discord when c is added as tonic.

3. Finally the two-note clang as consonance is a fact of direct sensory perception, conclusive in itself. But as part of the concordance it is a matter of *conception, of intellectually apprehended interrelations and mutual connexions*.

Even though this problem has not yet been totally clarified, and still further investigations, elucidations, and modifications are necessary, we nevertheless believe that the concept of concordance is by no means superfluous and has its significance for the theory of consonance.*

* In the Middle Ages the term concordance had a slightly different connotation than with Stumpf, in that the term consonance was employed for simultaneous, and concordance for successive, tonal patterns (see Johannes de Grocheo (1300), whose theory of music " *Theoria* " was issued by Johannes Wolf in the Collected Publications of the International " Musikgesellschaft ", Vol. 1). In accordance with this, Conradin understands by concordance two notes which, sounded immediately one after the other, have a melodic connexion. On the other hand, he employs the term consonance when two or more notes are sounded simultaneously and evoke one single perfect clang. On account of the variability of the melodic " connexion " in history and folklore, I find this definition of concordance inapt.

F. Consonance and Atonality

The consonance phenomena are independent of the material and stylistic peculiarities of music. Whether music moves in our traditional tonal system, or in the atonal, has no effect on consonance and dissonance as fundamental phenomena of musical acoustics. A consonant bitonal chord remains consonant and a dissonant one dissonant no matter what change may take place in the mode of musical expression, in the so-called tonal idiom. If the disciples of atonality attack the consonance principle on the score that the concept of consonance has changed in the course of time, their line of reasoning is altogether wrong. It is not a question whether the third was once found less agreeable to the ear than now; but how the grade of consonance of the third is *experienced* in comparison with stronger consonances or those of less degree. The third, as consonance phenomenon, has surely always been the same, even though its importance and tension differential in musical form may have undergone a change.

The application and full utilization of consonant and dissonant bitonal chords in music is an altogether different question. Here musical-æsthetic factors, which have changed very materially in the process of time, play a decisive role. In the epoch of the exclusively tonal major and minor systems in which the harmonic polarity of the dominant-tonic relationship represented the important factor, the centre of gravity lay with consonance. In atonal music the dissonance (above all, the second–seventh–ninth system) came strongly to the fore. Consonant intervals are avoided, while extremely sharp dissonances predominate (67, 87). However, this brings us into the realm of musical æsthetics, which has nothing to do with the problem of consonance and dissonance.*

G. More Complex Tone Structures

Up to this point we have spoken only of single notes and their interrelationships. Music is not concerned with single notes and their relations as expressed in isolated intervals and chords. But it has to do largely with more complex musical structures in the

---

* It should perhaps be mentioned that it is owing to the relinquishment of tonality that dissonance has largely ceased to be the tension differential in modern atonal music. Furthermore, the frequency of the dissonances has a certain blunting effect, which of course also affects the sharpness of the dissonance.

form of homophonic and polyphonic patterns. We will not go into the question of these more complex tonal forms, such as motives, melodies, movements, since they belong in the realm of general music theory, æsthetics, or the laws of musical form and style. Here we will study the more complex tone structures from the perceptive-psychological point of view; that is, from an attitude of observation that appertains to the domain of the psychology of music.

Psychology has raised the question of what is *directly perceptible* in an optical, acoustical, tactile object. Two different answers have been given to this question. The first is: the perceptive object consists primarily of elements out of which the organizing action of our mind forms a *complex whole*. According to this concept, the components, the structural elements, continue to exist in the aggregate; they are merely worked up into a logical whole. This, briefly put, is the underlying idea of the so-called *Complex or Association Theory* (the Evolutionary Approach).

The second answer is: the perceptive object, as a *unitary whole*, is a concrete fact. A melody or a sequence of chords, like an optical figure or an ornament constructed according to a consistent plan, appear to us as *unitary functioning wholes* which come about immediately, directly, without active assistance on our part. In the concrete whole the parts lose their individual independence; they merge wholly and entirely in the total impression (the mass). Their function depends on the perceptive object as a concrete unitary whole, and not (as the Theory of Association teaches) the whole on the parts. The totality, the homogeneous Gestalt, has its specific properties, its specific laws inherent in its own nature. True, the melody consists of single notes, just as a figure is made up of lines. However, the final product that is directly perceptible is a functioning whole, an individuality that cannot be apprehended from the parts.

This in a nutshell is the law of the *priority of the Gestalt*, of the primacy of the phenomenological totality which is the reverse of the law of the priority of the perceptive elements.

These considerations represent nothing new for musicians, as they know very well that the melodic totality is something else and something more than the sum of its parts. They know that a melody does not change when the notes are transposed an octave, a fourth, or a fifth. The melodic-rhythmic impression of a musical motive remains the same even when the motive is transposed to a key containing *none* of the notes of the original key. On the other hand, there are circumstances when the *mutation of a single note* can change the entire character of the melody. In a characteristic motive we need only raise or lower a note a semitone to produce an altogether different musical figure. The phenomenon of a change in the Gestalt is still more apparent if only a slight change is made in the structural whole; e.g. when the rhythm is altered but not the notes of the melody. In the latter case the melodic structure is totally and completely changed, though the notes themselves are unaltered.* The thematic inversion (such as occurs times without number in the fugues of Johann Sebastian Bach) is also of interest from the point of view of Gestalt psychology. See the E♭ minor Fugue of Part I of the Well-tempered Clavier. The variation is another case in point.

In general, it can be said that the concepts and rules of Gestalt psychology, which were originally developed or discovered on the basis of optical figures, are also valid for acoustic-musical figures, provided it is a question of music within the framework of our own occidental musical system, music that we know and with which we are thoroughly familiar. However, this is not true of totally foreign modes of musical expression. We must first accustom ourselves to exotic music and familiarize ourselves with the structure, before we are in a position to grasp it as a homogeneous Gestalt.†

* Only a totally unmusical person views a melody as a mere sum total of notes. For him, music is really nothing more than the sum of notes apprehended simultaneously or in sequence. Such an unmusical person hears notes, but perceives no melody.

† For information regarding the investigation and theories of Gestalt psychology, see works by von Ehrenfels, Benussi, Wertheimer, W. Koehler, E. Koffka, A. Gelb, F. Krueger, A. Meinong, P. Guillaume, A. Gemelli, A. Michotte, E. Rubin, D. Katz, G. Révész. For the musical side, see E. M. von Hornbostel and others.

VII

THE MUSICAL EAR

By musical ear we mean the ability to distinguish, apprehend, and recognize acoustic-musical relationships. By these relationships is meant the totality of elementary musical experiential material, chiefly musical pitch and tone quality, the intensity, the tone colour (timbre), the tonality, the key, the rhythmic and melodic relationships, and, last of all, intervals and chords of two or more tones.

A. Sense of Pitch

The necessary prerequisite to the musical ear is the *sense of pitch*; that is, the ability to recognize whether two notes are of similar or of different pitch. This ability can be tested by offering two notes, one immediately after the other, and requiring the observer to determine whether they are of the same or of different pitch. Such judgment is far easier than to determine which of the two notes is the higher. A practised observer, for instance, is able to discriminate two " a " tuning-forks with a difference of ½ vibration per second. But with this he is by no means always able to state accurately which fork is the higher. In the test, the notes are sounded either *successively* or *simultaneously*. When two notes are sounded simultaneously, the divergencies are easier to detect than when sounded in succession, because in the first case the beats or the dissonance of the two notes afford an admirable criterion for judging the difference.

It should be noted that pitch discrimination should not be reckoned as an essential feature of the musical ear. It is merely the necessary prerequisite to musical hearing.

B. Absolute Pitch

The ability to recognize notes in isolation instantly, to name them correctly without other aid, and to sing or whistle a designated note immediately is considered to be a special type of musical ear. This ability is called in general *absolute pitch*, to distinguish it from relative pitch, the ability to recognize and identify intervals. Other designations are also employed for the ability in question, such as absolute tone awareness and absolute tone memory. That person is gifted with *absolute pitch* or *absolute tone memory who without looking at the keyboard and without having heard other known notes shortly before is able to identify a note sounded on the piano by its correct letter name* (an " f ", let us say) ; *also the person who can sing the " f " freely from memory*. Both abilities usually go together. But there are persons who possess the first ability and not the second. There is no record, as far as I am aware, of the reverse case of a person who is able to sing any given note without at the same time being able to determine the absolute pitch of a tone.

Genuine absolute pitch is a special natural gift which is possessed by comparatively few persons. It is found oftener with men than with women. An investigation showed that 17.7% of the male music students and music lovers, but only 2.5% of the female, were gifted with genuine absolute pitch (154). According to an American report, 5% of a certain group of music students, orchestra-players, and piano-tuners in Chicago had genuine absolute pitch. Among the blind students, 14% possessed this faculty.

This special gift is not equally developed in all who have it. Differences are to be noted especially in respect to the *extensity of the tone domain* (region) in which the ability functions, and likewise in respect to the *timbre*.

There are certain persons whose sense of absolute pitch covers practically the entire musical range. Such an ear we call *universal genuine absolute pitch*. There are also persons who are only able to identify notes correctly within a more or less specific region. Upwards and downwards from this region, their judgments become gradually more indecisive and faulty till a limit is reached beyond which there can no longer be any question of absolute tone judgments. This more restricted faculty of pitch discrimination we call *limited absolute pitch*.

For the sake of completeness it should be stated that the tone region is also not wholly immaterial for universal genuine absolute pitch. The pitch judgments of persons with genuine absolute pitch are much keener in the middle part of the series (e.g. in the region of the small as well as the one-line and two-line octaves) than in the border zones. In the extremes, especially in the subcontra and four-line octaves, absolute pitch judgments are altogether unreliable.

With those gifted with absolute pitch, the degree of certainty and accuracy of judgment varies with the individual. There are fewer who have the ability to name or reproduce the heard tones correctly and without the slightest hesitation. The greater percentage also possess limited absolute pitch, only here we find confusion in the general pitch level and sometimes errors of a semitone.

The accuracy of absolute pitch judgment is further influenced by the attitude to standard pitch. If a person's ear is set to a definite aural standard (i.e. to the international standard pitch—440 cycles) he will find pitch deviations of 6–7% (scarcely an eighth of a tone) very noticeable, and this affects the accuracy of his judgments.

Among persons gifted with absolute pitch we find diversities in the extensity of the tonal domain in which notes are accurately identified, and other cases in which infallible judgment is also influenced by the timbre. There are those who have absolute tone memory independent of timbre; i.e. who have an *infallible universal ear for pitch*. Then we find others who only have a limited absolute pitch—a *special ear for pitch*—that is, only infallible for the familiar timbres; while others, again (and this is by far the largest group), have it solely for one timbre, usually that of the instrument played by the person in question.

Of the instruments, the notes of the piano are generally the easiest to recognize. Then come the violin, wood-wind instruments, brass instruments, and tuning forks; afterwards the notes of the human voice, and finally the clang of bells and glasses. It appears that notes with many harmonic overtones are more easily recognized than those with few. This explains why sung notes and sharper instrumental tones (which, as we know, have few overtones and in addition high dissonant harmonics) offer greater difficulties. In judging notes of instruments outside the range of their pitch identification ability, persons with limited absolute pitch occasionally make errors to the extent of a third, fourth, and fifth.

Absolute pitch seems to include not only the identification of notes in isolation, but also *keys*. If the absolute pitch for modes (key determination) is tested by primary chords, it is found that

C major and C minor take first place. In judging major triads, fewest errors are encountered with the C major triad. After the C major triad come the D, F, E, G, and A major triads, and then the others. With the minor triads that on C also holds first place. Nevertheless the difference between the C minor triad and the other minor triads is not so great as that between the C major triad and the other major triads. Here the order is C, F,

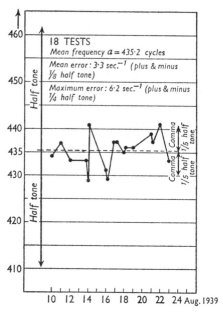

FIG. 22.—Standard Pitch Judgments (435 Cycles) of One and the Same Person Gifted with Absolute Pitch, Taken at Different Times.

D, E, G, A, then F♯, etc. (1). Sometimes the major and minor modes are confused. In this case the most frequent tendency is to mistake the minor triad for a major triad; i.e. to substitute the familiar for the less familiar. The percentage of errors amounts in general to not more than about 3–4% of the judgments (4, 95).

Genuine absolute pitch is a *natural gift* par excellence. It appears already in early youth and at once in a highly developed form. In musically gifted children one can find genuine absolute pitch as early as the third year. A musical prodigy whom I investigated manifested a universal genuine absolute pitch already at the beginning of his third year.

It is by no means incompatible with the innate character of absolute pitch that it requires *practice and experience* for its complete unfoldment and practical application. Persons with absolute pitch have training to thank for their ability to detect readily slight deviations from standard pitch. Here, on the whole, practice plays the same role as in colour recognition. We recognize colours as directly as persons with absolute pitch recognize musical notes. Nevertheless, apart from close concentration, accuracy of judgment depends mainly on training. If, for example, pure green is to be set on a spectrograph, the adjustments of an untrained observer will vary far more than those of a trained observer, though both recognize pure green

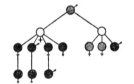

○   No absolute pitch.

◉   Absolute pitch observed.

●   Absolute pitch claimed. (Bachem, (4))

FIG. 23.—Genealogical Tree of a Family with Inherited Absolute Pitch.

instantly when they see it. The same is true in the tone domain. Van der Pol has shown that variations in individual judgments cannot be altogether avoided.

With systematic practice standard pitch can be identified so accurately that the average judgment error does not amount to more than 1/8 tone. Fatigue can also have a detrimental effect on the accuracy of absolute pitch. But the judgment error usually does not exceed a semitone.

And now a few words about the inheritance of absolute pitch. Recent investigations have shown conclusively that absolute pitch is *inherited* in numerous cases. In testing 103 persons with absolute pitch it was found that 40% of the cases were inherited. In many test subjects the inheritance could be definitely proved in three successive generations.

C. Regional Pitch

Now the question arises if there are other types of musical ear besides the aforesaid genuine absolute pitch. This question must be asked because certain experiences in demonstrations of absolute pitch are otherwise inexplicable. For instance, if I strike a note on the pianoforte and ask anyone possessing an awareness of the directional character in the pitch series, and familiar with the keyboard of the instrument, to repeat the note, he will do so, at least approximately; that is, with a minimum error at most. It has been found that even non-musicians are able to identify notes with an average error of a minor third. They need only have the most superficial acquaintance with the keyboard and the orderly succession of notes in the tonal system.

These experiences have made it clear that the capacity to discriminate pitch and identify isolated notes is by no means restricted exclusively to the group of persons who have the gift of genuine absolute pitch. There are many who are unable to identify the notes in the same way and with the same degree of accuracy as those endowed with extraordinary absolute pitch faculties. We can therefore only assume that in cases of this kind we have to do with a type of pitch identification (or recognition of notes with the unaided ear) that is of an entirely different character to the analogous ability possessed by the more gifted in this respect.

What is the nature of this pitch identification? Every tone has *one salient pitch*, and the pitch is something that is individual to the tone. Nevertheless, observation shows that the tones, in contrast to definite figures, words, names, objects, that appear as individualities do not owe this individual character to the pitch property. For instance, a C cannot be distinguished from a C♯ in the same way as a square from a triangle, or the world " bold " from the word " gold ", or the name " Peter " from the name " Paul ". Persons without genuine absolute pitch experience the note, not as an individuality, but as a *member of a group*, of a *tone region*, to which it belongs. The case is analogous to a progressive series of grey tints running from black to white in which each shade of grey has a specific brightness belonging to it alone, without the single nuances standing out conspicuously as individualities and impressing themselves on the memory as such. We can only designate to which category or nuance (region) the particular grey tint belongs (black, very dark, medium dark, dusky, medium light, light, very light, white).

This type of musical ear differs from the genuine absolute pitch characterized in Section B in that the judgment is not focused on the individuality of the note, but on its locus within a more or less specific tone region; in other words, on its regional (or locational) character (recognition of tone height).

The difference between genuine absolute and pseudo absolute (regional) pitch identification can be clearly demonstrated by comparing the tone judgments of both groups. The results of a comparative investigation carried out by A. Bachem on the basis of my theoretical expositions of the two kinds of pitch identification throw light on the situation (4).

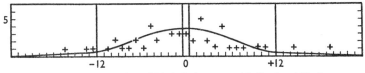

FIG. 24.—Distribution of Pitch Judgments with Regional Pitch.

The above diagram shows the results of the investigation of seven persons who identified a note given them on the piano a total of 45 times. The test note is indicated in the diagram by " O ". Every deviation of a semitone above or below is indicated on the horizontal axis by a plus or minus sign. The number of correct judgments is shown on the vertical axis. It indicates that the judgments were scattered over a wide area, both above and below the test area. Only three judgments were absolutely correct. Errors not greater than a semitone occurred five times; three of these were below, two above. The random distribution of the other 37 judgments extended from 20 semitones above to 14 semitones below. The average number of judgment errors, both above and below, amounted to 6 semitones; i.e. an augmented fourth.

A totally different picture is provided by an error curve for persons with innate absolute pitch. In 50 tests, 43 judgments fell on the test note and only 7 on notes in the immediate vicinity. Three of these were negative and 4 positive. In addition, the upper and lower octaves of the test note—i.e. notes which coincide with the test note in quality—received a substantial number of judgments: 9 negative and 12 positive.

These results confirm my contention that in genuine absolute pitch, notes are recognized by their timbre; in regional pitch, by their crude tone height. For while the judgments in genuine absolute pitch really only fell on the test note and its qualitatively identical octaves, in regional pitch the judgments covered an area of 24 qualitatively altogether different semitones. Since to a person gifted with genuine absolute pitch the timbre of the notes is especially defined—in fact, actually individualized—he can identify the notes with greater accuracy, while someone who is only gifted with regional pitch, and therefore only apprehends the musical notes on the basis of their " quantitative " characteristic, their tone height—i.e. their approximate locus in the musical range—is able to identify them only approximately.

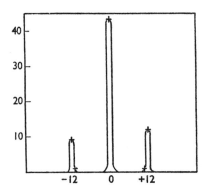

Fig. 25.—Distribution of Absolute Pitch Judgments.

The difference between the two kinds of musical ear can also be viewed from the *genetic* standpoint.

Absolute ear is a question of acoustical sense. It means that certain persons apprehend and identify the notes *directly*, without explicit reference to other notes, as a sensory object of individual dignity, of specific character. As everybody experiences the primary colours (including black, grey and white) directly and identifies them by name, so the person with genuine absolute pitch apprehends the individual notes of the musical note series directly as individualities, and associates definite designations (letter names) with them. He will no more confuse the note C with C♯ or D than anyone will confuse red or orange with yellow. The C character of a note determines its place in the musical note series. This explains why persons with genuine absolute pitch confuse notes of similar quality—i.e. equivalent notes such as C and c¹—

more easily than persons with regional pitch in which only the difference in distance is the decisive factor.

Compared with genuine absolute pitch, the capacity to identify notes according to their highness or lowness in the musical scale is of altogether different character. This form of spontaneous pitch identification is not based on a specific acoustic ability. Here it is rather a question of the employment of a *general psychological faculty* referred to the acoustical domain, which is natural to everybody.

Man possesses the gift of sensing disparate sensory impressions belonging to a *natural series*, usually of ascending character, as members of a linear series in a one-way direction and of arranging them in a spatial scheme. If we are offered a distinct red in various irregular shades of brightness and are instructed to arrange the shades of brightness in graduated order, then, on the basis of the inherent perceptual structure of the brightness-series, we will, as a matter of course, arrange the shades of colour so that they form a graduated series from light to dark, or vice versa. The *organizing principle* in this case is the increasing brightness. The difference in brightness of the colour nuances causes us to arrange these so that they form a progressive series in a one-way direction.

There is an analogous situation in the domain of acoustics. Here, too, the notes will naturally be apprehended as members of a progressive series in a one-way direction. The continuously changing pitch, which as *ascending moment* determines the arrangement in a linear series, is here the variable factor. When we once get a mental image of the note series ascending or descending in a one-way direction and associate this, for example, with the keyboard of the piano, then we arrange the tonal impressions to correspond to the spatial scheme of the keyboard. On the basis of the inherent sense of order, the position of the note struck on the piano will be given with more or less exactness, without relative pitch playing any part therein.*

According to this concept, regional pitch represents the special case of a generally valid *organizing action of the mind*, which is of decisive importance not only for the arrangement according to

* In order to avoid any misapprehension, I desire to emphasize here that in regional pitch, recognition of the note rests on the inherent sense of order, while with genuine absolute pitch only octave identification is conditional on this. Of course, persons with genuine absolute pitch arrange their tone judgments (based on timbre) in the same scheme.

intensity, quantity, volume of sensory objects, but also for that of abstract ideas, such as numbers, let us say. This principle is one of the foundations of ordered thinking. From this point of view, regional pitch can be considered an inherent gift—with some reservations. For it is based on the aforesaid inherent organizing action of the mind, which reveals itself even in little children and is governed by the need to arrange isolated objects as far as possible according to a definite organizing principle. If we assert that regional pitch, in contrast to genuine absolute pitch, is acquired, the statement is not altogether exact, but at least it does justice to the factor of experience. The effect of experience is shown by the fact that regional pitch is capable of development to a high degree, while this is not true of genuine absolute pitch, or at least only to a slight extent. The fact that regional pitch judgments generally increase in accuracy with maturation also points to the importance of experience and practice. A fairly reliable regional pitch was found in only 2% of the musical children under seven years of age, but in 5% of young persons between seventeen and twenty, and in even 20% of still older persons (20).

D. Ear for Standard Pitch

The analysis of pitch identification leads us to a third form of tonal judgment. As we know, there are many musicians who are able to recognize *one* note (more rarely several notes) exactly and to reproduce it spontaneously. Violinists memorize the one line " a " as tuning note; pianists usually the one line c (middle c). This ability has nothing to do either with absolute or regional pitch. It cannot rest on genuine absolute pitch because the identification is usually limited to one single note. Regional pitch does not come into consideration, since here every note judgment is absolutely exact in contrast to those of regional pitch. Many musicians are able to tune to, or reproduce, standard pitch with such precision that they give the impression of having genuine absolute pitch. This impression is increased still more by the fact that they are able, with the help of an aural or vocal standard and their reliable interval sense—i.e. their relative pitch—to identify the other notes rapidly and correctly.

If we now ask how such infallible judgment is possible without genuine absolute pitch, the answer is that this type of pitch identification must be a gradual, progressive *fixation of standard pitch in the memory* as a specific tone impression through experience and systematic practice. Accordingly, the note is not fixed in the memory qualitatively (timbre) or quantitatively (tone height), but as a tone individuality, as a homogeneous complex of quality, pitch, timbre, and ambient noise. It takes long practice, till some of the notes that are especially important for musical practice are so firmly fixed in the memory that at last they can be spontaneously identified without auxiliary aid and with an exactness bordering on that of genuine absolute pitch. This is analogous to painters, workers in mosaic, upholsterers, paperhangers, for example, who after long practice are able to fix colours and nuances of grey so firmly in their minds that they can pick them out accurately from similar shades.

The spontaneous pitch identification just described, which is based on long experience and is limited as a rule to one special note, we will call *standard pitch memory or ear for standard pitch*.

It is clear from these discussions that we must be very careful in the use of the term " absolute pitch ". Not all tone judgments that are so exact as to approximate performances of genuine absolute pitch can be taken as a manifestation of this rare gift. If we investigate the musical ear of a number of persons ostensibly gifted with absolute pitch, it will be found that all types of pitch identification are revealed. For every pitch judgment that relates to a spontaneous recognition and identification of notes in isolation can be classified under one of the three above-mentioned types of musical ear.

A test of 103 persons showed the following results: 7 experimental subjects had an infallible, genuine, universal ear for pitch; 44 had universal absolute pitch, which, however, did not embrace all instruments and at times did not exclude errors of a semitone, as well as confusion in octaves. Eight cases showed limited, and 5 borderline, absolute pitch, and in 7 cases both types were revealed. Regional pitch was found in 26 musicians. Here the errors varied between a semitone and a fifth. Finally, 13 cases were found to have standard pitch.*

* Singers usually take the lowest note in their range as their standard pitch. This ordinarily varies a semitone above or below.

E. Importance of Absolute Pitch

In musical circles, absolute pitch is usually considered a very valuable gift. Undoubtedly musicians possessed of this ability have many advantages in a musical and technical respect.

It is mainly singers who derive great benefits from absolute pitch. If, for example, they have to sing unusual intervals, it presents no difficulties for them, while for the others, no matter how musical they may be, big interval jumps lay a fairly heavy burden on the attention, at least. To the first it is immaterial whether they have to sing a third or an augmented fourth. If the intervals are sufficiently vivid, these persons depend on their well-developed intervallic sense. If this is not the case, then they choose another course, and sing the constituent notes of the third or the augmented fourth. Absolute pitch is also very helpful in sight and a-cappella singing. The advantages for violinists and conductors are self-evident. It can also be of some importance for the receptive side of music; i.e. for the understanding and enjoyment of music. Absolute pitch makes it easier to hold the right key in listening and singing. It enables one to follow the modulations, and thereby retain the initial key without having to strain the attention too greatly.

The opinion that absolute pitch, as such, is very valuable from the æsthetic point of view, and that persons so gifted are in a position to appreciate the beauties of music to a fuller degree than other mortals, must be disputed. Absolute pitch has just as little to do with the æsthetic experience of music as has colour memory with the æsthetic evaluation of painting.

It is also incorrect to assert that absolute pitch has a decisive effect on *productivity*, on free fantasy. In this connexion attention is called to an investigation that substantiated a certain correlation between absolute pitch and musical productivity. From these statistical findings the deduction was drawn that absolute pitch was to be viewed as a " sign or prognostic of an outstanding musical talent ". That this statement can lay no claim to general validity is beyond all doubt. Absolute pitch cannot provide a sure criterion for the presence of musical talent, because in the first place this is often revealed where there can be no question of real musical talent, and in the second place because it is by no means rare to find persons who are highly developed musically (composers among them) without absolute pitch. On the other hand, one cannot altogether deny the symptomatic importance of absolute pitch as sign of a highly developed musicality. Of 582 subjects investigated, 20 were found with absolute pitch, and of these 20, 17 belonged to the group of the very musical, the other 3 to the musical. Among the persons gifted with absolute pitch, we found no single unmusical case (117).

In my opinion, the connexion between musical ear and creative gift is something quite different. The correlation is probably due to the fact that musical persons gifted with genuine absolute pitch, inspired by the attention that they have attracted in their youth, and, owing to the advantages that absolute pitch offers them in their studies, are more apt than others to feel the irresistible urge to occupy themselves intensively with music. Absolute pitch is here no *conditio sine qua non*, but rather a (possibly decisive) motive for developing the available musical talent and for following music professionally.

Genuine absolute pitch also has its drawbacks. For instance, a singer or violinist with absolute pitch can become greatly confused if they have to sing or play a work a quarter tone too low or too high because the accompanying piano is out of tune. The same is also possible when a pianist gifted with absolute pitch is obliged to use a piano that is out of tune. They tell of a pianist with absolute pitch who had to play the first movement of Beethoven's C♯ minor Sonata on a piano tuned a semitone too low, and was therefore unable to capture in the musical pattern of C minor the mood values and emotional meanings which to her were inherent in C♯. She therefore played the work at the original pitch by transposing it to D minor, which of course involved tremendous technical difficulties.

F. Relative Pitch

Absolute pitch must be sharply differentiated from *relative pitch*, the *intervallic sense*. The difference between these two types of musical ear is that with absolute pitch the simple note is experienced and identified as a musical individuality, while with relative pitch the connexion between two notes is apprehended through its specific *intervallic character*. Consequently, in relative pitch it is not a question of the constituent notes of the interval.

Here the apprehension of the interval as an elementary musical entity plays the decisive role. *Under relative pitch we therefore understand the ability to identify a given interval correctly by name, or to transpose and sing it correctly at a different pitch level.*

The intervallic sense can be tested in the following way. A number of sequential intervals are offered, the subject being required to identify them by their musical name. Or one investigates whether the subject is able to sing a designated interval. If the test subject is untrained, then my long experience has shown that the more practical course is first to offer an interval, which the subject is required to sing back, and then to offer some other note on which the subject must sing the perceived interval. In this case it is a question of interval transposition.

Relative pitch is an inherent gift, and can be developed by practice. It varies with the individual. There are persons who can identify and reproduce the principal intervals with maximum precision but the other intervals much less accurately. The simplest is the fourth; the most difficult the minor sixth and the augmented fourth.

Intervallic sense is a specific musical faculty. In general, it is considered a safe criterion of musical aptitude, and justly so. The lack of intervallic sense, or failure to develop it, makes it almost impossible to understand music or respond to it æsthetically. If a person does not possess relative pitch, then he is perceptively insensitive to the melodic and harmonic structure of a musical composition and is unable to derive pleasure and enjoyment from the beautiful in music. Without intervallic sense there is no melody, harmony, tonality. In the last analysis, everything rests on relative pitch. Whatever may be the advantages of absolute pitch, in musical importance it cannot compete with relative pitch.

In recapitulation, the following may be said of the musical ear:

(*a*) First of all, a distinction is drawn between *absolute pitch* and *relative pitch*. The first is the *spontaneous* identification and reproduction of *notes in isolation*; the latter of *intervals*.

1. Genuine absolute pitch is innate, in many cases inherited. It manifests itself right from the beginning in a highly differentiated form.

2. Genuine absolute pitch is *universal* or *limited*, according

to whether the pitch perception covers the entire musical range or only the middle portion.

3. Genuine absolute pitch is either independent of the timbre or is limited to certain timbres. In the first case we speak of *universal absolute pitch*; in the second of *limited absolute pitch*.

4. People with genuine absolute pitch identify the notes on the basis of the tone quality (tone quality perception).

(*b*) Besides this differentiated pitch perception, there is a special form of spontaneous pitch identification in which the notes are only approximately identified; namely, according to the approximate locus in the tonal scale. This type of pitch identification we call *regional pitch*.

1. Regional pitch is an inborn faculty with everybody. It can be developed with practice and experience.

2. In regional pitch, judgments vary greatly with the individual.

3. Those who possess regional pitch identify the single notes on the basis of their pitch property, or, to put it more correctly, on the basis of *their locus in the pitch scale* (tone height recognition).

(*c*) The so-called *ear for standard pitch* is to be viewed as a special type of acquired spontaneous tone identification. It is limited to very few notes: usually to only one standard note (a^1 or c^1). The mnemonic fixation of this note, or these notes, requires long experience. Standard pitch is fixed in the memory by apprehending it as a concrete unitary whole.

(*d*) Finally, we have *relative pitch*, which is the identification, judgment, and reproduction of tone relations, of intervals. From the musical point of view this type of musical ear is the most important. Reliable intervallic sense also depends on practice and experience.

G. IDENTIFICATION AND ANALYSIS OF CHORDS OF TWO AND MORE NOTES

The ability to identify and analyse aurally chords of two and more notes (simultaneous intervals and complex chords) is considered to be a special type of musical ear. Here it is chiefly the perception of *unity* and *multiplicity*. Extremely unmusical persons identify two simultaneous notes as one note, whether they be consonant or dissonant. It even happens that they hear triads (such as perhaps $ab-eb^1-f^1$ or $g-ab^1-db^1$) as *one* note. Such unmusical persons do not even notice the duality when the prongs of tuning-forks are mistuned. People with an average musical ear generally have no difficulty in recognizing the duality or plurality of note complexes. Results obtained show that the accuracy of judgment depends on the degree of fusion of the two-note clangs and complex chords; i.e. the more dissonant they are, the better the judgment. Therefore such persons often perceive the octave as one note. Fourths and fifths are heard more rarely as unanalysable unities, while seconds and sevenths are always perceived as a duality. Persons with an average musical ear are also able to designate the number of component notes when chords are offered them. It stands to reason that with an increasing number of components and an increasing grade of consonance the differentiation of the notes in a chord becomes more difficult.

The analysis and identification of the constituent notes of a chord is also one of the problems of the musical ear. In the analysis, attention is first directed to the clang as a whole. At first no attempt is made to decompose the sound. This follows later on. Once the analysis is completed, the constituent notes come out distinctly in the tone complex. Analytical ability depends on the degree of concentration and on practice. In addition, the locus of the chords, the number of components, and the harmonic structure of the chord also play a role therein. Very consonant notes are much harder to discriminate in a note complex than dissonant ones. Persons of pronounced musicality are able not only to distinguish the component notes in a chord, but to perceive them as parts of a definite tone relationship. The more easily a person can retain a note in his memory or reproduce it spontaneously, the more reliable will be his judgments.

That analysis and the discrimination of component notes does not depend in the main on musical training, but chiefly on the inherent musical talent, is attested by the fact that musically disposed children, even before their first musical instruction, are able to analyse dissonant triads and tetrads with great ease (see Chapter XI).

Through this exposition of absolute, regional, and relative pitch, as well as the identification and analysis of chords, we have covered everything worth knowing about the musical ear. All other features that are treated elsewhere under the name of musical ear do not represent an elementary acoustical-musical ability. They fall under musical appreciation and the æsthetic contemplation of musical forms.

VIII

KEY CHARACTERISTICS

In the world of music the idea is fairly widespread that the different major and minor modes, like the divers intervals, have a specific distinguishing character, that in the keys as such there is an *inherent expressive value peculiar to the key*, which distinguishes them qualitatively one from another. This question was studied exhaustively by the Greek music theorists and mediæval musicologists who for the most part expressed themselves in a positive sense. Their point of view is justifiable if one considers that the Greek and ecclesiastical modes manifest just as great divergencies among themselves as do our major and minor modes as such. The Lydian mode represents an entirely different tone system from the Ionian, Phrygian, Æolian, Dorian. These differences come out clearly if we compare the four leading Greek modes (the so-called authentic modes) and the three plagal modes deriving therefrom.

TABLE 8

Greek and Ecclesiastical Modes

Greek name	Notes	Ecclesiastical name
Lydian	c–d–e–f–g–a–b–c^1	Hypolydian
Phrygian	d–e–f–g–a–b–c^1–d^1	Dorian
Dorian	e–f–g–a–b–c^1–d^1–e^1	Phrygian
Mixolydian . . .	B–c–d–e–f–g–a–b	Hypophrygian
Hypolydian . . .	f–g–a–b–c^1–d^1–e^1–f^1	Lydian
Ionian, or Hypophrigian .	G–A–B–c–d–e–f–g	Mixolydian
Æolian, or Hypodorian . .	A–B–c–d–e–f–g–a	Hypodorian

We see that every Greek and every ecclesiastical mode differs from the other in general pitch and in the sequence of tone steps (intervals); that is, in the ordinal arrangement of the whole and semitones within the octave, just as do our major and minor modes. The Greek Lydian mode, for instance, moves within the octave c–c^1; the Ionian, on the other hand, within the octave G–g. The first is formed by the notes c–d–e–f–g–a–b–c^1, the latter by the notes G–A–B–c–d–e–f–g. Accordingly, the sequence of scale steps (i.e. the alternation of whole and semitones) in the

Lydian mode is $1-1-\frac{1}{2}-1-1-1-\frac{1}{2}$, and in the Ionian $1-1-\frac{1}{2}-1-1-\frac{1}{2}-1$. Each mode represents, as it were, a characteristic melody in itself.

The musical Greek must have noted the differences in the diatonic modes (Modi), just as we notice when a work is played in the major or the minor. It was because of the structural and phenomenological differences of the Greek modes that the Greeks used the modes for very definite occurrences, convinced that the public would understand. The Dorian mode was used on solemn occasions, the Phrygian served to inspire the soldiers, the Lydian to evoke sadness and melancholy (our major mode!) and the Æolian accompanied the love-songs. It is therefore understandable that through this consequent linking of the *mode with the purpose*, each mode was associated with a definite emotion, a distinct mood.* Strange to say, in the Middle Ages the same emotive-conative associations were imputed to the Dorian ecclesiastical mode as the Greeks attributed to the Phrygian; and to the Phrygian ecclesiastical mode the same as the Greeks ascribed to the Dorian. Even from this it can be concluded that for the expressive character of the modes, tradition, and not the mode as a specific acoustical-musical form, was the determining factor.

In the problem under discussion it is not a question of the character of the Modi, of the modes, but of the key *within one and the same mode*. Within a mode, our scales differ only in *regional pitch*, i.e. in the octave defining the dominant and final. Otherwise they are all alike, since they represent the same frequency ratios. The step sequence is the same in all the major and minor modes; and, in accordance with equal temperament, all the semitones are equal. Nevertheless, it is frequently thought that the character, the mood, and with it the æsthetic effect of a musical work is greatly altered if a musical composition is transposed from one key to another; that is, if only the absolute pitch changes. There are musicians who go so far as to call every transposition a rank violation of the musical feeling and an unjustified interference with the composer's intentions. They are of the opinion, for example, that the C minor Concerto of Beethoven, or the A

---

* In the old Greek doctrine of Ethos, the definite effect imputed to each mode was a reflection of the tribal temperament. Dorian indicated: moral, austere. Phrygian, effeminate, weak, immoral, etc.

flat major Ballade of Chopin are *constitutionally* linked with these keys. They proceed from the assumption that in the choice of key the composer was guided by the inner mood of the projected composition or by the accompanying text or his own fugitive mental state at the moment. It was not by mere chance, they say, that Beethoven chose E♭ major for the Eroica, but because this particular key agreed best with the basic musical idea and the fundamental atmosphere of this symphony. No musician should therefore take the liberty of playing works (or of having others play them) even a chromatic semitone lower or higher than they were originally written.

Provided that every key within the same genera really possesses a specific expressive character—that, for example, one is expressive of gaiety, another of depth and richness and still another of passion—then with every transposition we run the risk of destroying the æsthetic effect intended by the composer. This would be valid for all musical works, but especially so for vocal compositions (Lieder, etc.) which, through the text, are even more strongly associated with a distinct atmosphere or mood. In these cases it would be indefensible to sing in C♯ major or D major a composition written in C major, to transpose songs for a lower or higher voice, or to perform a work on an instrument that is out of tune.*

The question whether the several keys actually have a peculiar character of their own has not yet been answered. Galley states in his encyclopædia that in general the minor modes have the character of sorrow and grief, whereas a happy atmosphere emanates from the major modes. Such descriptions are highly subjective and altogether unfit for characterizing the modes in view of the fact that the individual mood of the modes has changed greatly in the course of time.†

* That Beethoven was fundamentally opposed to the transposition of his Lieder "because of the absolute character of the modes" is explicable by the fact that he himself was gifted with absolute pitch (60).

† Proceeding from a musical psychological-kinetic point of view, E. Kurth has arrived at a sort of key characterization. He distinguishes three groups: a flat group, a sharp group, and finally the signature-less C major. The flat group signifies in a certain sense a decrease in intensity; the sharp group, through the repeated sharpening of the leading note, experiences an increase in tension. Kurth stresses the fact that the total musical experience of flat and sharp keys lies by no means in the exclusion or inclusion of the leading note. On the contrary, here we find novel, organically unified experiences in comparison with which the inclusion or exclusion of the leading note would be a cause rather than a phenomenological effect. It is to be assumed that such an experience depends very largely on the possession of absolute

The opposite point of view is also encountered occasionally; that is, the assertion that the characteristic trait of a key remains the same irrespective of whether the pitch of the nominal key is higher or lower, provided it bears the same designation. For instance, in the 17th century C major was considered just as virile, decisive, as today, though at that time C major lay between B and D as a result of a shift in chamber pitch.

If it is once realized that the normal or standard pitch has changed very greatly in the past hundred years, then we need not excite ourselves unduly over the transposition of musical works and lay any special weight on the presumable intentions of the composers in this respect. And this therefore justifies the question: how can we reconcile the traditional theory of the Ethos or characteristic traits of the modes with the fact that Mozart's C major Symphony, which at present is played about three-fourths of a tone higher than in his day, has still retained its C major character?

Granted that the choice of scale is not dependent on mere caprice, this by no means proves that the motive for the choice is to be attributed exclusively to the presumed character of the keys. It can also be that the composers prefer those keys that have been especially familiar to them ever since their youth. They hold firmly to these from habit and tradition, even when they have already overcome all technical and harmonic difficulties. They will improvise and compose in these keys quite involuntarily. That may perhaps account for the fact that in his eighteen piano sonatas Mozart chose C major four times, E major four times, and D major three times; and why in his twenty-one piano concertos he used no key with more than three sharps or flats. Table 9, listing the different keys of his works, may serve to illustrate this point.

This shows that in the 183 listed works Mozart only once used a key with more than three sharps, whereas he used keys with less than two sharps and two flats a total of seventy-nine times.

In the principal movements of Beethoven's piano sonatas he has also used no key with more than four flats, except in Op. 74, which

---

pitch or standard pitch. But even apart from this, the different characters of the modes within the genera cannot be explained by this group arrangement. And that after all is the important point.

TABLE 9
Mozart's Preference for Certain Keys

	|												|											
					Major keys.												**Minor keys.**								
♯♭	C	Db 5	D 2	Eb 3	E 4	F 1	F# 6	G 1	Ab 4	A 3	Bb 2	B 5	c 3	c# 4	d 1	eb 6	e 1	f 4	f# 3	g 2	g# 5	a 1	bb 5	b 2
18 piano sonatas *	4		3	1		3		1		1	3		1											
27 piano concertos *	4		4	4		4		2		2	5		1		1		1					1		
40 violin works	8		3	4	1	6		6		4	7				1					1				
8 piano trios	1			1				2		1	2													
6 violin concertos †			3			4		1		2	1													
27 string quartets	3		4	3				3		1	5		1		2					1				
8 string quartets	1		1	3		5				3	1		1							2				
49 symphonies	8		14	5				7			5													
183 works in all	29		32	20	1	22		22		14	29		4		4		1			4		1		

* Not included are the Rondos in D and A major and three piano sonatas of J. Chr. Bach arranged by Mozart as concertos. Sonatas 37, 39, 40 and 41 are included.

† Not included are the additional versions of several violin concertos, the Rondo in C major, Andante in A major and the Concertone for two violins in C major.

is in F♯ major. Of the other sonata movements, eleven are in keys with more than four flats or four sharps.

Besides habit and tradition, *technical considerations* can also play a part in the choice of keys; for example, the applicability of a wind instrument pitched to a definite key (B♭, A and high E♭ clarinets; F, E, E♭ and D trumpets; those used by the classical masters in C, B♭ and A; B♭ and E♭ cornets). Choice can also be guided by conventional motives; for instance, knowledge of musical literature, especially the study of the works of great masters, can lead composers to prefer keys used by the former for certain special musical forms.

It is obvious that this particular motive speaks more *against* than *for* the presumed character of the keys. In this question more weight might be laid on the *statements of the composers and professional artists* if they were not so contradictory. There are many artists, for instance, who are firmly convinced of the alleged distinctions in the character of the keys and claim that they can recognize every change in key on the basis of the key feeling, the fundamental character of the individual keys within the major and minor genera. On the other hand, there are at least just as many who frankly admit that they do not always notice when a familiar work has been transposed, provided of course that the change of pitch is slight.

In answering the above questions, the most reliable course, it seems to me, is to set the *declarations* of the musicians and the musically trained over against their *performances* and to ascertain if those who support the theory of the special character of the keys are really capable of distinguishing one key from another. In such a test those musical persons must be excluded who are gifted with absolute pitch, for they are able to recognize the keys on the basis of the individuality of the single notes. For this group of persons the C major scale will naturally produce a different effect than the D major, since the two keys are composed in part of notes and note combinations individually known to them. This is analogous to seeing a familiar picture with vivid colour effects under coloured lights, which distinctly alters the well-known colours.

In how far the statements of musicians and musically talented persons regarding the character of the keys can be considered reliable, in how far their statements coincide with their performances, can only be decided through systematic tests within the framework of a rigorous psychological experiment. We will give the results of such an experiment.

R. Hennig, a radical exponent of the theory of the expressive character of the keys, who dedicated an exhaustive work to the problem, maintained that he himself was able to recognize keys purely by their character, uninfluenced by subjective considerations and physical factors (53). Hennig was subjected to a practical test by O. Abraham in which the latter played triads to him on the piano in all the minor modes, supplemented by chords of the seventh, and he was then required to name the key of the chords. It turned out that he correctly identified only F♯ minor, and even this key *only on his own piano*; while he made numerous errors with all the other chords. Among other things he identified G♯ minor chords on his own instrument not only as G♯ minor, but also very often as F, E, or B minor, and on a strange piano even as F, A♭ or B♭ minor.

I have substantiated these findings on several musically trained persons. If the experiment is carried out meticulously, it will be found that many musical types will show an error of a half and a whole tone from the tonic, above and below. A strange instrument, less familiar timbres, high and low positions in the pitch scale, all effect the result. In these circumstances errors within the compass of a third or a fourth are no rarity.

These few experiments can lay no claim to answer the question conclusively, for the very simple reason that isolated chords are unsuitable as key determinants, since they admit of more than one interpretation. This would only be possible if harmonies, sequences, cadences, etc., were offered in the key in question and persons of unquestionable musical ability were required to identify the key. How such an experiment would turn out, we do not know. Nevertheless, there is no doubt that there are musical persons (in the main, professional musicians) who are able to identify keys correctly and recognize transpositions without having absolute pitch. How can this ability be explained if absolute pitch is left out of the question?

Divers theories have been propounded to account for this ability. One derives from Helmholtz and considers the apprehension of *timbre* to be the perceptive criterion. Helmholtz proceeded from the theory that the difference in character of the different scales on the piano is due to the difference in timbre, which in turn is linked with the hammer mechanism. He was of the opinion that the black digitals produce another quality of tone than the white ones owing to the somewhat shorter arm of the lever and the resultant difference in leverage. In the bowed instruments, the open strings, which are therefore richer in overtones, sound brighter than the other strings and give a brighter character to the keys in which they are much used. The natural notes of the wind instruments also sound brighter and different from the stopped notes. All this is supposed to have an effect on the absolute character of the key.

It is not difficult to prove the untenability of this hypothesis. We will only point to one circumstance. If timbre had a decisive influence on the phenomena or absolute character of the keys, then *one and the same key*, played on different instruments, might be expected to manifest a conspicuous difference; which, however, is inconsistent with experience. The consequences for the orchestra of such a concept should be clear to anyone.

Another point of view current among musicians is that the character or expressive mood of the key depends on the *number of sharps and flats*. In general, C major is considered strong and virile; G major (with one sharp) broader and brighter; D major (with two sharps) still broader and brighter, etc. Each sharp is supposed to increase the brightness and brilliancy, while each flat is supposed to make the key softer, more expressive. The implausibility of this point of view is clear when we realize that if this were the case a much greater difference would exist between F♯ major with six sharps and G major with one than between F♯ major with its six sharps and E major with four. And how is it, then, with F♯ major with six sharps and G♭ major with six flats, or with B♭ minor with five flats and A♯ minor with seven?

Another hypothesis that is not uninteresting psychologically but does not solve the problem is the following. It is not the key in itself, but its *letter name*—that is, the *image* evoked by the letter name—that is supposed to be the prepotent factor in defining the characteristic trait of the key. The sound images G♯, A♯, F♯ are " sharp " in character. D♭, E♭, A♭, on the contrary, are soft. According to this theory, the mood effect is described by the sound characters of the key names, which are simply *transferred* to the keys. This is the reason, therefore, why F♯ major, F♯

minor, etc., sound sharp and pointed, and A♭ major, A♭ minor, etc., sound soft. According to this concept, the sharp keys in general seem *by association* keen, bright, sharp; the flat keys, on the contrary, mild, soft, dark.

The possibility of the transference from the phonetic to the musical domain cannot be rejected off-hand. Nevertheless, this associative connexion is unable to explain the alleged variations in the expressive character of the keys—the key feeling—for the simple reason that here even in the best of cases it is a question of *group* characteristics (*all* sharp and *all* flat keys), and not of specific differences in Gestalt. For in the sense of this theory *all sharp* and *all flat* keys should have essentially the same character. It is difficult to understand why the sharp keys or the flat keys should exhibit differences among themselves. Furthermore, according to this theory, the key characteristic would only be apparent if one *knew the key in question beforehand.* The point can also be made that this type of phonetic association is cut to the particular measure of the German key names. It is by no means valid for the French and English designations: sharp, flat; dièse, bémol.

We have therefore seen that neither the statements of musical persons available to us nor the hypotheses advanced can solve the postulated question satisfactorily. But the problem nevertheless exists, for however we may interpret the divers statements and communications there is no doubt that certain musical persons are capable of identifying keys even without absolute pitch. The question now is what criterion guides them in their judgments? In my opinion the Two-component Theory also provides a satisfactory answer to this question.

Let us take a simple example. If we transpose a simple rhythmical melody from one key to another, this does not change the *acoustic-musical-temporal relationships.* Even the harmonic foundation of the melody from which we cannot emancipate ourselves, and through which the melody derives its deeper musical significance, is completely unaltered, no matter how it may be transposed. If through the transposition we still experience a change, it can refer to nothing but the *change of pitch of the individual notes,* or the shifting of the melody (key) either upwards or downwards. Now, if anyone recognizes that a work is played in the original or a transposed key, then this can be due to nothing but the perception that the mnemonically fixed general pitch of the composition has changed and the *harmonic function* of certain notes characterized by their absolute pitch have thereby undergone a change. (The harmonic function of the note E as component of the C major triad is, as everyone knows, quite different from the same note as component of the A minor chord.) But all this can only occur with the help of the *regional pitch ear*, which permits an approximate mnemonic fixation of the locus of the note in the pitch scale Although this ear (as shown by our discussion of the subject on page 99 ff.) is inexact, the function can be improved by practice to an error of only a semitone—at least in the middle register. This explains why a trained musician, even without absolute pitch, can immediately recognize the transposition of a composition a whole tone, while he will be uncertain and waver in his judgment when the rise in pitch is only a semitone. With long practice, professional musicians can memorize the pitch of isolated notes and the general pitch level of familiar musical works, so that they are able unaided to tell the original key from any transposition.

If, for example, a musician has fixed the standard pitch or the note c^2 firmly in his memory, then he is able, even without absolute pitch, to identify the various keys, since by taking the standard pitch as reference note, he can readily identify the tonic in question by means of his intervallic sense (relative pitch). This pitch identification has nothing to do with the so-called character of the keys.

It is manifest, therefore, that in cases where the key or the transposition is recognized, it is not a question of hypothetical differences in expressive character between the keys, but the *apprehension of a shift in pitch level of the whole composition* either upwards or downwards. This explains why the transposition is the more readily discernible, the greater the distance between the two tonics. In a transposition from C major to C♯ major a difference will be sensed far more rarely than in one from C to D major, or even one from C to G major. This also explains why most musicians recognize the keys more readily on their own pianos than on a strange instrument. The individual pitches of their own piano can be fixed in their memories better than pitches as such.

We have therefore come to the conclusion that the theory of key characteristics has very little foundation in fact. The original theory to the effect that the keys, as homogeneous tonal entities, have a peculiar expressive character of their own, which exerts a prepotent influence on the emotional and æsthetic effect of the musical work, cannot be substantiated either through observation and experiment or through tenable hypotheses. The consequences resulting from this theory also point to its untenability.*

It is altogether different if we merely ask how transposition and the mistuning of instruments can be recognized even without absolute pitch, for this question can be answered. In regional pitch we have a means of fixing the pitch-level of the notes, keys, and musical works. Through the arrangement of the keys and other musical patterns in the pitch scale they derive *different pitch characters* which makes it possible to recognize the transposition.†
This capacity makes it seem as though the key, as such, exerted a dominant effect on the total impression through its specific musical content. We must rid ourselves of this illusion and trace key identification, or the perception of transposition, within broad limits and without absolute pitch, to musical memory only ; that is, to the association of the musical pattern with its regional pitch.‡

* One consequence of the theory of key characteristics would be that the character of the key would change with a change in standard pitch. But this is not the case. We know, for example, that in the 17th and 18th centuries the expressive character of C major was described in exactly the same terms as today, though the " powerful, simple, virile " C major of Bach's time corresponded approximately with our C♯ major, and in the time of Mozart almost with our present D major.

† Besides absolute and regional pitch, there is still another possibility of fixing these notes and keys more or less individually in the memory. Here the agent of recognition is synæsthesia, or so-called " colour hearing ", which will be discussed in the following chapter. However, synæsthesia is of secondary importance to the problem of key characteristics on account of its rarity.

‡ E. Isler also arrived in principle at the same result. He, too, admits only one fundamental difference in the character of the modes (major and minor), but none in the transposition of the major and minor scales, etc. (38, 60). See also an article by K. v. Fischer in the *Schweizerische Musikzeitung*, 1943 (" Zur Tonartencharakteristik ").

IX

RELATION BETWEEN TONE AND COLOUR PERCEPTION

Tone as a primary sensation has nothing to do with colour as a primary sensation. A tone sensation in its phenomenological form is diametrically different from a colour sensation. At times they can arouse the same emotional reactions, linked together by associative processes. But as sensory impressions they admit of no comparison.

There are certain persons—at all events few in number—who automatically associate tones and tone qualities with distinct colours. Their identification of isolated notes is due not to the primary acoustic impression, but to the *optical*, mnemonic, or intuitive image associated with it. Such a reciprocal relationship between tone and colour is known in psychology as colour (or coloured) hearing (Synæsthesia). By *colour hearing* we understand the *fixed permanent association of acoustic sensations with optical images*. In persons with pronounced colour hearing, certain tonal stimuli always create *involuntarily, regularly, and constantly* the same colour sensations (so-called chromatisms or photisms). These chromatisms or photisms can be divided into three classes, according to type: *perceptual*, as though the colours were actually seen; *conceptual*, when the colour is envisaged as an ideated sensation; and *mental*, when the colour only comes to mind, when only its name is suggested to the conscious mind.

Colour hearing in music was described for the first time, as far as we are aware, by a certain J. L. Hoffmann (1786), who asserted that he automatically associated the tone qualities of the different instruments with definite colours. At the time of E. T. A. Hoffmann (1810) this phenomenon must have been already generally known, for otherwise it would be difficult to understand how he came to ridicule it in his " Kreisleriana ".

" Just at that time (he wrote) I was also wearing a suit that I once bought in the greatest ill-humour over an unsuccessful trio. The colour of it ran towards C♯ major, so I had a collar in E major colour put on it to pacify the spectators to a certain extent."

In the romantic period different musicians turned their attention to this " mysterious " synæsthesia. It often happened that composers characterized their musical impressions in terms of colour. For instance, Joachim Raff imagined the character of the instruments in terms of the following colours: horn green, trumpet purple, trombone violet, bassoon black. Liszt is also said to have exclaimed at an orchestra rehearsal: " Please, gentlemen, a little bluer if you please. This key demands it."

In belles lettres we also find a quantity of evidence pointing to colour hearing, among others Grillparzer, Moerike, Heine, Theophile Gautier, J. K. Huysmans, Rimbaud, Baudelaire, Maupassant. Whether these musicians and writers all really possessed colour hearing or merely desired to symbolize their æsthetic experiences through the expressive values of the different colours cannot be determined. It was therefore necessary to attack systematically the question of the connexion between tone and colour and above all to subject very pronounced synæsthetes to rigorous investigation. Bleuler, Flournoy and Claparède, Anschütz, Urbantschitsch, Binet, Pierce, Révész, Bos, Weinert, Lach, Wellek, and others have done successful work in this field.

The tests on synæsthetes have brought to light a large number of synæsthetic variants. There are persons with a very finely nuanced system of subjective colours for all the notes in the octave (including the enharmonic variants), as well as for all the major and minor modes, intervals, instruments, and vocables. In others synæsthesia is limited to the notes (tone qualities) with enharmonic distinctions. Many synæsthetes construct the " triads " and " melodies " from individual colour elements. They " see " a melody as tiny coloured dots in a dotted line like variegated glass beads on a string. Besides this analytical colour hearing, there is also a " synthetic " type. In this latter the chords and melodies are not formed from the constituent elements; but each entity appears in a definite colour, or colour nuance. Musical works, as such, are " dipped " as it were in one single colour—according to the key, for example.

A few examples of the phenomenon of colour hearing are given herewith. One experimental subject admitted associating the *vocal registers* with certain fixed colours.

Brown with a deep, dark voice.
Lavender with a soft, melancholy voice.
Yellow with a shrill, high voice.
Red with a high, ringing voice.
Blue with a fairly colourless voice.

Kandinsky, the painter, claimed that he sensed a similarity between " tone colour " and " colour tone ". He felt a constant relationship between:

Light blue and the tones of the flute.
Dark blue and the cello.
Green and the violin.
Red and the flourish of trumpets.
Vermilion and the ruffle of drums.
Orange and church bells.
Violet and the horn and bassoon.

There are persons who associate colour images with *single notes*. For instance, a synæsthete felt the following associations:

D and chestnut brown.
F and grey.
e and blue.
a and dark beige.
a^1 and light yellow toning gradually into blue.
f^2 and lemon-yellow.
c^4 and whitish-yellow.

The colour relationship is even clearer when definite optical images (coloured or colourless) are associated with the twelve notes of the *tempered scale*. For example, one test subject indicated the following associations between notes and colour:

c dull bluish-white.
c♯ colourless, shimmering.
d brownish-red.
d♯ dark blue.
e pure white.
f rich reddish-brown.
f♯ brown.
g medium grey.
g♯ orange.
a golden-yellow.
a♯ black.
b pale mixture of red and yellow.

Wellek investigated a synæsthete whose colour associations depended on the general pitch (158).

Octave	Great octave	Small octave	One line octave	Two line octave	Three line octave
c c♯ }	Grey	Yellow	Red	} White	} Blue
d	Green	Green	} White		
d♯ e }	White	Yellow			
f f♯ }	Red	} Brown	Red	} Blue-grey	} Black
g g♯ }	Blue		Black		
a	} Yellow	White	White		
b♭ b }		} Red	Red		

Finally, there are persons who associate certain colour images with certain *keys*.

	Major keys.	Minor keys.
F	Light green	—
C	Leaf green-yellow	Dark blue
G	Yellowish red	Red
D	Orange	Dark green
A	Bright red	Dark blue
E	Scarlet	Light green
B	Dark red	Violet (?)
F♯	Dark purple	—
C♯	Violet	Violet

With this person it was also found that the association of the colours with the keys depended on whether the notes were played on the piano or whether they were merely ideated. Although the test subject did not possess absolute pitch, she apparently could identify the keys on the basis of the associated colour images. She admitted further that the different composers, or the works of the composers, evoked certain colour images with her. For example, she associated Bach with orange and yellow, Haydn with blue, Mozart with light blue, Schubert with violet, Liszt with purplish-red, and Wagner with luscious green.

We must frankly admit that most of the colour hearing tests have not been carried out with the necessary precision. Therefore they do not furnish a clear and trustworthy picture of the constancy of type of the chromatism. As a rule investigators also failed to go into the question of how the co-ordinations arose, or in how far chance associations or automatic synæsthesia (secondary sensation in one sensory field produced by a primary sensation in another sensory field) played a part therein. There can be no doubt that colour hearing exists or that certain expressive values are associated with fixed colour relationships which may be co-determinants of the musical-æsthetic impression.*

Whether colour hearing should be viewed as a special type of absolute ear is open to doubt. The fact that tone and colour sometimes occur as an inseparable complex, that colour is experienced as a property of tone, would support this thesis. But it seems to me more correct to speak here of absolute colour memory because colour, not tone, is the primary sensation. The tone conforms to the individualized colour. In musical theory and practice, synæsthesia is of no importance, since it is only found in rare cases. It represents a unique phenomenon that is only of interest from the psychological point of view.

* The Ocular Harpsichord constructed in 1739 by the French Jesuit, Louis Bertrand Castel, was associated with colour hearing. In this instrument the seven colour bands of Newton's spectrum were made to correspond with the seven notes of the diatonic scale. Since then attempts have been made from time to time to accompany music with colour and figure complexes. In one of his orchestral works (Prometheus) Alexander Scriabine prescribed a " clavier à lumière ". Colour and sound also interested Berlioz for the " colour " that he sensed in each tonality (Fr. Gysi: *Musik und Farbe* in "Wissen und Leben ", No. 16, 1922).

PART III

FUNDAMENTAL PROBLEMS OF THE PSYCHOLOGY OF MUSIC

X

MUSICALITY

A. The Concept of Musicality

THE concept of musicality is one of the most controversial in the psychology of music.   In ordinary everyday language this concept has no concrete significance.   It is often used in the sense of " being musical " (fond of, or skilled in music) as antithesis of the concept " unmusical " (unskilled in, or indifferent to, music). This leads to a typological classification into the *musical* and the *unmusical*.   Such a classification is objectionable, since it is impossible to draw a strict line of demarcation between the two groups.   If the latter group is limited solely to the altogether unmusical, then the first group will be unwarrantably broadened. If only those persons who are especially musical are assigned to the first group, we then run the risk of allocating many musically talented persons to the group of the unmusical,   If, for example, we consider a marked *creative* or *interpretative* talent to be the essential element of musicality, then we must deny this quality to a large number of inherently musical persons, even to those who fully appreciate the ideal, formal content of music.

Among music theorists and music psychologists there are also those who, in defining musicality, lay the greatest weight on the so-called acoustic and acoustic-musical capacities (such, for instance, as the capacity to discriminate rhythmical and tonal relationships), on relative pitch, on an active melodic response, etc.   But we cannot arrive at a sure diagnosis of musicality on the basis of any such criteria.   Experience shows that a person may possess a goodly quantity of such attributes and abilities without necessarily being in a position to grasp music in its autonomous forms and effects.   It is quite another matter if these attributes and abilities are evaluated solely as *symptoms* of musicality.   In this sense they also represent valuable indices for the diagnosis of musicality.

But those who stress the *emotional side* of the musical experience, the sensuous appreciation of music, fall altogether short of the mark.   So long as music only has an emotional impact, delights or saddens us, affects us strongly, stirs our feelings, we remain in

the extra-æsthetic sphere of musical effects.   The musical person
in the true sense of the word seeks in music not only sensuous
reactions, not only dynamics, rhythm, volume, movement, content; but also the æsthetic, the *Apollonic*.   True, the æsthetic is
always clothed in the sensuous.   But the sensuous effect does not
constitute it.   There is, of course, music that only aims at exciting
the emotions.   But the object of such music is hardly other than
the rhythmical, melodic, harmonic, and dynamic content of
music that puts one in a joyous, happy mood, gives pleasure, keen
delight, and gratification.   This striving for sensuous effect, for
the *Dionysiac* side of music, is by no means unimportant.   It is
closely bound up with our feeling of life.   But this music is not *the*
music that transports us to the sphere of æsthetic experience.
The same effects can be evoked by other delightful events, such as
joy over seeing someone again, or pleasure in the beauties of
Nature.   We must hold fast to the thought that the musical-
æsthetic, the beautiful in music, which is the real heart of the
matter as far as musicality is concerned, has reference to the
autonomous emotional effect of music, to the *pleasure* deriving from the
specific musical-intellectual content and the *musical form* of the art
work, which in musical persons can arouse responsive feelings
and create an æsthetic experience.

The formulation of a pertinent definition of the concept of
musicality presents, as we see, great difficulties.   It is hard to
give terse, precise form to the fund of significations and characteristics.   It must therefore suffice if we establish the most
important properties of the musical person, though we lay no
claim to its being an exhaustive definition of musicality.   The
time has not yet come for a definitive definition.   For that we
should require a much more exact analysis of the musical person
and a formulation of the different types.

If we define musicality so as to take in all types and degrees
of the musical sense, independent of the time element and the
grade of culture, then we must count on the definition lacking that
concrete substance that furnishes criteria for diagnosing musicality.   From such a universal point of view, musicality can be
defined as follows: By musicality in general we are to understand
*the need and the capacity to understand and to experience the autonomous
effects of music and to appraise musical utterances on the score of their
objective quality* (*æsthetic content*).   But the combination of need,

experience, and competent æsthetic appraisal characterizes musicality just as it does any other form of artistic sense. Since this and all similar definitions afford no deeper insight into the nature of musicality, we will dispense altogether with a factual definition of the concept of musicality, and try to describe the musical person with reference to his musical utterances and behaviour towards music without for the moment considering the various grades of musicality and the intermediate types up to unmusicality.

In this sense that person is to be considered musical who is able to transfer his musical experiences to a sphere in which the art work is the object of purely artistic contemplation and radiates its specific artistic effects on the productive and re-creative individual. Not emotion, enthusiasm, love of music, a warm interest in it, but the *mental conquest of music as art characterizes the musical person.*

When we lay stress upon the word "mental", we would by no means imply thereby an "cerebral" activity in the learned sense. Here it is not a question of a higher, more perfect form of rational cognition, of an intellectual knowledge. Like everything in the sphere of æsthetics, the musical-æsthetic also can only be experienced and appraised. But such an experience is mental in character, since it cannot be assimilated passively, but must be inwardly digested and fashioned. Consequently it presupposes an intensive, heightened mental activity. Musical creations cannot be absorbed purely receptively. The perceptive subject has the task of co-ordinating what he has heard, of following the parts in their interrelations of harmony and modulation, of separating and keeping distinct the interwoven parts without thereby separating them from the whole. This all demands a mental attitude that is oriented to the formal indwelling values of the musical work, which enables an approach to the music (44).

If we would characterize the musical person especially with reference to his sensitivity to artistic quality and his capacity for an æsthetic evaluation of musical works as well as of their artistic performance, then we might add the following: The musical person possesses a deep understanding of musical forms and the structure or movement plan of the work. He has a finely developed sense of style and of the strict organization of musical processes of thought. He is able to follow the composer's intentions, even at times to anticipate them. It is also characteristic of the musical person to sink himself into the mood of the music and achieve a relation to it that has an effect on his whole spiritual being. He experiences the art work so inwardly and so profoundly that he feels as though he were creating it. This " creative " act is peculiar to the musical person not only during the mere æsthetic assimilation, but also in the interpretation of musical works. The possession of these qualities expresses itself in the ability to judge and evaluate the artistic quality of musical works. Musicality—this inborn property that requires (and is also capable of) development—irradiates the *whole individual*, and accordingly forms a characteristic trait of the *personality as a whole*.

In order to obviate any misunderstanding right from the first, it should be emphasized that the above description of musicality has reference to the person of very pronounced musical gifts and culture. It therefore represents, as it were, the ideal requirements. But it should by no means be deduced from this that persons who fail to exhibit all the aforesaid capacities have no right to be listed in the musical category. Besides the aforesaid optimum level of musicality, there are various degrees of musicality extending from this peak level down to unmusicality itself. However, in order to be considered musical a person must possess several of the above-listed properties and capacities.

Here we have only discussed receptive musicality, and not creative. The musicality of composers is so self-evident, their works furnish so many *points d'appui* for the diagnosis of their musical sense, their appreciation and feeling for art, that we can dispense with a test of musicality in this instance.

B. TESTING NATURAL MUSICAL CAPACITY

In its *pronounced* form, musicality can be definitely diagnosed without a special test for this purpose. But if we only wish to diagnose *musical aptitude*, then it is quite sufficient to seek symptoms that point indisputably to musical aptitude, determine its stage of development. Consequently it will not be our task to investigate musicality as a homogeneous, many-sided function. On the contrary, we must subject those capacities and performances to test that unquestionably derive from the musical aptitude, are a prerequisite to musicality, or can be deduced from it alone.

What is tested in this case is not musicality *per se*, but rather the *symptoms of an aptitude* for musical activity that permit well-founded conclusions regarding the existence and the degree of musicality. The point therefore is to measure, by means of previously determined and substantiated data, a number of acoustic and musical attributes and capacities that one can safely assume are intimately associated with musicality.

The first suggestion to measure musicality was made by the famous Vienna surgeon and music-lover, Dr. Theodor Billroth, in 1895, in his work, "Who is Musical?" He did not measure, but merely listed, the characteristics of the musical person that seemed to him to be important. The musically trained physiologist, Johannes von Kries, followed approximately the same lines in his little work under the same title (1926), in which he discussed in a stimulating, provocative way a fairly large number of sometimes important, sometimes unimportant, capacities (68). He arrived at the conclusion that, in the main, three properties are to be viewed as special " characteristics of musicality "; namely, a sense of rhythm, a musical ear, and musical memory.

The first systematic experimental measures of musical talent originated with Carl Seashore and myself (114, 136, 137, 138). The test battery carefully constructed by Seashore and verified by a very large number of test subjects had reference to auditory perception, vocal performance, the musical ear (pitch discrimination), auditory imagery, and musical feeling. Seashore laid special stress on pitch discrimination. He stated that the sensory capacity shows a high correlation with musical capacities.

In my opinion Seashore's tests designed to measure musical talent can be symptomatic for *musical aptitude* but not for *musical talent*. It would therefore be desirable to supplement these tests with several of the successful test batteries that I recommended. In my test battery the following acoustic-musical capacities can be evaluated:

(*a*) Rhythmical sense (has the lowest symptomatic rating).
(*b*) Regional pitch.
(*c*) Analysis of two-note clangs and chords.
(*d*) Capacity to grasp and sing a melodic line.

For the higher grades of musicality, the following capacities are to be considered:

(a) Relative pitch.

(b) Harmonic apprehension and response. In this test, subjects are required to sing or play back intervals or triads in their primary positions and inversions, judge their grade of consonance, and identify the key. Furthermore, they must show a capacity to grasp cadences and sing the progression of the individual parts.

(c) The ability to play familiar melodies from memory on the piano without accompaniment. Correct performance indicates a good melodic sense, good intervallic sense, and a good musical ear.

(d) Creative fantasy. Here a simple melody of familiar form is interrupted before the end, and the test subject is required to sing the melody from then on to the close. It is very instructive to have test subjects find suitable harmonies for songs.*

C. The Unmusical Person

Unmusical persons can be classified into two entirely distinct categories; namely, the *congenitally* unmusical and the *neurotically* unmusical. The first are the genuinely unmusical in the strict sense of the word; the latter the quasi-unmusical. Those representing the transitional types between the musical and the unmusical form a special group. These differ from the genuinely unmusical in having a rhythmic, melodic, and harmonic sense, even though they are unable to grasp the structure of a musical composition and evaluate it in terms of its æsthetic content. Up to a certain point these persons are capable of development in a musical sense. Through musical training, they gradually come into contact with music without, however, really attaining the sphere of the specifically musical in which the beautiful-in-music becomes an object of æsthetic perception.

The congenitally unmusical form no homogeneous, concrete group. On the contrary, they manifest divergencies of a fundamental character. The relatively best group of the congenitally unmusical (which can be called " non-musical ", to

* For a detailed description of my test batteries and methods, see the German edition of this work (" Einfuehrung in die Musikpsychologie," A. Francke Verlag, Berne, Switzerland), pp. 168–178, and the *Zeitschrift für Psychologie*, Vol. 85. C. von Maltzew, Rupp, Scheunemann, and Max Schoen have also occupied themselves with this question.

differentiate them from the pronouncedly unmusical) are those persons on whom music exerts at least an emotional effect. Music evokes in them emotive states, and they expect nothing more than gratifying emotional reactions. Their acoustic-musical capacities are very limited. True, they can discriminate consonant and dissonant chords. Yet their ability does not go so far that they can recognize chords or individual motives separated from their proper context. In thematic variations they also cannot identify the basic theme, because their sense of tonality is limited.

Among the pronouncedly unmusical we number the group of persons who are only susceptible to rhythm and dynamics. Such persons cannot distinguish between consonances and dissonances. Tonality for them is non-existent. Their memory of musical compositions is very inexact. They only recognize compositions with which they are very familiar, and even these only because of certain distinct features. They easily confuse different melodies of similar rhythm.

A fundamentally even lower group comprises those who have absolutely no rapport with music. They have no conception of its purport or significance. Music is as much of a puzzle to them as a mathematical formula is to those unversed in mathematics. It does not even have an emotional effect on them. Here there is no relationship between aural sensations and mood. Music's effect on them is hampering and annoying rather than pleasurable. Even so, the persons belonging to this group need by no means manifest an obvious lack of elementary acoustic properties and rhythmic sense. In fact, they can be extremely sensitive to differences in pitch and intensity, be able to repeat rhythmical motives correctly and execute rhythmical movements promptly. Wilhelm Busch's little couplet would seem to fit their case:

> Musik wird oft nicht schön gefunden,
> Weil sie stets mit Geräusch verbunden.*

Finally, there are also those who are totally lacking in the most elementary *acoustical prerequisites* to the appreciation of music—those, for example, who cannot even identify correctly the directional character of sequential intervals. They are completely indifferent to music.

* Many find music not one of life's joys,
  Because it's always linked up with noise.

We have no data regarding the percentile distribution of the unmusical among adults; but the figure will not differ materially from that among adolescents. Among schoolgirls, the unmusical represent about 10%. Among the school-children of Paris, Binet found 90% musical and 10% unmusical (12). Out of 1000 students, Schuessler found 50% good, 40% mediocre, and 10% bad singers. In a control check of 1000 students, 65% were found to be good singers, 30% mediocre, and 5% bad (133). On the basis of my long experience in measuring musicality (measured for intervallic sense, ability to reproduce sung melodies correctly, melodic memory), I would say 18% were unmusical.

In all these cases 'unmusicality is congenital.' Nevertheless, there are also apparently unmusical people who are not unmusical by nature, or at least are not as unmusical as they seem, or as they pretend to be. Here it is a case of *instinctive dislike of music*. Such persons develop a neurotic resistance towards any form of musical expression. They claim (according to Bernfeld) that they do not understand music, cannot see what others really enjoy in it (10). They manifest impatience and even hostility towards music and its exercise. In most cases this hostility can be traced back to some childish displeasure or disgust, such as failure of the first musical instruction, compulsory music lessons, an inferiority complex springing from some organic or intellectual deficiency or some error in upbringing, exaggerated ambition, family tradition, etc.

When we hear of a highly musical family in which one or another child is especially unmusical—in fact, openly balks at music-making—it is probable that it is a case of subconscious reaction that is forced on the individual through his helplessness as concerns the more musical members of the family. His attitude embodies on the one hand a longing to attain the proficiency of the others; and, on the other hand, envy and jealousy, which arouse resistance. The child tries to compensate for his inferiority by a certain feeling of superiority, by disparaging the value of music and musical activity. This tendency towards disparagement often passes all bounds. Everything that has anything whatsoever to do with music is rejected and consigned to the realm of the most primitive sensual emotions. Such persons do not even shrink from harming themselves if they can only harm the others thereby. This is often only a hostile attitude towards fictitious values. The parents and brothers and sisters do not actually have to be particularly musical. It is quite sufficient if they act as though they were. In this way they provoke an effective resistance on the part of the less gifted members of the family. The latter come into conflict with music in general and with all those who occupy themselves with it or are drawn to it emotionally.

Undoubtedly among the most interesting cases from a psychological point of view are those in which the grounds for the antagonism have yet to be determined. Let us take a case-history cited by Bernfeld in which a student who took a very active interest in music manifested nevertheless a certain lack of balance in his attitude towards it. Though he attended concerts assiduously, he denied the fact to his friend. After the concerts he was often depressed. For years he had tried to master music, but nothing much came of his efforts. It was found that " objectively " he was not unmusical. For instance, he could repeat melodies correctly, recognize dissonances, resolve chords, etc. In the course of his psycho-analytical treatment it was found that when a child of seven he had accidentally seen the violin-teacher kiss his elder sister. This situation, which formed the basis of a childish jealousy, had (according to psycho-analytical interpretation) awakened in him an insuperable hostility towards music which he could not overcome no matter how much he tried. The only thing left for him to do was to appear to be unmusical in order to justify his failure as a musician. Naturally the result of such an attitude is that the neurotically unmusical person gradually loses his natural musicality, and finally manifests all the characteristics of a congenitally unmusical person. Therefore even though such a person may satisfactorily pass a rigorous test of elementary musical ability, it cannot be predicated with certainty that he is capable of achieving anything in music, for it is possible that the emotional inhibitions towards music will have reached a degree that precludes any positive approach to it.

D. Musicality and Musical Training

Scientific investigation of musical aptitude has led us to recognize that the scale of individual differences is a very broad one as regards musicality. The differentiation is fairly marked between the groups of the extremely musical, the moderately musical, and the altogether unmusical. Through the empirical verification of the qualitative differences that refer more to behaviour and spontaneity than is evident in the crude data of mathematical speculations, we arrive at the conclusion, important both from the theoretical and the practical points of view, that *musicality* is not such a *general, demonstrable characteristic* of all mankind as, for instance, intelligence, educability, memory, etc. One finds a great many persons who are altogether unmusical, and an even greater number who do not even meet the most modest demands that we must make of a moderately musical person. Recognition of this fact has an important bearing on certain questions of musical pedagogy.

It is a regrettable fact that countless children who will never be able to accomplish anything in music are given musical instruction. After long years of fruitless study, they abandon music altogether and, disheartened by their failure, lose their appreciation of the advantages of musical education. On the other hand, we find only too many who, in spite of their musicality, have never studied music, and suffer bitterly all their lives from the want of it.

We have already gained a good deal when we are able to separate the musical from the moderately musical and the unmusical; when by means of tests we are able to predict with a large measure of probability whether a child has any prospects of success or not. Of course, it is a beautiful idea to want to enable everybody to enjoy to the fullest and most perfect measure the wonderful creations of music. But this must remain a pious wish, because the frequent lack of musicality prevents its realization. Just as persons with no mathematical aptitude can never understand the beauty, profundity, and elegance of a mathematical deduction, in spite of regular instruction and indefatigable industry, so, too, unmusical persons never grasp a composition, are never able to understand its compositional and its structural plan, no matter how hard they may try. But since music has a tremendous effect even without deeper comprehension, we must seize every opportunity to bring people into touch with it. Even where there is no pronounced musicality, music will make a lasting impression and raise the " Ego " into a sphere that is ordinarily closed to it, uplift it above the empirical world, and free it from the heavy burdens of existence.

XI

MUSICAL TALENT

A. Aptitude and Talent

Before we take up the question of musical talent, we must be perfectly clear as to what we mean by talent. This is all the more important in view of the fact that in everyday language, as well as in science, the word talent has several connotations. Sometimes it is synonymous with aptitude, disposition; another time one understands thereby a mature capacity expressing itself in achievements of value. These two things should not be confused and reduced to a common denominator. On the contrary, the two concepts—aptitude and talent—must be kept distinct one from the other.

By *aptitude* we understand that *inborn capacity of a person that enables him to* realize and develop certain general or specific types of behaviour, properties, and capacities. If we speak of a musical, scientific, technical aptitude or of a special disposition for foreign languages, mathematics, etc., we mean by this the *native latent endowment*—in other words, the fitness to give concrete and effective expression, through maturation and intellectual growth and development, to certain valuable properties and capacities.

Aptitude signifies merely natural propensity, a potential ability by means of which certain properties, capacities, and productive powers may be realized through the operation of environmental factors and the systematic training of the personality. If we assert that an individual possesses the necessary and intellectual prerequisites to noteworthy accomplishments in music (given favourable developmental conditions), we mean by that chiefly the measure of the aptitude. It is well known that other factors, such as environment and heredity, mental equipment, will-power, morality—in a word, the total personality—also play an important role. The greatest aptitude is not sufficient in itself if goal, plan, determination, zeal, passion, and study are not called into play at the right moment and in the right way. On the other hand, given a harmonious combination of spiritual and material circumstances, even a mediocre musical capacity is capable of outstanding accomplishments.

Aptitudes are labile, diffuse, undefined, not sharply differentiated. They manifest themselves principally in the form of direction of interest, and also in a marked educability and a relatively rapid progress in the field indicated by the aptitude.

While *aptitude* indicates *fitness for performance*, talent indicates *capacities far above the average* in a *special field of human activity*.

No one is, or ever has been, capable of exceptional accomplishments in several unrelated fields. Talents that have achieved great success in different domains have seldom evinced productive powers in more than two directions. Among such cases is Leonardo da Vinci, whose genius manifested itself in two great fields: painting and technique. Otherwise it is a question of domains that are intimately associated one with the other. Michelangelo, who was painter, sculptor, and architect in one, remained in the realm of representational art. Descartes and Leibniz, who made an immortal name for themselves as philosophers and mathematicians, did not go beyond the boundaries of the abstract sciences.

The opinion is very prevalent that special hierarchies of talent appertain not only to the great comprehensive domains of science and art, but also to the special fields within these domains. In conformity with this point of view, one assumes a specific talent for drawing, painting, and modelling, and a specific talent for modern, classical, and Semitic languages; in fact, even special talents within these fields. The same is true in the sphere of music, in which interest in, and inclination for, a distinct branch of music or a definite form of musical expression are ordinarily attributed to a special aptitude or talent.

In my opinion, in each of the *great* domains of science and art there is one *homogeneous talent that covers the entire field*. This viewpoint is at variance with the prevailing conviction that creative work in the special, essentially independent provinces of science, art, and technique is linked with special talents. This contrariety of viewpoints can be eliminated if a distinction be drawn between *type* and *direction* of talent. By type of talent we understand an integral homogeneous capacity in a distinct field, an innate disposition of work expressing itself in creative activity. In the course of the individual life, such a preformed special talent can, as a result of inner and outer factors, take different *directions* characterized by an increased interest for a special field, and by a special attitude of mind and manner of thought, of fantasy, of mental imagery. This lends a special structure to the original homogeneous talent which can easily give the impression of a particular type of talent.

The oneness, the organic totality, of the creative talent manifests itself in all departments of human activity. This is especially evident in the realm of music. With very few exceptions, the great composers wrote in nearly all genres. Henry Purcell, the leading exponent of English opera, composed not only an opera and a large number of stage works that were styled operas, but also church music, arias and incidental music for plays, songs, chamber music, works for solo instruments, etc. Mozart's compositions included church music, symphonies, operas, choral works, Lieder, chamber music, concertos, and compositions for piano, violin, and flute. Beethoven wrote church music, choral works, symphonies, chamber music, music for solo instruments, an opera, and ballet music. Schubert, the song composer *par excellence*, in spite of his short life wrote church music, choral works, symphonies, chamber music, Lieder, and music for the piano. Debussy composed chamber music, choral and orchestral works, and music for the piano and the voice. Béla Bartók wrote chamber music, choral and orchestral works, music for the voice and solo instruments, opera, and ballet. The same is true also of Kodaly, Ravel, Stravinsky, Richard Strauss, and many others.*

From my point of view, there is no ground for assuming special talents for the principal branches of music. Everything seems to point to the fact that one-sidedness, the limitation of creative activity to a special genre or field, is due to direction of interest, to special training, to the influence of an inspiring personality, to the specificity of physical environment, to the general intellectual background and the fundamental disposition of the person in question. In the productive musician, the specializing of the creative activity is largely due to disposition as well as to the attitude towards work and life. The person's fundamental

---

* Just how far this is generally valid depends on whether it can be satisfactorily proved that factors other than a very special direction of talent influenced the so-called one-sided composers (Chopin-piano and Wagner-opera) in their choice of field.

temperament can be lyrical (subjective-sensitive) or epic-dramatic (active-emotional). These fundamental moods and sensations, these vital emotions, reveal themselves in the artistic performances in all provinces of art. We can therefore easily understand how it is possible to speak with equal justification of lyrical poetry and lyrical music, or of dramatic literature and dramatic music. Here it is by no means a question of analogies. On the contrary, the common designation rests on the common fundamental mood, on the unity of source from which the lyrical and dramatic works in the different arts have sprung (119).

B. Variants of Musical Talent

In music we must differentiate *two types* of talent; namely, the *creative* and the *reproductive-interpretative*. The latter is subdivided into instrumental-virtuoso talent and talent for conducting.

Although the creative and the reproductive-interpretative talents are sometimes combined in one person, they still represent two highly independent, and by nature altogether distinct, types of talent. This is shown by the fact that the two do not usually go together. None of the great organists, pianists, violinists, and conductors, with few exceptions, were distinguished composers. Even though they often engaged in creative work, they nevertheless very rarely succeeded in producing works of high value in a musical sense. Their compositions lack originality, show the influence of really great composers, and knuckle to current taste. Eminent instrumentalists find it difficult to produce anything outstanding, for the simple reason that virtuoso performance on any instrument demands such great subordination, such an inward absorption in a composition not one's own, such a degree of self-control, and such specialized technical training, that there is scarcely any energy left for the development of a creative gift.

In contrast to the above, it happens much more often that eminent composers distinguish themselves at the same time as executant artists. This is explained first of all by the fact that any kind of musical training postulates the playing of some instrument, and training in composition and creative activity are scarcely possible without the command of at least one solo instrument. Furthermore, with young musicians, circumstances are rarely such that they can devote themselves exclusively to composition at the beginning of their careers. Most of the composers have also revealed their talent as reproductive artists. Bach, Handel, Haydn, Mozart, Chopin, Schumann, Mendelssohn, Mahler, Bartók, etc., first attracted attention through their interpretative gifts. Several of the great composers remained true to their instruments throughout their lives, and in their day won just as much fame through their virtuoso performances as through their compositions. For instance, Johann Sebastian Bach and Rameau were the most celebrated organists of their epoch. Chopin and Liszt were fêted as virtuosos just as much as composers. In olden times, when playing and composing, singing and writing went hand in hand, this combination was found far more frequently than it is today. However, in those days such extraordinary demands were not made of the executant musician as is the case today. The same is still true among musicians of primitive races.

C. Premature Emergence of Musical Talent

(a) *Reproductive-interpretative Talent.* We have already stated that musical aptitude shows itself clearly at a very early age. It is significant that, of all the arts, music is the only one that manifests itself during childhood. Although its premature emergence is almost exclusively limited to technical-instrumental abilities, there are also cases where even young children reveal real artistic qualities.

In this connexion I should like to point out that we must be very cautious in judging the instrumental performances of talented children and young persons. For youthfulness and charm, the unusual technical facility, can make such a strong impression on us that the incongruity between technical talent and real musicality escapes us. In judging such children, interest for the out-of-the-ordinary plays a greater role than musical-æsthetic judgment. We are only too prone to attribute a higher artistic value to the interpretation than it warrants. The marvellous technique and the captivating charm of such youngsters have an uncommonly suggestive effect.

In the performances of really gifted children and young people we realize that the works have not been merely learned by rote, but that the compositions of the great masters are played with a high degree of musical intelligence. Gifted children play delicately and softly and with flexibility when art calls for it; and forcefully, with precision and passion, when dynamic accent is required. They know perfectly well when the melodies have to be played with a singing, legato tone and when they must be accented, declaimed.

(b) *Creative Talent.* The emergence of musical-creative talent in childhood is much rarer. Haydn is one of the few great musicians in whom the creative talent also manifested itself very early along with admirable pianistic ability. The same was true of Mozart, who is said to have written charming pieces for the pianoforte before he was six years old. Unfortunately, these works have not survived. We have a series of minuets dating from his sixth year that are notable for their purity of form, simplicity, and the clarity of the melody, and point to a creative gift. To what extent Papa Mozart was a collaborator cannot now be determined. The Minuet in F major of 11th May and that of 5th July, 1762, are especially well done. In 1764—that is, in his eighth year—he wrote six sonatas for piano, violin, and cello as well as symphonies for small orchestra.*

Schubert is said to have written a series of songs and piano-pieces also at a very early age. At all events, in 1811, when he was fourteen, the attention of Salieri, the influential Viennese conductor, was attracted to him by the Lied, " Hagar's Klage ". Schubert's rapid development as a composer and his tremendous productivity are astounding. Up to his eighteenth year he wrote, among other things, over 100 Lieder, as well as a number of works for the stage, masses, string quartets, sonatas, and miscellaneous works for the pianoforte. The creative talent also developed very early with Chopin. He is alleged to have written piano pieces at the early age of eight. His first works were published comparatively late. The Rondo in C minor (Op. 1) appeared in 1825, when he was fifteen. In his twentieth year,

---

* Among Mozart's early compositions between his sixth and ninth years, the following in particular manifest his extraordinary talent:

Sonata for piano and violin (1762–64), Op. 1, K. 6.
Sonata for piano and violin (1763/4), Op. 1, ♯2, K. 7.
Sonata for piano and violin (1763/4), Op. 2, ♯1, K. 8.
Sonata for piano and violin (1764), Op. 2, ♯2, K. 9.
Six sonatas for piano, violin, and cello (1764), K. 10–15.
Symphony (1764/5), K. 16.

during his residence in Vienna and Paris, Chopin was already a mature composer with his own characteristic style.

In most cases it is found that the early emergence of the creative gift falls in the first half of youth, and only in exceptional cases during the age of puberty; i.e. before the thirteenth and fourteenth or after the eighteenth year. It is therefore characteristic of the creative musical gift that it emerges of necessity during youth. Among the eminent musicians there is scarcely one whose talent manifested itself for the first time after adolescence.

Although all kinds of instrumental talent emerge through natural law at the beginning of youth, their *full development* does not take place in this epoch by any means, but only in the period between the twentieth and thirtieth years (adulthood).

Of Johann Sebastian Bach (*b.* 1685), who began to compose in his very early youth, we have organ compositions dating from his eighteenth year, which, however, give no hint of his genius. We find the earliest evidence of his great gift in the cembalo work " Caprice on the Departure of his Brother Johann Jakob " and in the Præludium and Fugue in C minor for organ. In the field of organ music and cantatas Bach attained his full mastery at twenty years of age, but he only achieved his real greatness towards the age of thirty-seven. Handel (*b.* 1685), who gave evidence of his reproductive gifts at the early age of eight and began to compose at eleven, wrote his first opera, " Almira " (still under Italian-Neapolitan influence), at nineteen, his " Rinaldo " at twenty-six. The period of his great operas began with " Radamisto " in his thirty-fifth year. With Haydn (*b.* 1732) the productive talent awakened in his sixth year. Although he is numbered among those in whom technical and creative capacities manifested themselves simultaneously, he first gave evidence of his talent in his first quartet, written at the age of twenty-three. But his great art only began when he arrived at the end of his twenties, the time when he wrote his first symphonies (No. 1 in D major, 1759; and No. 2 in C major, 1760/61). Although Mozart (*b.* 1756) wrote his first opera, " La finta semplice ", in 1768, at the age of twelve, he did not attain his opera style till the age of twenty-four, when he opened the brilliant period of his creative work with the opera " Idomeneo " (1780/81), which was still strongly under Italian influence, and his masterpiece " Die Entführung aus dem Serail " (1781–82).

His genius only came to full flowering in his twenty-ninth year, when he wrote his greatest works, the pearls of opera literature, in rapid succession: " Figaro ", " Don Giovanni ", and " Zauber-flöte ". Beethoven's creative attempts from his twelfth and thirteenth years were still wholly insignificant. He was between twenty-five and thirty before he disclosed his real creative gift. About this time (1795) he wrote the three piano trios (Op. 1) and the three piano sonatas (Op. 2), as well as his first symphony (1799), which still showed the influence of Mozart and Haydn, though it formed the point of departure of a developmental cycle that reached its culmination in the " Eroica ", written at the age of thirty-three. Schumann (*b.* 1810) wrote his first more important piano pieces at the age of twenty. At thirty he was the mature artist. His symphonies and his chamber music date from the period subsequent to his thirtieth year. Wagner (*b.* 1813) began to compose very late. At twenty he wrote his first opera, " Die Feen ", which was of no artistic value. His opera style only developed during his thirties with " Fliegender Hollaender " (1841) and " Tannhäuser " (1845). Brahms's musical talent manifested itself very early. His first work (F♯ minor Sonata) dates from his nineteenth year. As for Liszt (*b.* 1811), we know that his talent first took a purely reproductive direction. He began to compose at eleven. The " Huit Variations " date from 1825. His great development did not take place till after his thirtieth year. With Mendelssohn (*b.* 1809) and Schubert (*b.* 1797) it was a question of one of those rare cases in which the creative talent is fully developed already during youth. Mendelssohn began to compose at the age of eleven. At twelve he wrote his first opera. At twelve (1820) he had already completed a number of works, and when scarcely seventeen he wrote the " Midsummer Night's Dream " Overture, which none of his later works surpassed in artistic quality. Schubert resembled Mendelssohn in his rapid development and tremendous productivity. By the time he was eighteen he had composed operas, church music, choral works, three symphonies, piano sonatas, and over 100 Lieder.

The question why music, of all artistic talents, has the distinction of early emergence and rapid development is not easy to answer. One reason can be, however, that there is no art the exercise of which is so independent of all life experience and the maturation of the personality as is music. In addition, the musical creative activity has much less to do with the functions of thought and speech than the reproductive work in any other field of art. Music creates its forms and material wholly out of itself. Consequently in his development the executant musician is bound very little to knowledge of other kinds. If we also add that music is anchored in the emotional world, in a sphere to which youth also has free access, then the early emergence and rapid development of the musical talent find a logical and consistent explanation.*

D. The Musical Prodigy

In this connexion I should like to say a few words about the so-called musical prodigy. And by prodigy we mean a musically talented child whose performances far surpass those usually expected of a child of his age. What is manifested in such relatively outstanding performances, however, is for the moment only a premature artistic development, and does not yet justify such a designation. Even when a child's musical performances surpass not only those of his companions but also of the normally talented adult, this is still no indication of an especially marked talent. Neither the unusually rapid development nor the relative super-normality can justify the epithet " prodigy ".

The " wonderful " element in the case lies neither in the emergence of the musical talent in childhood nor in the rapid pace of its development, but *only* in the singular *creative ability*. Consequently the fundamental prerequisite is always the creative formative power, irrespective of whether it takes the direction of productive or reproductive talent.

Now the important question arises as to how a child who is apparently very highly gifted in a musical way is to be judged with respect to the significance and evaluation of his more than average musical capacities.

If we can compare a child's accomplishments with the artistic performance of eminent contemporary artists, without any regard

* In the history of the plastic arts, talent is not manifested as early as it is in music. The number of painters who attained the zenith of their artistic powers during youth is extraordinarily small. Dürer's " Self Portrait ", dating from his thirteenth year, and the famous Mohammed etching of Lukas van Leyden, allegedly dating from his fourteenth year, are among the exceptions (115). In the reference quoted I also cited cases from the literary world (Rimbaud, Chatterton, etc.) and the field of mathematics (Pascal, Evariste Galois, Leonhard Euler, etc.). See also (119).

to his chronological age—as was possible with Haydn, Mozart, and Liszt—then one needs no special methods by which to evaluate his gifts. We appraise his talent (in terms of greatness) by the same standard by which we evaluate masters. But we must proceed differently when it is a question of youthful performances that do not completely meet the demands to be made of works of real artistic quality. In such cases the musician must let the music psychologist judge the talent. Here we cannot be guided exclusively by musical-technical and æsthetic principles. Psychological and psycho-genetic motives must be taken into consideration. In judging the ability to compose, circumstances must be borne in mind that would never enter into the question with adult composers. The errors caused by lack of knowledge have little to do with a child's talent. Fertility of mind, inventiveness, purity of form, and the urge to create are to be appraised. Clean harmony, transparent form, correct movement-plan, contrapuntal accuracy can be mastered through study and practice, but an opulent musical temperament, imagination, taste, poetic élan are advantages that no one can acquire. It therefore follows that youthful works must always be judged as a whole. Here it is extremely important to compare works dating from different epochs of the artistic development so as to be able to gauge the progress also. We must proceed in the same manner when it is a question of a child virtuoso. The chief considerations here are the style, the mastery, but above all else the *creative* in the interpretation and the all-round musicality. So in cases where the existing artistic achievements can furnish neither an adequate basis for measuring the talent nor sufficient guarantee for prognosis, the most outstanding musical attributes and characteristic personal qualities are also essential factors in the judgment.

I had an opportunity of observing an especially gifted child from his fifth to his thirteenth years and of investigating the development of his musical talent (116). The youngster composed his own melodies with accompaniment when barely five years of age. At seven, when I began my investigations, his musical ear was already extraordinarily developed. He possessed genuine absolute pitch, and of an accuracy and certainty completely independent of timbre. He identified tones of the piano and stringed instruments with the same certainty as tones of wind instruments, bells, and glasses. In the analysis of chords, scarcely anyone excelled him. He analysed consonant and dissonant chords absolutely correctly. The following is an example of some of the chords given him for analysis.

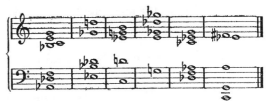

Ex. 13.—Analysis of Dissonant Chords.

The child showed especial facility in transposing. In his seventh year he transposed one-part compositions and simple

Ex. 14.—Theme to Test Visual Memory.

music in several parts into all keys and without a mistake. For instance, he transposed Bach organ preludes and several two-part preludes into different keys at the prescribed tempo. He also

Ex. 15.—Modulation.

transposed the Rondo from Beethoven's G major Sonata (Op. 19, No. 1) into F♯ and C♯ major at sight, with equal proficiency. His musical memory was astounding. One illustration will exemplify this. To test the lad's visual memory, I offered him the theme given in Ex. 14, with directions to read it over but not to play it. After reading it through eight times (which took six and a half minutes) he was able to play the theme on the piano without a mistake. Two years later I asked him to play it for me. He did so at once without an error, and also wrote it out correctly.

Ex. 16.—Serenata.

Ex. 16.—Serenata (continued).

The modulation from D♭ major to E minor given in Ex. 15, dating from his tenth year, will give some idea of his precocious musical talent.

Ex. 16 gives an example of his original work; namely, the *Serenata* written in his eighth year. It leans more to the style of

Ex. 17.—A Composition by Mozart Dating from his Eighth Year.

Composed on May 11th, 1762.

Ex. 18.—A Minuet Composed by Mozart at Six Years of Age.
(*Used by permission of The Boston Music Company.*)

Composed on July 5th, 1762.

Ex. 18.—A Minuet Composed by Mozart at Six Years of Age.
(*Used by permission of The Boston Music Company.*)

the Mozart epoch. The melody of the little work is pleasing and admirably characterized through its simplicity and naturalness. The middle part, which leads back so smoothly into the recurring main theme, and the pretty design of the trill in the third bar, are worthy of note.

I have treated this case at some length because I investigated it myself. Naturally this child's accomplishments could not be compared with those of the great masters who were also prodigies in their time.   The above compositions, written by Mozart and Beethoven in their early childhood, will exemplify this.

Ex. 19.—Theme and Variations Written by Beethoven in his Eleventh Year.

The creative gift of both children is clearly evident in these works.   The perfect harmony, transparent form, correct structure, melodic élan—all qualities of the elect musician—can be found in these little compositions.

E.   Blind Musicians

I must not omit to call attention to the creative and reproductive-interpretative (re-creative) talent of *blind musicians*.

It is unnecessary to prove that no distinction can be drawn between the sighted and the blind in respect of musical aptitude. There is no doubt whatever that, on an average, musical aptitude and talent are to be found just as frequently among the blind as among the sighted.   However, the fact that the blind, on the whole, distinguish themselves less frequently by exceptional musical accomplishments does not mean that they are less talented than the sighted.   It is unquestionably owing to outward circumstances and the difficulties of musical education which make it hard for them to choose music as a profession.   Of course these difficulties have been eliminated in part, since easily readable Braille scores have become available for the blind, and the relatively large number of transcripts of the works of the great masters in this system of notation now makes study easier.

It is perhaps not uninteresting to know that the first music notation for the blind derives from J. J. Rousseau, who was himself a composer. The system of notation now generally in use originated with Louis Braille, and in character is similar to his well-known embossed-dot system. As in the ordinary Braille notation, the blind read the system of dots with their finger-tips. Here the unit consists of two vertical rows of three dots in the form of an upright triangle. This arrangement permits the transcription of all the musical symbols. Since it is nevertheless a little laborious to read the Braille notation, in teaching the blind one occasionally employs the method of dictating or playing over the compositions. But here, of course, a good musical memory is the primary requisite.

The two directions of musical talent, the creative and the re-creative, are found among the blind just as among the sighted. Those instrumentalists who have achieved the highest mastery in the virtuoso command of their instrument furnish convincing proof of the latter gift. Among these are to be mentioned the celebrated organists, Paumann and Labor, and also the Hungarian pianist, Imre Unger.

As to the original creative power of blind musicians, music history furnishes a number of illustrations. Francesco Landino (Florence, 1325-1397), who became blind as a child, was not only one of the outstanding masters of the Florentine ars nova of the 14th century, but at the same time he was the chief exponent of this period of the Trecento madrigal, which also influenced French, Spanish, English, Dutch, and German polytonality of the 15th century. The autographs of a large number of his compositions have been preserved. Several examples are contained in Johannes Wolf's historical works. It is worthy of mention that a certain cadential formula (Discant clausula or clausula cantigans), a form of the harmonic turn in common usage in ecclesiastical and secular compositions of the 14th to the end of the 15th century, bears Landino's name; i.e. the Landino Sixth (30). In a picture by Giovanni del Prato (Paradiso degli Alberti) we see the blind Landino playing at an aristocratic gathering in Florence. The picture depicts the powerful effect of his organ-playing on young and old; in fact, even on birds.

VIII. Accidentals. — Key Signatures

42. Accidentals are placed before the note or the interval sign which represents it, thus:

Sharp ⠩ Double sharp ⠩⠩ Natural ⠡

Flat ⠣ Double flat ⠣⠣

43. To indicate the key signature, it is necessary merely to write the required number of accidentals by placing once, twice or three times in succession the accidental sign in question. When the key contains more than three accidentals, their number is indicated by a figure preceding the characteristic sign.

Example:

The signs used are the following:

Fig. 26.

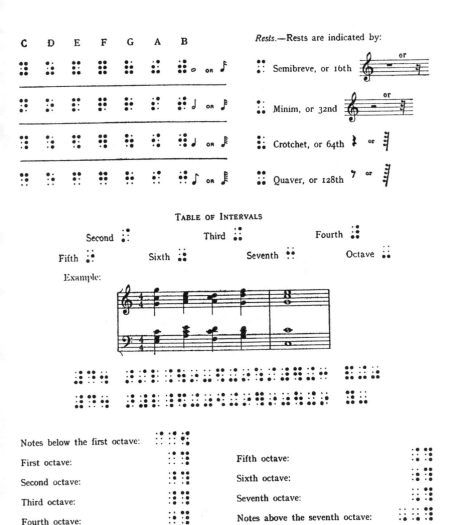

C D E F G A B

Rests.—Rests are indicated by:

Semibreve, or 16th

Minim, or 32nd

Crotchet, or 64th

Quaver, or 128th

TABLE OF INTERVALS

Second   Third   Fourth

Fifth   Sixth   Seventh   Octave

Example:

Notes below the first octave:

First octave: Fifth octave:

Second octave: Sixth octave:

Third octave: Seventh octave:

Fourth octave: Notes above the seventh octave:

The figures indicating the number of beats (upper number on the inkprint copy) are taken from the series formed by points ⠆ while the figures representing the value of the beats (lower number) are taken from the series formed by points ⠒

Example:

FIG. 26 (*continued*).

(Reproduced by courtesy of the New York Library for the Blind.)

Conrad Paumann (1410–1473), who had been blind from birth, lived in Nuremberg in the 15th century. He was a highly esteemed organist and theorist. His work "Fundamentum organisandi" (ca. 1452) achieved an extraordinary, though not altogether justified, acclaim. Above all, there is no evidence that the compositions and musical exercises published in this work are by him.* The assumption that Paumann was the author of the German lute tablature is also founded on error. Nevertheless, this blind musician exerted an enormous pedagogical influence on his contemporaries.

The Spanish master, Francesco da Salinas (1513–1590), who was blind from childhood, was one of the greatest musicians of the Renaissance. His masterly organ-playing was famed far and wide. He gained high repute in the musical world through his seven works on the theory of music.† At the last (from 1537 on) he was professor at the University of Salamanca. Johannes Wolf, a leading expert in the field of musical historical research, considers Salinas an authority of the first rank on theory and regards his "Musica" as a mine of musical knowledge even today.

Finally I should like to mention a blind musician of recent date; namely, Josef Labor (1842–1924). He was a virtuoso pianist and organist, and was reputed to be the best organist in Austria. He also made a name as a composer. It is interesting to note that we find Arnold Schönberg, the well-known composer of impressionistic tendencies, among his pupils.

F. Relationship between Mathematical, Musical, and other
Types of Talent

It can be said in general that there is no conspicuously positive correlation between musical and other artistic or scientific aptitudes. This finds its explanation in the specific nature of the musical aptitude, which makes it so independent of other types of talent. Statistical findings show that as a general thing, musical persons manifest a second specific aptitude no oftener, or at least

* It is possible that this work was written by the renowned organist, Georg von Putemheim.

† De musica libri septem, in quibus ejus doctrinae veritas tam quae ad harmoniam quam quae ad rhythmum pertinet, juxta sensus ac rationis judicium ostenditur, 1577.

not much oftener, than unmusical persons. There are even types
of talent that actually have a negative correlation to the musical.
In the case of pronounced musical talent, these types of aptitude
are more frequently lacking than not.

Before we take up the relation of the musical to other types of
talent, we should like to refer to the tests of K. Bartsch, who
investigated the relationship between musicality and general
intellectual capacity. His surveys covered 200 moderately
musical pupils of the Teachers' Seminary. Bartsch could find no
clear-cut relationship between musical aptitude and the general
intellectual ability as testified by the term reports. He found that
intellectual ability in the pronouncedly musical coincided ordinarily with that of pupils of moderate musical talent. Expressed
numerically, the ratio between musical and unmusical was
46·3 to 47·7. H. Schüssler reached another result. With pupils
of the elementary and intermediate schools (200 musical and 200
unmusical) he found that, ordinarily speaking, the unmusical
showed a lower efficiency level in school subjects. The results
were 15% better with the musical than with the unmusical. The
last results agree with the opinion of most musical pedagogues,
who maintain that with pupils of pronounced musical aptitude,
the musical abilities usually keep pace with the universal intellectual capacities. It has been shown, namely, that pupils of the
intermediate and higher schools who receive good term reports in
instrumental-technical and musical-theoretical subjects also
usually excel in the general scientific branches.

Haecker and Ziehen, in particular, gave exhaustive study to the
question of the correlation between musical talent and other types
or directions of talent. The two investigators found a clear
relationship between musical talent and drawing or literary
talent, at least in the case of males. In males an aptitude for
drawing was found combined with outstanding musical talent a
little oftener than with deficient musicality (19% to 12%). In
the case of females such a correlation does not seem to exist. Here
18% of the especially musical and 17% of the unmusical showed a
pronounced aptitude for drawing. It was also found that the
relationship of the literary talent to the musical is more intimate
than that of the talent for drawing. With males 21% of the
musical and only 7% of the unmusical showed literary talent.
Among the females there was also no correlation here. Eleven

per cent of the musical and 8% of the unmusical showed a talent for poetry (46).

The question concerning the correlation between *musical and mathematical talent* arouses special interest, since there is a prevailing opinion that there is a peculiarly intimate relationship between these two types of talent. Here we must keep two problems distinct: the first is what relation pronounced musical talent bears to the mathematical; and the second, what relation pronounced mathematical talent bears to the musical. It cannot be decided offhand, for instance, whether there is a mutual, or only a unilateral, correlation between these two types of talent.

The statistical investigation of Haecker and Ziehen furnishes us with data on the first question. This covered 227 musical and 72 absolutely unmusical males, and 142 musical and 90 absolutely unmusical females.

As far as males were concerned, it was found that in only 2% of the cases was a very pronounced musical aptitude linked with distinct mathematical talent, while 13% of the unmusical manifested mathematical ability. According to this there would actually appear to be a negative relationship between musicality and mathematical aptitude. The question could not be answered with respect to females, because the number of those with mathematical talent was infinitesimally small.

Following the heredity investigation of Heymans and Wiersma, Pannenborg investigated the correlation between musicality and a number of other intellectual capacities on the basis of a heredity inquiry as well as a biographical investigation of twenty-one eminent musicians and a school test of 342 musical boys and 152 musical girls between the ages of twelve and eighteen (94).

Pannenborg was able to verify the findings of Haecker and Ziehen. Of 52 test subjects of very pronounced musical talent, only 15·4% showed mathematical aptitude. Of the remaining 371 persons of average musical talent, the percentage proved to be not much less. It showed 12·3% having mathematical talent. Predilection for mathematics was found with 13·7% of the boys and 11·8% of the girls; whereas mathematical ineptitude was found with 33·9% of the boys and 36·8% of the girls.

The biographical investigation of great composers also led to completely negative results. Feis in his work on the genealogy of musicians arrived at the same conclusions. A short time ago I also investigated this question with *professional musicians*, the results of which I published in the Swiss *Journal of Psychology* (1946) under the title, " Relationship between Musical and Mathematical Talent " (117). My findings agreed with the aforesaid reports, only the percentage of the mathematically talented musicians was still lower. We found mathematical aptitude, or interest in mathematics, in only 9% of the musicians.

The second and far more interesting question is whether mathematicians are more musically gifted than exponents of other special branches and professions. It has been persistently maintained for hundreds of years that mathematicians are ordinarily more musical than non-mathematicians, though it is just as easy to find mathematicians without any trace of musicality.

Since the meagre experiential background and the paucity of cases in which the two talents were incorporated in one person gave no ground for asserting a correlation between the two types of talent, we decided to arrive at an answer through the *statistical method*. To this end a detailed questionnaire was sent to a large number of Dutch mathematicians and physicists (including 200 scientists engaged in productive work), with the request to fill it in very meticulously. The questions were formulated so as to establish beyond a doubt whether the respondent were musical or not; in fact, so that the answers would even indicate the degree of musicality. Physicians and writers were also included for comparative purposes. Seventeen questions were presented to the respondents, so as to get an idea of the direction of their musical interest, their musical training, musical activity, their ear, and their inherited capacity. The questionnaire read as follows:

INQUIRY REGARDING MUSICALITY

There is a very prevalent opinion, shared also by numerous mathematicians, that there is a very intimate connexion between music and mathematics, as well as between musical and mathematical talent. Since this problem is important from the point of view of psychology, and especially so from that of the psychology of music, we have decided to investigate the alleged correlation more systematically. We are therefore addressing ourselves to you with the request to answer the following questions in detail, and to return us your reply. Should you be in doubt whether the given answer is correct (in the sense of the questionnaire) please place a question-mark after the answer. Should the results of this investigation be made public, the names of the respondents will not be revealed. You will receive notice when the results are published. We thank you in advance for your kind co-operation, which is of great value to us.

PSYCHOLOGICAL INSTITUTE OF THE UNIVERSITY
OF AMSTERDAM

_____   _____

Name of respondent   Address

Do you classify yourself among the bona fide mathematicians, the mathematical physicists, or the experimental physicists? ....

GENERAL QUESTIONS   ANSWER

A. Are you interested in music?
B. Do you consider yourself musical? (Very musical; musical; moderately musical; unmusical.)

SPECIFIC QUESTIONS

GROUP 1.

1. Do you play, or have you played, any instrument? (Piano, stringed instruments, wind instruments.)
2. Do you sing, or have you ever sung? (Solo or in a chorus?)
3. Do you play in an orchestra or any other musical ensemble, or have you ever done so?
4. Do you improvise or have you ever improvised on the piano or any other instrument?
5. Do you compose, or have you ever composed?
6. Have you had regular musical instruction?

GROUP 2.

7. Do you often go to concerts?
8. What type of concerts do you prefer? (Solo, chamber music, orchestra, oratorio?)
9. What composers interest you especially?

GROUP 3.

10. Do you readily recognize a musical composition again?
11. Are you able to sing melodies or motifs correctly that you have heard several times?
12. Are you able to _recognize_ and _name_ the principal intervals (octave, fifth, fourth, major and minor third)?
13. After hearing an interval, can you sing it in a _transposed_ key? (For instance, after hearing the fifth c–g, can you sing the same interval from e♭, that is, e♭–b♭?
14. Have you absolute pitch?
15. If so, does it cover the entire tonal range or only the middle portion? or is it limited exclusively to the standard pitch note a¹?

GROUP 4.

16. Do you know whether your father or your mother showed an aptitude for music in either the productive or the reproductive form?
17. Do you know whether your father or your mother showed an aptitude for mathematics or the natural sciences?

18. Do you believe that there is a conspicuous relation between mathematics and music?
19. Do you believe that mathematical talent is usually combined with musical aptitude?
20. Are you interested in the mathematical basis of music?

*   *   *   *   *

Table 10 furnishes an authoritative survey of the percentage of musicality among the members of the higher professions.

TABLE 10

Frequency of Musical Aptitude among Mathematicians, Physicists, Physicians, and Writers

	Musical	Unmusical	Total
Mathematicians . . .	76 (56%)	59 (44%)	135
Physicists	116 (67%)	56 (33%)	172
Physicians	98 (59%)	67 (41%)	165
Writers	78 (71%)	32 (29%)	110
Grand total . .	368 (63%)	214 (37%)	582

The above table shows that in these groups 37% on an average are either absolutely unmusical or have only a very slight musical aptitude; i.e. one-third of the persons belonging to these professional categories are practically unmusical. The most striking result of the investigation is that the mathematicians (productive as well as receptive) do not show a *higher percentage of musicality* than the other professional groups. One might easily claim the reverse, since we find a higher percentage of musically talented persons in the other three groups than among the mathematicians. The prevailing opinion that mathematicians are ordinarily more musical than other groups of intellectuals has therefore been exploded by this investigation.

Now the question arises why the thesis that mathematicians in general were more musically gifted than others was so persistently defended for centuries, in fact for thousands of years. There are, in the main, two reasons for this. First of all, *tradition* plays a role in the matter. For thousands of years it has been taken for granted that there is an intimate relationship between mathematics and music. Even in the time of Pythagoras, Plato, and Aristotle, music and harmony were considered to be a mathematical discipline. The Theory of Intervals and the controversy over the enharmonic and chromatic genera had greatly engrossed the Greek musical theorists. In " The Republic " Plato prescribed a course for philosophers in the mathematical subjects, such as arithmetic, geometry, astronomy, and music (40). Of course, by music he means here the mathematico-physical construction of the intervals or the scales. This tendency was current down to the time of Euler, who promulgated a Theory of Consonance based on mathematics. In fact, we can find distinct traces of this mathematico-physical attitude even with Helmholtz.

But this is wrong as a result of confounding the *mathematical basis* and *physical causation of intervals and the tone system* with music *as an art*. This error has been the source of the greatest misunderstandings, which are still current, especially among certain musically talented mathematicians. There can no longer be any doubt whatsoever that music is *not* mathematics. Mathematics is a *science*; that is, the science of space and number, the science of the infinite. Music, on the contrary, is an *art*, and that particular art that is associated with sound. The fact that the tone system can be characterized by certain physical acoustical relations that are expressed in numerical ratios does not have a prejudicial effect on the type of relationship existing between mathematics and music. Where it has to do with number and volume, mathematical considerations play a role. This is also the case in the theory of music, in so far as the latter is concerned with the physical basis of the musical elements and the purely formal structure of the elementary patterns (tone, volume, tempo, interval, rhythm, phrase). The applicability of mathematics to acoustical-theoretical problems in music explains why mathematicians occupy themselves with these matters.

The relationship between music and mathematics takes on another aspect when we investigate musical creations in detail and in their entirety with respect to their schematic structure and the arrangement of parts, just as poetical works are analysed with respect to their metre, their rules of versification, their embroidery, etc.

A. Speiser, leaning on the authority of A. Lorenz, recently pointed to the significance of musical symmetry, arrangement of parts, repetition, and the rigorous Gestalt laws, and showed among other things how melodic formulæ or patterns of the higher order (such as a, a, b; a, a, b; c, c, d with the time-outline 1, 1, 2; 2, 2, 4) arise from the basic patterns (e.g. a, a, b with the time-outline 2, 2, 4). Without underrating the value of such efforts, which undoubtedly furnish important contributions to the theory of musical form, we should like to point out—with reference to our own problems—that the analysis of units of musical form and their symbolization through letters and figures has nothing to do with mathematics or geometry.

A further circumstance that presumably contributed to the genesis of this prejudice was the fact that cases of precocious emergence of talent occur in the two fields; that is to say, in music and in mathematics. This fact also certainly contributed to the assumption of an intimate relationship between the two essentially divergent talents and fields.

Through the unequivocal statistical findings and the historical and theoretical considerations interlinked therewith, I believe I have clarified the problem of the relationship between mathematics and music, or between mathematical and musical talent, and removed the misapprehensions that have existed for centuries.

XII

DEVELOPMENT OF MUSICAL CAPACITY

IF we would gain a correct picture of the development and efficiency of musical talent—i.e. its capacity for work and achievement—it is well to make a sharp distinction between that of children and adolescents in general, and that of the especially gifted.

A. METHODS OF RESEARCH

For the investigation of the musical evolution during childhood there are, in the main, three methods at our disposal; namely, *systematic observation, experiment,* and the *use of a questionnaire.* The statistical method is not a method in the strict sense of the word. It is a procedure, the function of which is to co-ordinate and summarize the experiences and findings of the three indicated methods for the purpose of determining general legalities.

Systematic observation has reference to the description of spontaneous musical utterances of the child, and is employed mostly by those in constant contact with children; i.e. by parents, close relatives, teachers, and private tutors. In collecting the observation material, the facts that have been actually perceived must be kept strictly separate from their *interpretation.* This is an important aspect of the matter which is very frequently transgressed. The observations are usually taken quite informally during daily intercourse with the children. Everything touching the child's behaviour towards music is closely observed. The material is then arranged chronologically and according to certain subject categories. In this method one can follow a definitely outlined schema with a list of specific questions and directions. It is impossible to say in advance when the free and the charted procedures should be used. Everything depends on circumstances and the questions involved. In general, free observation is used in individual cases. Its object is the detection of personal peculiarities and constitutional factors. This is the purpose of most of the memoranda and diaries that report on the acoustic and musical performances of children, usually within the framework of their general intellectual development. The musical utterances are thereby considered an integral part of the childish personality. One tries to clarify the influences to which the child is subjected and under which his development takes place, and to comprehend the strange interrelations of the awakening functions. The best-known works on child psychology (Preyer, Stern, Scupin, etc.) treat musicality in early childhood from this general developmental psychological aspect (101, 135, 144). The works of Richet, Stumpf, Révész, and Guernsey deal especially with the musical development of individual children (45, 116, 125).

Experimental research is employed to test the various musical capacities and types of behaviour. Here children of different ages are investigated as to their musical ear and tonal memory, their ability to analyse chords, their free fantasy, etc. The aim of experimental research, on the one hand, is to obtain reliable comparative information regarding the individual musical capacities and their relationship to each other; and, on the other hand, to follow the general course of the development. Here a primary requisite is that the majority of the children reveal a more or less developed musical sense. This requirement is justified since, as already mentioned, there are few absolutely unmusical children.

In the *questionnaire method* a mass of material suitable for statistical evaluation is systematically collected. Questionnaires are distributed containing a list of questions that must be answered very carefully. The inquiry can refer to the actual person of the respondent (such as: Have you an ear with a good sense of pitch? Do you play any musical instrument? Do you compose? etc.); or it can be addressed to an intermediary for the purpose of obtaining information regarding others.

B. Emergence of Musical Capacity

The investigation of the development of musical aptitude starts with a test of the first emergence of the musical sense. The research conducted by Haecker and Ziehen provides us with information on this point. Here intermediaries were requested to furnish data regarding the first discernible indications of the musicality of the children. They were given a list of questions which they had to answer in great detail. Although the number of children investigated was not sufficiently large (441 in all) to provide generally valid conclusions, we still believe we are justified in assuming that the findings give a correct picture of the situation in general.

It has been found that in the great majority of cases the musicality of musically talented children is revealed already at a very early age.

TABLE 11

First Emergence of Musical Aptitude

Age	under 2	2	3	4	5	6	7	8	9	10	11	12	13	14	15	16	17	18	19	over 20	Total
Boys	18	28	30	18	37	26	15	19	16	30	3	16	9	8	2	3	2	0	1	3	284
Girls	17	18	10	13	16	12	11	12	13	20	1	7	2	2	1	1	0	1	0	0	157

The above table shows that approximately 50% of the boys and girls revealed musical aptitude long before school age; namely, between the second and sixth years. In the others, musicality was first manifested in the years immediately preceding puberty. The first emergence during puberty occurs only in very rare cases. On the basis of this investigation it can be stated that musical aptitude of boys and girls usually betrays itself unmistakably in various utterances and performances before the beginning of puberty. This is all the more evident if the findings of the above table are co-ordinated into five-year periods and the percentages of frequency compared.

TABLE 12

Musical Aptitude of Children and Adolescents

	2 to 5	6 to 10	11 to 15	16 to 20	Total
Boys . . .	131 46·1%	106 37·3%	38 13·4%	9 3·2%	284
Girls . . .	74 47·1%	68 43·3%	13 8·3%	2 1·3%	157

A far more important question than the date of the first emergence of musical aptitude is that touching the *evolution* of this aptitude during childhood and adolescence. In the main, the following can be said in answer thereto. First of all one notes a gradual heightening of the individual musical capacities in the child. The first climax is reached towards the tenth to the eleventh year. At the beginning of puberty, which falls about the twelfth to the thirteenth year, important fluctuations are observed which cloud the picture of the development. Soon after this the evolution of the musical capacities sets in again, a little slowly at first. It then progresses rapidly during the period of puberty.

Table 13 requires no further elucidation. The first jump takes place between the ninth and tenth years—that is, in the so-called pre-puberty period—the second between the eleventh and fourteenth, or during actual puberty.

TABLE 13

Evolution of the Musical Capacity during Adolescence

Age . . .	8	9	10	11	12	13	14
Ability to sing a melody back (imitation) . .	80%	89%	94·3%	83·3%	97·6%	97·7%	94·3%
Memory for melody	10%	14·3%	19%	25·7%	29%	54·3%	59%
Analysis of a fifth .	13·3%	15·7%	23·3%	27·7%	44·3%	49%	77·7%
Analysis of a major third . . .	50%	51%	75·7%	72·3%	91%	90%	96·7%
Discriminability .	37·7%	44·3%	61%	73·3%	75·7%	81%	84·3%

C. Stages of Developmental Cycle

The presence and development of the musical sense was investigated predominantly by the method of free observation. This was the procedure employed by Werner and Schuenemann, who endeavoured to bring out the characteristic musical utterances of children at different étappes of the developmental cycle (134, 159a).

The *first year of life*, according to Schuenemann, furnishes no criteria of the musical disposition of the child. The young child seems to be very sensitive to acoustic stimuli. His attention is caught by noises just as much as by tone complexes. Among the acoustic stimuli are those that titillate the child and those that excite it and make it cry. It is not content to react to acoustic stimuli. Its delight in musical sounds can be so great at times that it even seeks the source of the sound. It happens that children try as early as their first year to imitate a pitch with their tender voices. Interesting as infantile vocalization and musical reactions before the speaking period may be from the evolutionary-psychological point of view, they nevertheless have practically nothing to do with musical apperception.

In the *speaking and play period*—that is, between the *second and fourth years*—music as such now begins to enter into the child's world of activity and mood. Music visibly delights children; above all, that to which they can play, dance, and sing. With them, as with primitive people, music and movement go together and cannot be divorced one from the other. In this period, for biological reasons, rhythm seems to be more important than melody. Even in the second and third years (i.e. in the first period of speech development) many children begin to sing little airs of their " own invention ". Of course these melodies are little more than series of sounds related to the child's activity at the moment. At first the words have no direct connexion with the melody. However, text and music gradually begin to be inseparably connected. The self-devised text is not constant, the words are often replaced by others of their choosing. The same is true when they sing back a melody. Here, too, one can observe the most varied modifications; for instance, whole passages will be omitted, familiar phrases take the place of difficult ones, the direction will be changed, and so on. It is by no means rare to find children who are able to repeat correctly tone sequences, melodies, and intervals even in their second year.

According to Werner the incipient form of the child's " melodic " utterance is a tone that runs through a number of indefinite tone steps in a descending portamento. In the child's third year the falling motive (in which a note is held at approximately the same pitch and is connected with a second lower note) develops from this pre-musical stage.

Ex. 20.—Pre-melodic Form Dating from the Third Year.

The rising-falling tone sequence is characteristic of the second developmental cycle which begins about the age of three and a quarter years.

Ex. 21.—Rising-falling Tonal Pattern Dating from the Fourth Year.

The presence of two or more peaks in the melodic invention is a relatively late cycle. It is not found earlier than the end of the child's fourth year. The original ontogenetic form of the melody is the minor third. It is the source of music.

La la la   La, la, la   la la la   La, la La, la la, la, Gross - ma - ma !

Ex. 22.—The Alleged Ontogenetic Primary Form of Melody.

The minor third retains its ascendancy during the whole development of the child (Ex. 22). The song with the range of a whole or half tone is a secondary manifestation. His assumption that the major third and the diminished fifth (the last through doubling of the minor third) arise from the minor third is untenable, in my opinion.

In children with musical talent the singing of self-invented melodies that " exhibit the first beginnings of musical form " replaces such babble songs as early as the *fourth year*. In these melodies, as in the repetition of heard melodies, one also finds uncertainty in general pitch, intervals, keys, and motives. The tone steps sometimes resemble our intervals. Sometimes they are only approximations of the fixed intervals. It is very significant to find some children revealing a sense of tonality even at this earliest stage of musical activity.

The two following examples represent original melodies from this developmental stage. The first is a melody with words by a little girl of four. The song is bitonal and employs the interval of a minor third. The second example is also by a child of four. It is more complicated and involved and clearly reveals a sense of tonality.

I should now like to make a comment as regards the first epoch of musical development. Evolutionary psychology has endeavoured to draw parallels between the *child's* musical utterances and the *music of exotic races*. This tendency, which netted certain results in different departments of human activity such as speech, thought, and drawing, also found its adherents in musicology. An attempt is made to prove that the so-called phylogenetic evolutionary series (i.e. the general development of music from its beginnings up to a definite stage of development) has its parallel in the ontogenetic evolutionary series (i.e. the individual development of the child). Investigators were convinced that the étappes through which the human race has passed in the development of music (up to a certain point) would be found again, in principle and schematically, in infantile musical utterances. However, fruitful as this " biogenetic " point of view may be in biology, it must nevertheless be applied with the greatest caution as soon as an intellectual activity such as music is

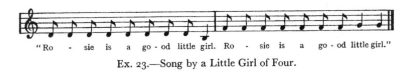

"Ro - sie is a go - od little girl. Ro - sie is a go - od little girl."

Ex. 23.—Song by a Little Girl of Four.

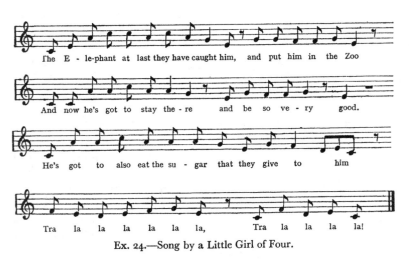

The E - le-phant at last they have caught him, and put him in the Zoo

And now he's got to stay the - re and be so ve - ry good.

He's got to also eat the su - gar that they give to him

Tra la la la la la la, Tra la la la la!

Ex. 24.—Song by a Little Girl of Four.

involved. We should not allow ourselves to be influenced by outward similarities between exotic music and the self-invented melodies of children, and these should by no means be made the basis of far-reaching theories. That primitive, biologically predicated necessities often lead to similar sound reactions (such as the ruling factor of rhythm, for instance) is a phenomenon that has nothing to do with music. Since with a child, as with primitive man, rhythm is an extraordinarily important life factor, inasmuch as it governs movement, speech, mime, and play, it is quite natural that similarities are to be found in certain activities of children and the primitive races.   But this is also true of the " descending trend " of the melody, which is deduced as argument, and in my opinion is nothing more than the natural result of the vocal mechanism which, after tension and the strain of holding, necessarily leads to the relaxation of the vocal chords. So long as we do not have more material on the songs of primitive peoples and so long as similarities and dissimilarities between spontaneous children's songs (free of environmental influence) on the one hand, and songs of primitive peoples on the other are not carefully investigated and compared, this question of genetic parallelism cannot be satisfactorily answered.

The *sixth year* is supposed to be decisive for the development of the child.   The close application and concentration that slowly set in as a result of natural evolution and school instruction are also clearly reflected in the children's behaviour towards music. They listen to the piano, are always about when there is any music, have their favourite songs played over and over again, and try to play familiar tunes on the piano.   Children's songs are no longer sung at haphazard, but are controlled, supplemented, and improved.   However, the tendency towards variation and alteration still exists, only these mutations are no longer so capricious as formerly.   In this period a gradual transition from playful, natural music-making to conscious assimilation and correct reproduction of musical impressions is unmistakable.   In the repetition of familiar songs, the children still easily lose the key.   But little by little the decisive importance of the tonic gradually comes to the fore, especially with children of pronounced musical aptitude.

The tonic becomes the centre from which the melodic movements flow and to which they again return.   The feeling for tonality takes root and opens up the way to musical-æsthetic enjoyment.   This gives us the fundamental prerequisite to production and reproduction (creation and re-creation), even if within narrow limits.   If children are offered a familiar melody, and are then required to sing some low note outside the melodic span, they will generally sing a note in the tonality of the melody they have just heard (fundamental, third, and fifth).

At first, harmony arouses no great interest.   Children find every harmonic accompaniment equally good, whether consonant or dissonant.   Usually they do not even notice the difference between major and minor. Of course there are also some who during this period prefer minor chords to major chords, in fact who even harmonize their melodies on the piano. Here thirds have the preference at first; later on sixths, fifths, and even harmonic triads are encountered.

Ex. 25.—Harmonized Accompaniment of a Melody.   (Boy of Eight and Three-quarter years.)

Ex. 26.—Harmonized Accompaniment of a Melody.   (Girl of Ten years.)

The same thing is true of the self-invented melodies of children as of the alleged primitive words of childish speech. Strictly speaking, children invent no *new* melodies, no *new* forms. They only connect up the familiar, imitating it, abbreviating it, schematizing and altering it.

The period between the *ninth and twelfth years* is the most important for musical development. Psychological investigations therefore gain in importance, since the children are not mentally capable of comprehending questions and tasks put to them and of reporting their own self-observations. The only thing is that at this age children are often greatly under the influence of their music lessons, and for this reason their development is of greater interest to musical pedagogy than to the psychology of music.

D. Development of Musical Talent in Maturity and Advanced Age

The problem of the relationship between talent and age is a psychological one, and touches in principle every field of artistic and intellectual endeavour. My experiments and tests have therefore covered every branch of art and every field of science and technique, including the more generalized talents of public life. In the present instance, however, I shall restrict myself to the creative musician, though I should like to point out that the phenomena and laws appertaining to the progressive evolution of the creatively gifted individual are materially the same in every branch of activity.

In this problem three questions come up for discussion. First, the genesis and growth of the creative gift during childhood and adolescence. Second, the development or deployment of the gift during maturation. And finally the fate of the creative talent in senescence.

I have already treated the first question in detail, showing that the creative talent, in many fields of artistic and intellectual activity, manifests itself in early youth. Those instances in which it reaches its peak or one of its peaks at the close of adolescence provide clear and distinct evidence of the evolution of such talent during youth. It would be instructive to compare the youthful works of gifted individuals not only one with another, but also with the later works, and to draw deductions therefrom regarding the process and speed of evolution. Here the field of music is especially fruitful because musical development proceeds very rapidly and is plainly discernible. Corresponding comparative investigations can also be carried out in the history of art, even though in this latter field the number of analogous cases is few in comparison with music, especially since youthful works in the field of representational art are now for the most part lost.

In the field of science, attention should be directed especially to the achievements of those young mathematicians who furnished irrefutable evidence of talent between their seventeenth and twenty-fifth years. I imagine that such a comparative investigation would provide important data regarding the nature of the different types of talent and the individuals so endowed.

The second question, which touches the development of the

creative gift with advancing years, has been given little attention to date, though it is important from a psychological point of view to know during what life-epoch most (or the greatest) of the intellectual achievements ordinarily fall.

⸙In general, creative mental power increases continually from youth up to the critical age. We shall not go wrong in placing this epoch between the thirty-fifth and fiftieth years. Peak achievements generally fall within this period: the life-span during which the individual creates his most important works, or at least attains the peak of his quantitative efficiency.⸙ Aristotle remarked in his " Rhetoric " that the acme of mental efficiency lasts from the thirtieth to the forty-ninth year. At the end of the 18th and the beginning of the 19th century, this golden time of mental virility and productivity was put somewhat earlier. Helvetius, in fact, asserted that all the ideas of which man is capable and that have their source in external impressions date from the life-span up to the thirtieth or at most to the thirty-fifth year, and that all later contributions are merely a development of these early ideas. In his " Parerga and Parlepomena " Schopenhauer makes the claim that the maximum energy and the greatest mental potential manifest themselves in adolescence—at the latest up to the thirty-fifth year. However, later years, and even senescence, are not without their intellectual compensations. That which a gifted mind is destined to contribute to the world is amassed in youth. But only time and years can make the mind master of the material. Youth remains the root of the tree of knowledge. But it is the crown of the tree that bears the fruit.

Psychological observations and historical facts have shown that maturity is distinguished by full physical and psychical vigour as well as by maximum endurance with the minimum of fatigue. This is explained by the parallelism that exists between the biological periods of growth and decline, and the efficiency curve.

The importance of middle age as regards productivity is confirmed by a statistical survey by Harvey Lehmann (77). According to Lehmann's findings, the zenith of creative activity is more often found between the thirty-fifth and fortieth or the fortieth and forty-fifth years than between earlier five-year periods. However, this fact is only true for a certain type of creatively gifted person, and then more as regards the quantity than the quality of the achievements. For there is also another type in which the performances mount continually in the course of the life-span, and reach their zenith relatively late; that is, in the latter half of life. Here music history furnishes us with numerous examples.

It is also interesting to note that in the process of centuries, the date line of intellectual maturity, as well as the boundary line of physical and mental activity, have risen in comparison with earlier estimates. The increased span of life we owe mainly to improvements in medical skill and hygiene. The later maturity is due to the heightened demands now made on executive and creative musicians. In recent years these demands have been noticeably lowered; unfortunately, not to the advantage of artistic development. But this is apparently due to a lack of outstanding artistic personalities, a situation for which the war and the unfavourable political and economic conditions in the cultivated nations of the world are to blame.

Thus we come to the third epoch of life. Here the question is in what way the productive gift manifests itself in senescence. May we speak here of a gradual reduction of the intellectual power? Or do we come nearer the truth when we assert that there is no necessity for the ageing person to lose his creative talent, even in senescence, provided he does not suffer any of the physical and mental impairments that are frequently the concomitant of advanced age?

We attach very great importance to the study of this question, since our conclusions are diametrically opposed to the consensus of opinion that senescence necessarily implies a decrement in production.

The psychiaters are inclined to picture the penultimate phase, the pre-senile period, as a period of decline. It is pointed out that this period varies in different cases, but it is assumed that diseased conditions tend to arise in the decade between sixty and seventy which superinduce a decline in the physical and mental powers. For instance, a narrowing of the intellectual horizon, a loss in spiritual riches, more limited interests, an egocentric isolation. In addition, there are the diseased bodily changes (such as atrophy of the cells in arterio-sclerosis) that lead to specific ailments of senescence and are probably not without effect on the spiritual–mental condition of the ageing person.

" Senectus ipse morbus ", says an old Roman proverb—" old age in itself is illness ".

In advanced age (seventy-one to eighty), and especially during so-called senescence (eighty-one to ninety), these concomitants of old age have an increasing effect on the bodily condition as a whole. The ageing person is supposed to lose gradually his mental elasticity, his initiative, originality, and self-criticism, and to find it difficult to grasp and assimilate new fields. Furthermore, the subjective feeling of age and of " growing old " is often met with even in the fifties. On the other hand, it has been found that in those fields of skilled and professional work in which development or deployment of the mental powers is the salient issue, the period of maximum efficiency is usually ten to twenty years after the climacteric, so that it is by no means exceptional to find the most important works and achievements falling in the fifties, and even in the sixties. That highly gifted persons show a constant, and even a gradually increasing, efficiency during a period of life which, on purely physiological grounds, is usually marked by a decline of the vital forces, is comprehensible if we take into consideration the tremendous compensatory effect of the mind and the will-power. Cases are known where the mind has overcome bodily illness or a life-long malady.

The history of art and science shows unequivocally that, as a rule, age implies no decrement, above all no decline, in the general mental qualities and productive power of highly gifted persons. One might rather maintain the contrary; namely, that in all fields of intellectual endeavour, highly gifted individuals, as they grow older, manifest a heightened productive efficiency, usually in quality, but also very frequently in quantity. Not a decline, not a dissolution, but development, progress, greater maturity, is observed. The ageing talent enjoys full freedom and intellectual vigour in its insular world of reality.

A few examples will suffice to illustrate this unexpected result. Georg Philipp Telemann, who manifested a fabulous creative activity from his twelfth year up to the time of his death, wrote his finest musical works in the last years of his life, when he was already over eighty. Handel composed his greatest masterworks—the oratorios—between the ages of fifty-six and sixty-seven. He wrote the " Messiah " in twenty-four days when he was fifty-seven. He did not give up his creative work till he lost his eyesight. Rameau actually only began to write operas when he reached the half-century mark. He composed his last big operas between 1757 and 1760 (i.e. between his seventy-fourth and seventy-seventh years). He also did not discontinue his most important theoretical works till the year 1760, or four years before his death. In the last period of his life (i.e. from his forty-ninth year to the time of his death at sixty-five) Johann Sebastian Bach composed many consummate masterpieces. At the beginning of this period he wrote his B minor Mass, his purest and most sublimated creation. This was followed by a large number of magnificent works, such as the "Easter Oratorio" (1716), the "Musikalisches Opfer" (1747), the revision of the Passion according to St. Matthew (1747–1748), the "Chromatic Fantasie", the second part of the "Wohltemperierte Clavier", the great cantatas, and finally just a year before his death, the "Kunst der Fuge". Haydn was already over sixty-five when he wrote his two greatest works, "The Creation" and "The Seasons". Beethoven wrote the "Missa Solemnis", the A♭ major and the C minor Sonatas (Op. 110 and 111) and the Thirty-three Variations (Op. 120) between 1821 and 1823, and his last five great Quartets (Op. 127, 130, 131, 132, and 135) between 1824 and 1826; i.e. up to the year before his death. Verdi composed "Aïda" at fifty-eight, "Otello" at seventy, and "Falstaff" at seventy-five. Gabriel Fauré wrote his greatest work, the Piano Quintet (Op. 115) and the String Quartet (Op. 121), at the age of seventy-nine. In the last five years of his life, Béla Bartók (who died at the age of sixty-five) wrote the "Divertimento" for String Orchestra, the "Contrastes" for piano, violin and clarinet, the Violin Sonata, the Concerto for Orchestra, the Piano Concerto, and the sixth string quartet.

I should now like to add some illustrations in other fields of art. Michelangelo worked on his greatest creations and the cupola of St. Peter's in Rome up to his death at eighty-nine. Leonardo da Vinci completed his famous picture, Anna Selbst-dritt, shortly before his death. Titian worked on his celebrated portraits of Charles the Fifth and Philip II up to his eighty-first year. His last self-portrait and the Pietà also date from his last years. He died in his ninety-ninth year. In the last years of his life—namely, between the age of sixty-one and sixty-three—Rembrandt only painted three canvases, but all of these works rank with his greatest achievements: the Self-portrait in the Royal Museum in Amsterdam, the " Prodigal Son " and the " Family Group " in Brunswick. Dante wrote the " Divine Comedy " in the last years of his life. Goethe completed the second half of " Faust " in his eighty-second year. Dostoievsky wrote " The Brothers Karamasoff " two years before his death, which took place at the age of sixty. Anatole France wrote his well-known work, " La révolte des Anges ", at seventy, and Bernard Shaw his " St. Joan " at sixty-seven.

Even though the above-cited examples provide no conclusive proof that the late works of great talents are marked by an exceptionally high niveau, and even less that gifted individuals very often do not produce their greatest works (i.e. the works to which they owe their fame) till very late in life, nevertheless they do show that age is not necessarily accompanied by a decrement in productive power and a reduction in mental elasticity. No matter how great the physical decline may be, it does not of necessity exert a detrimental effect on the mental virility and productive power of the individual.

The prognostic importance of this evidence lies in the fact that every highly gifted person has the chance not only to maintain his previous level during senescence, but to swing himself to heights which even he himself had never envisaged.

This evidence is not at variance with the findings of experience to the effect that great artists and writers usually find their style in middle life and develop a notable activity even at this epoch, sometimes producing works of great significance, as I have already shown above.

Another question closely associated therewith is whether the works of great masters and scholars produced at an advanced age conform with their earlier accomplishments with respect to the presentation of fact, style, mode of expression, manner of performance; or whether characteristics are manifested in the epoch of physiological decline that are not found in the earlier works. On the basis of an analysis of late works and those produced in senescence by eminent artists, an effort has been made to establish those traits or features that particularly characterize these performances. In the works produced after sixty, let us say, it has been found that greater stress is now laid on the general and universal, while a strong urge towards simplicity and lucidity can be noted. The persuasive power of such data is, however, greatly reduced through the confusion in concept resulting from the identifying classification of " late works " and " works produced during senescence ". Works produced at a very advanced age were frequently not studied as such. Instead, those works were taken which after a long, intensive, systematic preliminary labour came to fruition in the last phase of the creative activity of the master in question; in other words, the late works. Which is erroneous. For we know that the period of full artistic maturity depends on the personality as a whole. The peak of development need not therefore coincide with the chronological age. For this reason, clearness and illumination, inwardness, complete harmony between form and content are not necessarily distinctive features of senescence, but of the original and fully matured artistic personality as such. Whether such features are true in general of the late works can only be established with certainty if they can also be found in the late works of distinguished artists who died comparatively young. Accordingly, it must be shown, for example, that the late works of such masters as Mozart, Schubert, Molière, Schiller, Verlaine, Pushkin, Vermeer, van Gogh (who died in early life) are characterized by the same features that we also find in the late works of a Handel, Haydn, Goethe, Petrarch, Cervantes, Titian, or Rembrandt.

These facts authorize the assertion that there is no fixed comparative relationship between senescence and productivity. In most cases originality and depth of creative power decline with advancing age; i.e. between forty and fifty. On the other hand, a large number of the geniuses and highly gifted only attain the zenith of their creative power and development at an advanced age. It seems as though the passion of youth fulfils a different function in creative activity than the maturity and the lucidity of intellect of later life. In this latter period the creative individual can lift himself above the rank and file, isolate himself, and devote his entire energy to an impersonal goal. He pays less attention to the vicissitudes of everyday life. He takes less and less active part in the aims and activities of the community. And even the urge for recognition and fame gradually declines. This spiritual attitude favours reflection and a sustained attitude, and with this, productive work directed to high aims.

It is impossible to state exactly when the tension between person and work begins to lapse.   This depends on various factors—some physical, some mental; and not least on the intellectual tendencies, the temper, of the age.   If the career of a highly gifted person, through a fortunate destiny and his own way of life, is not disrupted by physical and mental crises, there is no ground for assuming that the ageing individual (and even the senescent) will lose his productive imaginative powers.   This indefeasible fact should keep us from the over-hasty deduction that gifted individuals such as Mozart, Schubert, etc. (who died in early life) had reached the peak of their creative work in spite of their comparative youth.   According to Charles Bühler, there are cases in which a person who dies in early life has already inwardly run his course, when the entire normal span of life has been concentrated into an abnormally brief period of time.   The lower limit of this period is put at twenty, the upper at forty, in the event that seventy is considered the normal span of life.   Which in my opinion is too high.   In such instances, the life phases, which in normal circumstances require years, pass unusually quickly, so that the talented person can carry out all his plans during his youth.   The possibility cannot be denied, at all events, since many careers have reached their zenith very early—between thirty and forty years.

But such cases do not entitle us to assume that a great talent that is cut off in early life has actually completed its life's mission in the short span of days allotted it.   Such an assumption is only justifiable if the efficiency and achievements of the gifted individual have already declined appreciably before his death—provided of course that he was in perfect health.   But, even so, we should be cautious in formulating an opinion, for history records numerous instances of talented individuals who, after a long gap in creative work, suddenly and quite unexpectedly deployed once more all their full creative power.   Take Verdi, for example.   After his great successes with " Rigoletto ", " Trovatore ", " Traviata ", and " Ballo in Maschera ", there were three periods in which he composed practically nothing; e.g. between his forty-sixth and fifty-eighth years (a period of twelve years), between " Aïda " and " Otello "—that is, between his fifty-eighth and sixty-ninth years—and finally between " Otello " and " Falstaff ", or between his sixty-ninth and seventy-ninth years.

As for geniuses who draw from the original sources of their talent, it is unjustifiable to assume that their creative life will be concentrated within a fairly brief space of time. It is highly improbable that artists and scholars whose production shows a rising curve during youth should suddenly cease to produce anything of importance from a more or less accidental moment on. Let us assume, for instance, that Shakespeare had died before " Hamlet ", Beethoven before his last quartets, Mozart before " The Magic Flute ", Leibniz before " Théodicée " and the " Nouveaux Essais ". Would it not, then, be quite unwarranted to assert that they had given expression in their already published works to everything of which they were capable? And if Kant had died at the age of Spinoza—that is, at forty-four—before he had become acquainted with the idea of transiting causality (cognition and causation) as developed by the philosopher Hume, he would scarcely have made a place for himself in the history of philosophy, and would only have remained one of the many unimportant dogmatists deriving from the Leibniz–Wolff school. Or have we the right to assume that Purcell with his thirty-seven years, Chatterton with his eighteen, Raphael with his thirty-seven, the mathematician Galois with his twenty-one, and the physicist Hertz with his thirty-seven years had really achieved everything of which they were capable? It can never be foreseen whether a talented person may not at some later period of life produce an intellectual achievement of which he was deemed incapable; that is, if his previous works are taken as a criterion. If the production of a creative personality is cut off by an untimely death, it indubitably represents a great loss to humanity.

The marvellous age of a Goethe, a Leonardo, a Bach (who reached the peak of their achievements at an advanced age)— men whose creative genius remained untarnished to the very end of their lives—evidently points to the fact that the urge for growth and self-development—the source of all cultural and intellectual achievement—can, in union with superb gifts and great moral strength, overcome physical impairments and enrich humanity with unexpected treasures.

XIII

INHERITANCE OF MUSICAL CAPACITIES

A. Native Endowment and Environment

We find over and over again that blood relations, especially parents and children, grandparents and grandchildren, manifest similar traits. These family resemblances are not limited to physical likenesses only, but also extend to the psychical and mental qualities, such as temperament, character, intelligence, and talent. It was natural to trace connaturalness or resemblance of the physical and intellectual constitution of blood relations to *heredity*, to *transmission of the hereditable latent predispositions of the progenitors to the descendants.*

These resemblances can only be viewed as factual inheritances if their origin can be indisputably traced to heredity. However, in numerous cases a compelling proof of this cannot be proffered, for the principal reason that ostensible resemblances between blood relations may also be due to another powerful factor; namely, to *environment*, i.e. to the operation of the material and intellectual surroundings in which the individual grows up and develops. According to this concept, the psychical family resemblances owe their origin solely to corresponding geophysical, social, and traditional factors. Such a one-sided theory of environment is unmistakably at variance with the fact that related as well as unrelated individuals show great dissimilarities, in spite of the *same environmental influences*. A convincing example of this is the case of monosygotic twins who, irrespective of the uniformity of outward circumstances, manifest striking differences one from the other. It is also well known that individual members of a pronouncedly artistic family, though they live under similar environmental conditions and are subjected to the same influences as the other children, often have not the slightest leaning towards the artistic activities of the parents.

On the other hand, numerous cases can be cited that teach us that with similarity of disposition, differences in environment have no effect on the development of the individual. It has been observed that brothers and sisters reared in an orphanage resemble psychically their brothers and sisters brought up in other surroundings.

But a pure theory of aptitudes does just as little justice to fact as a pure theory of environment. Can the local distribution of scientific and artistic talents, for example, be explained solely by heredity? Heredity can never explain the fact that polytonality began in France (Abbey St. Martial in Limoges in the 12th century and the School of Cambrai in the 15th century), then appeared in Italy (Ars nova in the 14th century) and afterwards in England (Dunstable, Lionel Power, John Benet in the 15th century), to come to full flowering later on in the Netherlands in the 15th and 16th centuries (Dufay, Obrecht, Okegheim, Despres). Especially favourable regional, social, and cultural circumstances must have contributed to this. The same is true as regards the *chronological frequency* of talents; e.g. with reference to the historical fact that during the Renaissance a surprising number of talents emerged in all domains of art. Furthermore, the choice of profession and the direction of interest within one family—as for instance that of the great Bach family of musicians, which serves as an illustration of artistic inbreeding, as paradigm of the inheritance of musical talent—cannot be traced exclusively to heredity. Children of less musical talent in this family of musicians ostensibly selected the profession of music only because family tradition, musical environment, the guild spirit, and, last but not least, the prestige of the great Johann Sebastian Bach all played a part in this choice. The same can be said of the family of Johann Strauss (senior), whose sons and grandchildren (among them his famous son Johann) all became conductors and composers of dance-music as a result of especially favourable outward circumstances.

Accordingly, the pure environmental theory and the pure theory of heredity or aptitude are equally limited. The latter disregards the development predicated by environment, the first overlooks the fact that predisposition forms the necessary prerequisite to any development. Environment can only have an effect on *existing aptitudes*, either as a help or as a hindrance. On the other hand, natural aptitudes require environmental influences for their development.

The individual brings the natural aptitudes for his development with him when he comes into the world. The environment furnishes the stimuli for development. Aptitude and environment together make up the sum total of the individual (96).

In most cases the part played by both factors can only be estimated with more or less probability. In the conspicuously talented as well as the conspicuously untalented, the factor of heredity is to be rated higher than environmental influences. Take Beethoven, for instance, whose great natural musical gift exerted a more decisive effect than environment, including his education and training and the course of instruction. Perhaps the dominating influence of talent is shown even more clearly in the case of artists whose productive power comes out during their childhood in creations of value. With Mozart, environment and education can account for much. But the fact that he was already able to compose notable works between his tenth and twelfth years can only be explained by a congenital disposition. The same will also apply to Johann Sebastian Bach, with whom environment, family atmosphere, professional traditions, on the one hand, and hereditable factors, on the other, had a decisive effect on his artistry. The evidence that change of environment often has no noticeable effect on performance also points to the pre-eminence of the talent factor.

The fact that we occasionally meet with cases where aptitude is not seemingly traceable to the transmission of the hereditable quality on the part of the parents or grandparents *but appears to arise spontaneously in the individual,* seems to argue against the theory that aptitude is a matter of hereditable disposition.

So far as the aptitude of the children derives from both parents (or both grandparents), it might really be expected that the degree of the inherited properties would depend on the proportion in which they are found in the parents. According to such an assumption, children of a very musical father and an unmusical mother should manifest moderate musical talent. But the science of heredity teaches us that certain inherited properties and capacities very frequently show an *alternating quality*; that is, either the property of the one or the other parent will dominate among the descendants. From the hereditary-biological point of view, both forms are possible; i.e. the mixed and the alternating. In children of unequally gifted parents, sometimes there is a mixture of the two parental properties, and again we find the property of the father alternating with that of the mother. In reality, however, *alternating heredity* seems to be the rule in the domain of psychic heredity. There are properties, in fact, in which a mixture is never found, and this is especially *true of musical talent.*

B. Inheritance of Inborn Musical Capacity

With respect to the problem of the inheritance of inborn musical capacity, we have the findings of two very systematic investigations. The one we owe to the Dutch scientists, Heymans and Wiersma (56), the other to the German investigators, Haecker and Ziehen (46).

Heymans and Wiersma had a large number of educated persons (423 in all) describe (on the basis of a questionnaire) the mental and emotional characteristics of both parents and all children springing from the union. Among the questions presented was also that of the *musical ear,* which the researchers quite rightly considered to be a particularly important index of musicality. The following table summarizes the results of this inquiry.

TABLE 14

Inheritance of a Musical Ear

	Percentage of the children		
	Musical ear		Indefinite
	Good	Bad	
Both parents with good musical ear . .	84·0	10·4	5·6
One parent with good musical ear; the other with bad musical ear . . .	59·4	35·9	4·7
Both parents without musical ear . .	29·7	62·5	7·8

The heredity comes out very distinctly. We see that 84% of the musically talented and 10·4% of the unmusical children derived from parents of equal talent. With untalented parents the ratio is reversed. Here the percentage was 29·7% musical and 62·5% unmusical children. We are struck by the fact that parents divergent in respect of musicality give birth to a comparatively large number of musically talented children (59·4%). Is this latter finding not at variance with the laws of heredity? By no means. The cause is to be sought in the well-known phenomenon of heredity, whereby the *positive qualities dominate as a rule over the*

negative to a great degree. This is also true here. In heredity, the good, well-developed musical ear of the one parent triumphs over the poor, undeveloped ear of the other. The fact that with parents of unequal gifts almost a third of the direct descendants have a good musical ear must be mainly laid to the credit of the grandparents.

The inheritance of a musical ear comes out even more clearly in the following summary.

TABLE 15

Inheritance of a Musical Ear

	Very good	Good	Bad
Fathers	13%	42%	30%
Mothers	12%	46%	23%
Sons	17%	45%	27%
Daughters	18%	52%	19%

The general biological fact of the alternating occurrence of talent was also corroborated by the investigations of Heymans and Wiersma. Parents of unequal talent have more talented (59·4%) than untalented (29·7%) children. And they have more untalented children than parents of equal talent (10·4%).

The investigations conducted by Haecker and Ziehen have reference exclusively to *musicality*. The two investigators asked their test subjects several questions regarding their musical aptitude and activity, among others whether the subject in question was considered to be an extremely musical person or not, what musical instrument he played, whether he sang or composed, whether he recognized musical compositions again on hearing them, whether he had an especially good memory for pitch and intervals. The test subjects were graded into five classes, according to the degree of their musical aptitude (extremely musical, very musical, moderately musical, un-musical, absolutely unmusical). Four hundred and eighty-five musical persons were examined in this heredity test. The answers were very carefully evaluated, so that the findings can be considered absolutely authoritative. Table 16 summarizes the findings that are of interest to us here.

The comparison of the results of both tests shows an altogether astonishing agreement. This agreement indicates that the musical ear (which was the subject of the Heymans–Wiersma test) is just as trustworthy an index of musicality as the musical capacities envisaged by Haecker and Ziehen.

As regards inheritance, the Haecker–Ziehen tests also showed the extremely high alternating tendency of the parental talents. With parents of equal musical talent the chance that a child will be very musical is 85%, about 60% when the parents are unequally talented, and still as high as 25% when the parents are without talent. The predominance of the positive cases (extremely musical) over the negative (moderately musical and unmusical) also comes out very clearly. Furthermore, it is found that the musical disposition is inherited to a greater degree from

TABLE 16

Inherited Musicality

	Percentage of the children		
	Extremely musical	Moderately musical	Unmusical
Both parents extremely musical .	85·6	6·5	7·9
One parent musical, the other unmusical	58·6	15·0	26·4
Both parents unmusical . . .	25·4	15·9	58·7

the *father* than from the mother. The number of cases in which the maternal influence is decisive is appreciably less. As regards the inheritance of musical aptitude by musically productive individuals, 22% of the seventy-four test cases were influenced biologically in a positive sense by the father *and* mother, 25% by the father alone, and only 12% by the mother.

The communicated findings refer to persons of average musical talent, but not to outstanding musicians. The question is therefore warranted in how far these findings are valid for the inheritance of musical aptitude by professional and creative artists. Since it has been found that the inheritance of musicality is to be viewed as a *general* biological phenomenon, there is not the slightest reason to assume a deviation from the universal law of heredity for any group of musical persons. Quite to the contrary. The statistically verified laws must be valid *a fortiori* for eminent professional musicians.

It is quite another question whether those inheritance laws are also verifiable by biographical data on eminent musicians available to us. This is certainly not the case, and for the simple reason that the biographies show gaps and inaccuracies about the progenitors, especially in the maternal line. Nevertheless, it is certain that, in spite of the deficiencies of the biographical data of musical history, there are so many examples of direct inheritance of musical aptitude from the parents that the laws of heredity in the field of music cannot be questioned. In illustration thereof a number of distinguished musicians whose musical talent was undeniably inherited are listed herewith in alphabetical order. Here in all cases the talent was inherited from the *father.*

Bach, Boieldieu, Beethoven, Bellini, Bennett, Bizet, Boccherini, Brahms, Bruckner, Cherubini, Couperin, Fétis, Manuel Garcia, Johann Hiller, Liszt, Loewe, Lully, Malibran, Mozart, Offenbach, Adelina Patti, Puccini, Rameau, Reger, Rossini, Scarlatti, Schröder-Devrient, Schubert, Sembrich, Spohr, Johann Strauss, Richard Strauss, Pauline Viardot, Vivaldi, Robert Volkmann, Weber.

Besides the father, who plays the dominant role, the *mother* is occasionally the carrier of the talent, as for instance in the case of Gounod, Grieg, Mendelssohn, and Rubinstein.

Even if individuals show no evidence of hereditary influences, this by no means affects the general validity of the law of heredity. We must take into consideration that the statistical findings cannot claim to be valid for every individual case. The large-scale statistical and genealogical-statistical methods only show collectively valid regularities. Therefore the science of heredity demands that every individual case that seems to lie outside the laws of heredity should be specially examined. One must investigate what factors retarded the hereditable influences or veiled their manifestation.

C. Frequent Occurrence of Notable Talents in One Family

An especially interesting phenomenon in connexion with the inheritance of intellectual qualities is the frequent occurrence of notable talents in the same family. Here we must assume that the hereditable tendencies have such a potent force that even though they may remain latent in an intermediate generation for some reason or other, they are able to crop out again in the succeeding generation with the same energy as before.

Cases of families of more than average talent were collected and examined by different investigators in the field of heredity, in particular by de Candolle, Feis, and Galton, among others (26, 36, 42). The genealogy of the great Bernoulli family of mathematicians is celebrated, since in three generations alone it produced eight notable mathematicians, some of them world-famous.

In the history of music we are most familiar with the noted Bach family, in which great musical art was hereditary for more than 200 years. The period in question extended from the beginning of the 17th down to the middle of the 19th century. Hans Bach, the great-grandfather of Johann Sebastian Bach—already a professional musician—died in 1626, and Wilhelm Friedrich Ernst Bach, grandson and last male descendant of Johann Sebastian, died in 1845. Nearly all members of the

TABLE 17

Pedigree Table of the Bach Family (152)

Johannes (Hans) Bach, † 1626
" der Spielmann "

Johannes 1604–1673 Organist	Christoph 1613–1661 Town Musician	Heinrich 1615–1692 Organist
Georg Christoph 1642–1697 Cantor	Joh. Christoph 1645–1693 Musician	Joh. Ambrosius 1645–1695 Musician
Joh. Valentin 1669–1720 Cantor	Joh. Christoph 1689–1740 Organist — Joh. Ernst 1683–1739 Organist	
Joh. Lorenz 1695–1773 Organist — Joh. Elias 1705–1755 Cantor	Tobias Friedrich 1695–1768 Cantor — Joh. Christoph 1702–1756 Cantor	
Line continued to 19th century	Line continued to 20th century	

Joh. Christoph 1671–1721 Organist	Joh. Balthasar 1673–1691 Trumpeter	Joh. Jakob 1682–1722 Oboist	*Joh. Sebastian* 1685–1750

m.: I. Maria Barbara Bach			II. Anna Magdalena Wilcken	
Wilh. Friedemann 1710–1784	Karl Philipp Emanuel 1714–1788	Joh. Gottfried 1715–1739	Joh. Christoph Friedrich 1732–1795	Joh. Christian 1735–1782
			Wilh. Friedr. Ernst 1759–1845 Cembalist	

family were cantors, organists, town musicians, conductors, and composers. In seven generations there were more than 700 descendants, and among these, eleven eminent composers and artists holding an honoured place in the scrolls of musical history.

Besides Johann Sebastian, his four sons (Johann Christoph, Wilhelm Friedemann, Karl Philipp Emanuel and Johann Christian) are also worthy of mention.

In addition to the Bach family, there is also a long list of other musical families. Especially notable are the following: the Couperin musical dynasty gave France a number of admirable organists and the great François Couperin. For more than 200 years four succeeding generations of the Couperin family were engaged in the field of music with great success. The first member of the family to achieve fame in this respect (Louis) was born in 1626. François Gervais, the last professional musician in the family, died ostensibly in 1830. Francesco Baglioni was an Italian singer. His son was a violinist, and his five daughters were singers. In the Bohemian Benda family there were three generations of musicians. All this family, to the number of twelve, were well-known instrumentalists, composers, and singers. The families of Lully, Dussek, Batka, and Kreutzer (Rodolphe) also produced a very large number of notable musicians.

Another outstanding example is the Dutch Brandts-Buys family, in which we find no fewer than five generations of musicians. The founder of the family was Cornelius Buys (1757–1831). His son, Cornelis Alyander Buys (1812–1890), was organist, composer, and conductor. Four sons of the latter (Marius Adrianus, Ludwig Felix, Henry, and Adolph) distinguished themselves as organists and conductors. Jan (1868–1934), the son of Marius Adrianus, made a name for himself with his orchestral works and operas. Johann Sebastian (1879–1939), the son of Felix, was a music critic. The son of Marius Adrianus, Jr. (Johann Sebastian, known as Hans) born in 1905 and therefore a representative of the fifth generation is a many-sided musician.

In addition, I should like to point out that many highly gifted men do not marry, and those who do usually have very few children. Not infrequently they have no children at all. Statistics have shown that the male descendants of gifted men usually do not extend beyond the third generation. It is maintained that intellectual discipline, with its almost infallible

TABLE 18

Pedigree Table of the Brandts-Buys Family

Corn. Buys Czoon   Aleida Brandts
1757–1831
Trumpeter
later organist

Cornelis Alyander
1812–1890
Organist, Composer
Court pianist to King Willem III

Marius Adrianus Sr.	Ludwig Felix	Henry François Robert
1840–1911	1847–1917	1850–1905
Organist, Composer	Composer-conductor	Conductor

Jan W. Frans	Marius Adrianus Jr.	Johann Sebastian
1868–1934	1872	1879–1939
Organist, import-	Organist, Composer,	Music Critic
ant composer	Conductor	

Johann Sebastian
called Hans, *b.* 1905
Pianist, Organist,
Composer, Conductor

degeneration phenomena, is not conducive to propagation of the family. The families continue in the female line, while the male line gradually dies out (105).

D. Relationship Between Talented Parents and their Children

In connexion with the problem of heredity, there are still two questions that must be answered. The first is: how can we explain the fact that *highly gifted musicians rarely spring from extremely musical parents?* Does not the general law of heredity presuppose a synonymous correlation between parents and children?

By no means. Statistical investigations have already shown that there is no correlation between *the quality and the degree of talent*, especially since a certain percentage of pronouncedly musical children even come of unmusical parents (perhaps even of grandparents who were not especially musical). But the decisive point is to recognize that the inheritance does not refer to *trained properties* (acquired skills), to manifest talents and achievements; but only to *inborn native endowment, to natural traits* that are the basis of those manifest abilities. A distinction must be drawn between acquired, realized abilities, on the one hand, and congenital, dispositionally present capacities, on the other; just as biologists do when they speak of phænotypical (manifest) and genotypical (dispositional) properties. Only the *potentiality* of musical activity is inherited, but not the effective performance, which, like all phænotypical characteristics and actual capacities, is only developed during the lifetime of the individual. What the individual acquires through work, industry, study, education, interest, and last but not least through his inborn nature and character is, and remains, his property. His descendants may profit from it. But they cannot receive it as a gift of nature.

For hereditary-biological reasons alone, we cannot expect any considerable correlation between parents and children in respect to the *extent of the talent*. The cases in which the manifest achievements of the parents and the children closely coincide (for example, in certain families of artists) are among the exceptions, and require a special explanation.

The second question that must be put is this: why do talented parents often have less talented, and even untalented, children?

This question is also to be answered in the sense of the preceding—namely, that parents do not transmit their talent, their efficiency, to their children; but only the natural trait, a talent germ that must first be cultivated. In addition, there is still a special circumstance that works against the transmission by heredity of high-powered latent capacities. This is the phenomenon known in the theory of heredity as *regression* (atavism). The Law of Regression or Reversion can be formulated as follows: If the parents are above or below the general average, then that will also be true of the children, though to a far less degree. That is to say, the children of highly gifted parents seldom attain the niveau of the latter, while children of moderately talented parents show a greater congenital talent in comparison with them.

XIV

CREATIVE WORK

THÉ query has often been raised whether there is any justification for viewing musicians typologically as a class unto themselves, or whether it would not be more correct to allocate them a place in the general typological system. Both points of view have much in their favour. On the one hand, the basic forms of personality that are ranged according to the principle of conspicuous character traits or temperament are so general, and take in so many essentially disparate types, that they also seem suitable for characterizing musicians. On the other hand, it cannot be denied that the course of education, the direction of the talent and interest, the specific professional work, and furthermore the special inner and outer conditions play such a tremendous role in the development and differentiation of musicians that one finds a certain similarity among them. But since the individual diversities of character, of temperament, of mental attitude, of way of life, far exceed the characteristics musicians have in common, it is hardly possible to draw up a special typology for them. It is impossible to reach a decision in the matter, all the more so since today there is a complete lack of any preliminary research on the question.

But the subject on which some clarity has recently been achieved is the *productive* activity of musicians. Musical biographies, as well as the correspondence and utterances of eminent musicians, and, last of all, their manuscripts, orient us in the main on their creative activities. The manuscripts can inform us regarding the nature and method of work, at times also concerning the unfolding of musical fancies and ideas, as well as the relationship between fantasy and systematic work, and no less regarding musical improvisation and its instrumental and vocal realization.

Another equally important system of investigating the process of musical creation is the use of a questionnaire. In this, productive musicians are requested to furnish a report regarding their experiences and self-observations (introspective reports) touching their creative work. This detailed inquiry can be supplemented later by tests and spontaneous reports.

We find two apparently totally different concepts concerning the nature of creative work in general and of musical creative work in particular. The one lays paramount stress on the spontaneous musical inspiration welling up from the *unconscious*. Here the artist is represented as an *original force*, as it were, who brings forth musical ideas in more or less final form through the action of his unconscious. In this the conscious mind plays only a secondary role, the conscious mental work serving chiefly to give fixed form to the inspiration and to develop it further. The musical ideas revealed through the unconscious are, it is maintained, of an improvisational character at first, and are then modified and supplemented in accordance with the artistic intention.

The proponents of this theory are convinced that the unconscious is the fountain source of all creative power, the unconscious being usually taken to mean the divine, supernatural, incomprehensible. Of course by this one does not intend to deny the importance of brain-work, but admits, on the contrary, that the inspiration, the inspirational ideas, achieve their final form solely through intensive conscious work. It is believed that the essential in the creative act lies in the mysterious power of the unconscious, and it is assumed that this force operates during a spiritual state in which conscious activity is switched off, as it were.

This point of view, which can be called the *metaphysical*, finds expression in the utterances of poets and writers, artists and philosophers. The entire literature of artists' personal confessions and correspondence manifests the tendency to raise creative man above everything earthy. Everywhere we find reports of the strange intoxicated state of the creative mind during the period of inspiration; that the individual has the feeling of not acting of his own volition, but of being merely a tool of a higher world order, a vessel (in the words of Goethe) " found worthy to receive a divine inflow ".

> " Everything takes place involuntarily to a high degree (said Nietzsche) but as in a tempestuous feeling of freedom, of unconditionality, of power, of divinity."

We find the same in principle with musical æsthetes and musicians such as Schumann, Brahms, Berlioz, Hanslick. Brahms once wrote that " that which in general is called invention, i.e. the thought, the idea, is simply a higher inspiration for which the artist is not responsible, for which he can claim no credit ". Mahler was of the opinion that " the creation and the genesis of a work is mystical from beginning to end since one—himself unconscious—must create something as though through outside inspiration. And afterwards he scarcely understands how it happened."

No objections can be raised to these descriptions of the experience. They express correctly what artists directly experience at the moment of inspiration. The sudden eruptive emergence of the musical ideas, the apparent passivity of the productive artist, a peculiar intoxicated state, and the element of compulsion that defines the whole creative process are found time and time again.

The other concept of creative work pays special consideration to the *psychological factors* on which the ideas, the inspirations *depend*. It raises the question whether it is necessary, for the understanding of musical creation, to assume forces which seem to lie outside the productive personality and cannot be comprehended empirically, or whether musical inspiration can be explained in a natural way; that is, empirically-psychologically, and can be deduced from the creative process and its antecedents, concomitants, and consequents in their entirety. O. Selz (140) and J. Bahle (5) have taken an energetic stand for the latter concept by pointing out that unconscious action and creation are not peculiarly characteristic of the creative individual. Bahle asserts that creative work does not begin with the inspiration; that, on the contrary, even before the inspiration a whole series of processes dependent on special circumstances take place which condition the inspiration, such as experience, study, tradition, experimentation. According to this point of view, inspiration does not initiate the productive activity. It really represents the *climax* of a long activity. Of course, it has the peculiar tendency to burst forth suddenly and unexpectedly. But this does not mean that it came to birth without preliminary labour.

Both contemporary and older composers furnish numerous testimonies for this *psychological theory*, since they show that the so-called spontaneous, unprepared inspiration presupposes a long occupation with the material. In Haydn's biography we read how he toiled and moiled over the composition of the "Creation", and how he often grew desperate because he could not find the right thing. Mozart said of Haydn's string quartets that they involved incalculable labour, though in hearing them one had the impression that they were created in a state of least resistance.

It is quite erroneous to believe that the Overture to "Don Giovanni" (which Mozart is said to have written in one night) sprang up out of an unprepared soil as a result of divine inspiration. This immortal work had occupied Mozart's thoughts for a long time, and in both mood and form, in fact even to the orchestration itself, it was ready in his mind long before he put pen to paper. This by no means belittles the achievement. It only brings it back to the basis of rational understanding. Mozart once wrote to his father: "You know that I am knee deep in music so to speak; that I busy myself with it all day long; that I like to speculate, study, ponder."

We know of Beethoven that everything that strikes the listener as the creation of a moment had been very laboriously worked out. The duet between Marzelline and Jacquino in "Fidelio" was conquered bar by bar, as it were. There are eighteen different versions of several of the opening bars of the Florestan aria. The wonderful Adagio of the Ninth Symphony also did not come to Beethoven suddenly. We know that the theme of this Adagio already appears in earlier sketches. Haydn also apparently planned the theme of "Gott erhalte Franz den Kaiser" (Austrian National Anthem) long before the composition. Speaking of Beethoven, Romain Rolland wrote that "whoever tries to find the clue to the secret of creation sees with a shock how dearly the genius has to pay for his wonderful conquests. For it costs him an inhuman and boundless effort of the will to satisfy and arrange the angry elements in art so that when he has subjugated them at last, he finds himself—bruised and beaten— back in the world of every day."

The same can be said of Schubert and Schumann. Schubert numbered his Erlkönig "Opus 1", which would lead us to believe that his genius manifested itself suddenly in an overpowering way. In point of fact, however, he had already composed 100 songs and a number of quartets, even though they had not yet been published. Schumann made numerous sketches for his quartets exactly as painters are accustomed to do for their pictures.

> " Do not estimate the power of reflection too lightly (wrote Wagner). The art-work that is produced unconsciously belongs to periods that are far distant from our own. The art-work of the crowning period of cultivation cannot be produced otherwise than consciously."

Stravinsky also said exactly the same thing:

> " For me as composer, composing is a daily routine which I feel called on to carry out. As every organ deteriorates if it is not kept in running order, so too the abilities of the composer decline and petrify if he does not make a constant and zealous effort to keep himself in practice. The layman thinks that in order to create, one must await an inspiration. But this is an error. I am far from repudiating inspiration. Quite to the contrary. I consider it to be a moving force that belongs to every human activity and is by no means a monopoly of the artist. But this power only unfolds when it is set in motion by an effort and this effort is—work. Just as appetite comes with eating, so too work evokes inspiration, in the event the latter is not present from the beginning. But it is not a question of inspiration alone, but of the result: the art-work."

The two concepts characterized above—the metaphysical and the psychological—are understood and represented as opposites in the literature of psychology and musical æsthetics. If we look into the matter more closely, it will be found that they are by no means contradictory, but really supplement each other.

It must be pointed out first of all that both concepts accord a decisive formative importance to musical inspirations. But where the metaphysical theory lays weight on the unconscious and attributes to the latter a very special creative force, the psychological theory characterizes creative production as the result of long, inner, sometimes conscious, sometimes unconscious, processes in which intensive work, a conscious attitude, a prepared plan, and special interest play the leading role. The one viewpoint emphasizes the " idea ante rem ", as it were; the other the " idea post rem ".

The proponents of the psychological theory also attribute a creative role to the unconscious and similarly the apostles of the metaphysical theory by no means underrate the importance of the brain effort, the work, the industry, the study, the preparation, the conscious conception. We find that all writers and musicians who are usually cited as apostles of the metaphysical theory also fully appreciate, and even stress, that which the disciples of the empirical psychological concept defend so positively. Most of the artists who occupy themselves with this problem can be brought forward as witnesses both for the *metaphysical* and the *psychological* point of view. Goethe, for instance, says in one place: " Every productivity of the highest order, every significant *aperçu*, every invention, every great thought that bears fruit and brings results is under no one's control, and is above everything earthly." Then again he writes: " Every true *aperçu* is one in a train of processes (i.e. derives from a result and leads to a result). It is a middle link in a great ascending chain of productivity." No one will find anything contradictory in the two statements. The same Nietzsche who said of inspiration that " everything happens involuntarily to a high degree, as in a tempestuous feeling of freedom, of unconditionality, of power, of divinity " had the following to say of the working methods of the artist:

> " It is to the interest of the artist that others should believe in sudden suggestions, so-called inspirations; as if the idea of the art-work, the poem, the underlying thought of a philosophy shone down from Heaven like a divine ray. All great men were great workers, indefatigable not only in invention but also in rejection, sorting out, revising, and arranging " (89).

But what is the actual difference between the two concepts? The metaphysical theory stresses *inspiration*, which, it contends, bursts forth unexpectedly, suddenly, without ostensible or demonstrable preparation and gives aim and direction to creative activity. The psychological theory, on the other hand, seeks to explain the *course*, the *process of development* of creative activity, and tries to fit inspiration into this scheme. The champions of the metaphysical theory cannot imagine inspiration without assuming mysterious forces that are never manifested in a conscious state. On the other hand, the proponents of the psychological theory believe that the genesis and unfoldment of musical ideas can only be explained by the assumption of supernatural forces.

What differentiates the two concepts one from another is, in my opinion, the assumption or rejection of the *miraculous*, of the impersonal, of the inexplicable, in artistic creation. The argument consequently is not over the *fact* of the inspiration in itself, but over the *interpretation* of this fact, over the genesis of the creative thought.

I believe that the antagonism to the metaphysical theory is mainly directed at the *concepts* it employs, and not so much at the interpretation, the point of view itself. If, for instance, we understand the words supernatural, divine, miraculous, not in a metaphysical but a metaphorical sense, and take them to mean that it is a question of ideas—inspirations that are far above ordinary heights of achievement and represent something unique, something not consciously conceived—then no objections can be raised to these ideas. That can also be said of the frequent occasions when we find that the *demonstrable* basis of the productive inspiration is incommensurate with the greatness of the creation. But if we mean that the creation is produced without preliminary work of any kind, or that supernatural forces play a role in the integrating process, we bring this process into a sphere that can no longer be controlled and lies outside the range of scientific research.

Perceived under a genetic attitude, the psychological theory has furnished us with much very interesting and valuable insight into the stadia of the creative process; but it seems to me that it does not lay hold of the *real problem* of creative activity, to say nothing of solving it. In both theories and also in their synthesis it is largely a question of the forces and factors of the productive work, and not of the *creation* itself. Of course in certain cases the ideas of value (as far as plan and tendency are concerned) can be traced to recollections, linkages, traditional forms of expression; none the less we must concede that significant inspirations are independent of already familiar forms to a very great degree. Recollections, analogies, undoubtedly play an important role in the creative process. But they cannot be made responsible for the subject content, the originality, the greater genuineness, and the value of the inspirations. If such factors were alone decisive, then we might expect that the great masters of music nearly always had ideas of value suitable for artistic development. For it may be taken for granted that they did not fail to take full advantage of the inspired mood for intensive work. We know that this is not the case. The production of the great masters does not consist exclusively of great creations. Even in one and the same work we can find portions that are more, and less, significant; more, and less, successful. We also find musicians who have produced only very little of outstanding value, in fact who have produced only one work of really great stature. (Mascagni, for instance, and to a certain extent Bizet also, who besides his wonderful " Carmen " only wrote a few notable musical works such as the " Arlésienne " Suite, " Djamileh ", " Les Pêcheurs de Perles "). And still it is difficult to assume that during their lifetime they only once experienced those stadia that are considered a prerequisite to musical creative work.

There are limits to the investigation of the productive process. The hope of being able to comprehend the successive processes of creative work is vain. Many roads lead from the explorable to the inexplorable which are not practicable for our brains and our analytical powers. There is no doubt that the forces that govern original creative work, that lead the productive effort to the topmost peak, that give almost unlimited scope to mental life, cannot be grasped in their multiplicity through observation and introspection.

A genetic investigation of creative work is able to establish the factors of the musical productive process and also to determine those stadia of realization that run from the first conception to the completed work. But to the *concrete* question *how* the artist arrives at certain musical ideas, at certain leading motives, at his original themes, and why he arrives at just these and no others, it can provide no satisfactory answer. The psychological motive may indeed furnish the impulse for the creative act; in many instances, perhaps determine the idea. But it can by no means be viewed as a really adequate causation. No matter how precisely we may be able to follow the whole long inner preparatory process, how convincingly we may be able to describe the stages of development of a composition, there always remains an unbridgeable cleft between the preparatory process and the original inspiration of value. The connexion is established by the *genius* of the artist who, through the happy coincidence of divers circumstances and through the work in the unconscious, supplies the connective link. And it is in this leap—which often surprises the productive artist himself—that the unexpected, the involuntary, lies. Both mental activities (conscious work and spontaneous unconscious inspiration) are operative in composing. The one can never lead to a consummate artwork without the other. Naturally the productive fantasy does not hover in the ambient. It is like a stream that grows broader and mightier through constant new influxes. It draws its material from experience, from the acquired skills, from the associated actual conditions. But all this cannot constitute and explain the new, original, unique (19, 119).

The mental activity of the creative genius is also subject to certain general laws. Nevertheless the content, the original creative idea *per se* is, and remains, a direct utterance of the productive mind for which in reality there is no explanation and for which none is required. It is, so to speak, a natural phenomenon which, though it has its first cause within us, cannot (and perhaps for that very reason) reveal its ultimate roots to us. Even as we do not notice how we grow and alter, even so little do we experience the genesis and growth of our thoughts and visions springing from the interplay of mind and mood. If one wishes to call this " miraculous ", one is at liberty to do so. But it is no more miraculous than the transformation of the bud into a flower.

XV

RECEPTIVE AND PRODUCTIVE MUSICAL ACCOMPLISHMENTS OF THE DEAF

IT may seem paradoxical to speak of deafness in a work on the psychology of music. But if we stop to consider that neither congenital nor acquired deafness (i.e. deafness arising during lifetime) nor hardness of hearing necessarily imply the loss or alteration of the acoustic-musical capacity, it will be clear that deafness, or an appreciable reduction in the acuity of hearing, represents a special problem in music psychology.

Musicality's essential independence of the function of hearing is evident in two directions. First of all, it is a recognized fact that normal hearing—the unimpaired condition of the sensory auditory apparatus—in no wise guarantees the reception of musical patterns and the development of fertile musical latencies. People whose hearing is intact can be altogether unmusical. This is shown by sudden neurotic inhibitions, which can result in serious disturbances in musical apprehension and activity without the hearing being affected. When an eminent pianist was seized by an attack of musical amnesia (clouding of the memory for musical content) during a concert, it was absolutely impossible for him to go on with his playing. He found himself obliged to interrupt his artistic activities till after a short time he had regained his former abilities.

The contrary case, when gradual deafness or impaired hearing has no effect on musical apprehension and enjoyment, also speaks for musicality's independence of the function of hearing.

Several historically verified examples will serve to prove that hardness of hearing—gradually increasing deafness, in fact—need have no detrimental effect on the creative ability.

Beethoven's ear malady began in 1800 (in his thirtieth year). Eight years later he was already very hard of hearing, and by 1819 he was stone deaf. We know through his Conversation Books that from this time on communication could only be held with him in writing. Nevertheless, from 1819 till his death in 1827 he wrote his greatest works such as the " Missa Solemnis "

(1818–1823), the Ninth Symphony, the six last string quartets (1824–1826), and the piano sonatas in E major (Op. 109), A♭ major (Op. 110), and C minor (Op. 111). We will therefore come fairly near the truth if we say that Beethoven composed his works from Op. 60–65 (1808) to the last (the Quartet in F major, Op. 135, written four months before his death) in a period of acute hardness of hearing or total deafness.

Robert Franz, the sensitive Lieder composer of the 19th century (1815–1892), never enjoyed especially acute hearing. According to his own statements, he lost his auditory perception for notes above e^3 in his twenty-fourth year as the result of an accident. His condition grew worse as time went on, aggravated by a peculiar sort of irritability towards many sounds. In 1871 he became totally deaf. After his deafness he gradually lost the power of auditory imagery, till suddenly his eyes did vicarious service for his ears. " Now (he wrote in 1882) I perceive tonal differences far worse than formerly and I sense through the eyes exactly as I formerly did through the ears." He continued as follows: " My songs and rearrangements (works of Bach and Handel) were all, without exception, written during the period of my ear malady." Franz wrote about 360 songs. If one dates his total deafness from 1871, then it will be found that he composed the greater part of his songs (which rank with the finest creations of German Lieder) after the complete loss of his hearing, so that he never heard most of them.

After a period of aural disease, Friedrich Smetana (1824–1884), the well-known Bohemian opera composer, became totally deaf in 1874. He perceived subjective tones, and was constantly worried and irritated by ringing and noises in his ears. This condition lasted for several years, and it was in such harassing circumstances that he wrote his string quartet in E minor and a long series of orchestral and operatic works. " I never heard a note of all these works (he wrote in a letter) and still they lived in me and through mental imagery alone moved me to tears and to sheer ecstasy." Of the eight operas that established his fame, five were written after the beginning of his total deafness; namely, " Dve Vdovy " (Two Widows) in 1874, " Hubicka " (The Kiss) in 1876, " Tajemstvi " (The Secret) in 1878, " Libuse " (Libussa) in 1881, and " Certova Steňa " (The Devil's Wall) in 1882. Then there is also Gabriel Fauré who after being hard of hearing for many years finally became stone deaf at the age of sixty-five (1910). After this date he wrote a Quartet for strings published posthumously and two piano Quintets which are reckoned among the greatest works of their class. These few examples, which could be supplemented by numerous others, refer exclusively to musicians who before their deafness had an especially sensitive musical ear.* Now the question arises whether it is to be assumed that those who are deaf from birth or early infancy also have musical aptitude in spite of their lack of hearing and can have any sort of connexion with music.

First of all, it is extremely improbable that the *musical disposition* is much less common with this group of deaf-mutes than among those with normal hearing. For example, there is no reason for assuming that in a musical family the inheritance of musical traits differs biologically in any way with a child born deaf than with his brothers and sisters with normal hearing. That the congenital capacity, through elimination of the aural function, will gradually recede is apparent on the face of it. But the need for acoustic-motory experiences does not necessarily have to disappear altogether just because of this. This we see by our recent experiments with deaf-mutes.

That scientific literature altogether failed to take into consideration the latent musical disposition of deaf-mutes is explained by the fact that deaf-mutes were never investigated concerning their rhythmical-musical sense. Furthermore, they had no opportunity of expressing themselves in this respect. One proceeded from the erroneous hypothesis that because access to the specific acoustic musical world was completely closed to the deaf, any attempt to bring this world nearer to them was hopeless from the outset. If we go into the question a little deeper, then we shall find that the musical world is not hermetically sealed to the deaf. Although they are totally deprived of the acoustic material (the necessary prerequisite to musical perception) they still apprehend certain elements of music such as rhythm, tempo, intensity, and, above all, the vibration stimuli that accompany sound movements.

* As regards the interpretation of this sensory vicariousness experienced by Franz and Smetana (visual resources as a substitute for the auditory) it can only refer to a more highly sensitized " mental " hearing. Musical experiences have nothing to do with optical musical notation or optical images. The representative role of the eyes in Franz's case must therefore have rested on pure delusion.

What are the vibratory sensations, and in what way are they able to some extent to replace sound sensations with deaf-mutes?

If we touch a vibrating tuning-fork or string, we perceive not only a tactile sensation, but, in addition, a strange feeling of vibration. Every periodic vibration that attains a definite frequency and intensity arouses in us not only a tone sensation, but also a *sense of vibration*. These vibratory sensations play a great role with deaf-mutes. In speech instruction (the so-called articulation instruction of deaf-mutes) the pupil, as we know, lays one finger on the teacher's larynx while he places another on his own, and in this way tries to imitate a sound purely by motor impulse till he feels the same vibration in both fingers. In this way the deaf-mute learns articulate speech with the aid of vibratory sensations, and in this manner facilitates his contact with normal persons (64).

The sense of vibration, which, like the tactile sense, is distributed over the entire body, reacts to all tonal and noise stimuli. Through the vibratory pulses, deaf-mutes distinguish silence from noise, the various music instruments one from another. With close attention they are also able to apprehend the rhythm and loudness of musical notes, and even to discriminate them as regards pitch, with more or less accuracy. It is shown that the lower the note, the deeper the vibratory sensations are localized in the body. Notes of the double bass, cello, bassoon, horn, etc., are localized in the chest; those of the violin, flute, etc., in the head.

The rhythmic-dynamic effects of music experienced through vibratory sensations are employed with success in gymnastic exercises with deaf-mutes. By laying one hand on the tambourine held in the other hand, the deaf-and-dumb child apprehends the vibrations generated by the notes of the piano. In this way children are enabled to apprehend soft and loud, short and long notes vibrationally. Movements of the arms, legs, head, and trunk are practised in connexion with the series of vibrations, which develop gradually into rhythmic gymnastics. These gymnastics linked with music make a strange impression on the outsider, since one knows that the children do not hear a single note.

It seems that the vibratory sensations are able not only to order the rhythmical movements, but also to facilitate a certain access to the æsthetic sphere, though only to the lower regions. The famous Helen Keller (deaf and blind) stated in her autobiography that music moved her very deeply, but her statements regarding her " musical " (really her vibratory) sensations made no impression at the time. To me also her reports seemed a little mysterious until some years ago I had opportunity, quite by accident, of making the acquaintance in Berne, Switzerland, of Eugen Sutermeister, a deaf-mute clergyman, who was totally deaf, and yet insisted that he was passionately fond of music and that music afforded him great pleasure. He went to concerts, had his favourite composers, criticized the works. We subjected him to a rigorous investigation (120). It was found that he actually was able to identify the musical works according to their mood and to recognize those that he had frequently heard. Further acoustical tests showed that with this deaf-mute the most important conditions for musical enjoyment, as well as for the recognition and identification of the musical work, were the *rhythm, intensity, and tempo*. Through practice he had acquired the ability to sense differences in the vibratory sensations to a very fine degree. Although the richness of vibratory sensations in no way approaches that of the musical clang as regards pitch, quality, tone colour, tempo, and intensity, nevertheless the perceived vibratory sensations must still have been very abundant and have rendered valuable service in recognizing and identifying the compositions.

It requires no further comment that the musical effect which penetrates the consciousness through vibratory channels can have no relationship with the musical impression that is imparted through *acoustical* mediums. Even the rhythmic, the dynamic—in fact, even the temporal—are manifested in another form than in music, since they are neither borne by musical ideas nor are they clothed in acoustic-musical elements. Although the deaf do not grasp the ideational content of the musical work, do not experience the specifically musical, do not hear the notes, yet they seem to be very deeply moved by music. In this aporia lies the psychological and therapeutic-pedagogical significance of music for the deaf and dumb (121).

How can we explain this? The powerful sentiently perceptible vibration pulses and the vasomotory effects engendered by them evoke in deaf-mutes sensuous moods of a positive nature. Those who hear are also strongly conscious of these emotional reactions. That music exerts a fascinating effect on the musically untrained, even on the unmusical, is a familiar fact. Of course we understand that here it is not a question of æsthetic reaction, since the æsthetic is remote from the sensuous effects that take place in the vital sphere. The purely sensory effect of music rests, on the one hand, on the sound and the rhythm; and, on the other hand, on the vibratory or vasomotory effects of the sound. When we say that music is stirring and moving, that it induces rhythmical bodily movements, this should be taken more literally than was formerly thought. Here we have to do with the direct effect of strong vibrations on the vasomotory system of the body, which (with the hearing) determines our emotional reaction. With deaf-mutes it forms the prerequisite to, and in fact the whole content of, their " musical " experience.

We with normal hearing are also affected by vibrations, like any resonating body. To these vibratory sensations we can also attribute a portion of the " deep " effect of organ music and choral singing in an auditorium with excellent resonance, and also of the stirring effect of fortissimi. In my opinion this also has much to do with the practice of ending a musical composition with a dynamically brilliant movement or strongly accented chords.

If we wish to arouse moods in the deaf that can speed up the rhythm of life, stir their emotions, then we expose them to music. It then depends on the interrelationship of the rhythmical and the dynamic whether the emotional reaction is varied, or the reverse. Here everything rests on the right choice of music, not on its artistic but its vibratory value. One must ascertain by experiment what pieces generate strong and lasting emotional reactions when translated into vibrations. This is supported by the fact that in the pre-school years, as experience shows us, music makes its greatest impression through dynamical and rhythmical contrasts. These induce definite motor reactions of a direct emotional nature such as beating time, movements of the body, phenomena that can also be observed with deaf-and-dumb children.

Access to the specific acoustical-musical world is completely closed to deaf-mutes. Nevertheless, as I have here shown, certain aspects of the world of music are accessible to them. The principal object of the rhythmic-dynamic education of deaf-mutes is a gymnastic-clinical pedagogical one, it is true, but this does not eliminate the Dionysiac effect of music.*

* I should like to call attention to a special application of music in the education of deaf-mutes in the United States. Sarah Harvey Porter (100) tells of a school band in an American institute for deaf-mutes. Of the thirty-one boys and girls that made up this remarkable band, nineteen were stone deaf, the others partially deaf. However, I am not convinced of the pedagogic value of this experiment.

XVI

PATHOLOGY OF MUSICAL PERCEPTIVITY

BESIDES congenital deafness and that due to organic disease, there is a special form of deafness that is of psychogenetical origin. Although in this case the individual's organ of hearing is perfectly intact, the patient does not hear or understand speech and music. His attitude towards the world of sound is that of an actually deaf person. The analysis of such phenomena of psychic deafness has shown that they are often the result of *infantile traumata*, especially an after-effect of childish phobias and anxiety complexes. It happens, for instance, that nervous children, in order to avoid a reaction to music and noises in general and to human speech in particular, instinctively pretend to be deaf in their early childhood. This neurotic condition can become permanent so that the patient fails to react to the perceived speech-sounds over a long period. We can gain some idea of this psychic inhibition if we consider that sometimes the normal individual can so accustom himself to the surrounding noise and confusion that it does not disturb him in his intensive mental work. Such a person knows nothing of the conversation going on round him; in fact, he takes no notice of what is happening in his immediate surroundings. A similar deadening of tone and speech-sound perceptivity is found to an increased degree and in permanent form in psychotic deafness (deaf-mutism). Such a condition can be corrected by psycho-analytical treatment, provided the physician is successful in uncovering the psychogenetic causes and in awakening the patient's interest in speech and music. In this case the psychically deaf person, with constant systematic practice and after a relatively short time, begins to hear and grasp in a perfectly normal manner the musical notes and the human speech-sounds which until then were involuntarily repressed.

This complex pathological question is of no interest to the psychology of music, though there is another neurotic phenomenon that is. This is the inability to recognize musical sounds, and is known by the collective name *Amusia*. The concept of amusia has undergone changes during the last decades. Formerly all those persons were called " amusic " who are not only unmusical in the ordinary sense of the word, but for whom every form and aspect of music is strange and incomprehensible. Even today amusia is frequently taken to mean this complete indifference to music. By " amusia ", however, we are to understand disturbances in, and lack of, *musical perceptivity* which, analogous to aphasia, are apparently the result of damage to certain brain-cells. Consequently that person is " amusic " who has *lost a former musical ability so that he is no longer capable of correctly perceiving or reproducing notes and musical patterns.*

Musical history reports frequent cases of amusic disturbances and defects among musicians. The assumption that these disturbances and defects arise more frequently among the musically gifted than others is an error. They are only observed and discussed to a greater extent because the musician suffers more keenly from them and sees himself obliged to give up his professional activity.

It would lead us too far afield to go into the various forms of amusic disturbances. It will suffice here to call attention to the most important types. In the main, two principal groups can be distinguished; namely, the motorial and the sensorial. *Motorial* amusia is when the patient loses the ability to *reproduce* melodies or musical pieces accurately, though he grasps and understands the music correctly as before. In a person suffering from motorial amusia, musical perceptivity remains perfectly intact, but the ability to reproduce music, including its interpretation, is destroyed. The patient is perfectly aware that he is singing or playing the piece incorrectly, and yet he is unable to rectify the errors (64).

The most diverse disturbances will be found in motorial amusia. In one case, for instance, the patient with a full understanding for music could play or sing melodies, but could not perform them in the proper rhythm. Another patient was able to sing isolated notes correctly, but not a melodic sequence. A violinist suffering from amusia played the first five notes of the G major scale correctly. All the rest, however, were wrong. It also happens that patients suffering from amusia can sing after a fashion but cannot play. We have to do, not with amusia, but with an aphasic condition when the patient must first hear the words before he can sing a familiar song and tries in vain to capture the melody if one gives him the title only.

In contrast to motorial amusia, *sensorial* amusia (which is also known as *deafness to music*) is characterized by the patient having completely lost the *understanding* for simple melodies, and even more so for complex musical patterns, though his ear for notes and noises is later shown to be intact.   Notes are correctly reproduced and the rhythm correctly grasped.   However, the most familiar song is not recognized, much less reproduced.   Sensorial amusia sometimes breaks out very suddenly.   An opera-singer was once seized by it while singing on the stage.   He no longer understood what was sung or played.   He was completely stalled, and could not bring forth a single correct note.

In most cases amusia is accompanied by speech disturbances; i.e. while the ear for notes, clangs, vocables, is completely unaffected, understanding for music and speech is lost.   The patient hears everything, but understands nothing.   He is unable to recognize either familiar folk-songs or the most ordinary words.

An entirely different type consists of *disturbances in the perception of isolated notes*.   Such auditory defects are called *Paracusis*, or disordered hearing.   There are four distinct types of paracusis.   In *diplacusis binauralis echotica* the given clang (with binaural hearing) is heard twice over as a result of a disease of the one ear— first with the healthy ear and afterwards with the diseased ear.   The sensation is re-echoed, as it were.

In *diplacusis monauralis echotica* the diseased ear hears the monaural clang (unchanged) twice in succession, the second clang being an echo of the first.   In the clinical form of *diplacusis binauralis disharmonica* the diseased ear hears notes within a definite region of the scale either higher or lower than the normal ear, so that a dissonant double clang is the result.   A patient suffering from this disorder, for example, hears the note g as g with the healthy ear.   With the diseased ear, however, it sounds about g♯.   In most cases the difference is not more than about a quarter or half tone.   But there are cases on record in which the pseudo note is a fifth, even an octave, higher or lower than the normal note.   This phenomenon is quite rightly designated " disharmonica ", since the difference is almost never a pure interval, so that the two-tone clang is always dissonant.

I found a special type of paracusis in a very musical man to whom I have already referred (p. 72).   I called the pathological phenomenon in question *diplacusis qualitatis*.   The domain of the

tonal series to which the diseased ear reacted comprised all notes
between g♯² and d♯². Below g♯² and above d♯² tone perception
was normal. The patient heard *all* notes within the paracusic
area—that is, between g♯² and d♯²—as g♯. On closer examina-
tion it was found that this pseudo note g♯ agreed with no g♯
note in the tonal series. It was neither a g♯¹ nor a g♯², but
simply *a g♯ quality* at the *pitch* of the objective note. I mean by
this that when a² was sounded, the patient's diseased ear heard it
as g♯. When c³ was sounded, he heard a g♯ at the pitch c³.
The pathological process merely changed the *quality* of the note,
but not the pitch along with it. Even with persons of normal
hearing, the g♯ quality is found at various pitch levels, as G♯, g♯,
g♯¹, etc. In the aforesaid patient this was so in *all* pitch degrees
of the tonal domain between g♯² and d♯³. This pathological
phenomenon furnishes important proof of the independence and
dissociation of the two musical characteristics, quality and pitch.
For it has demonstrated that the usual correlation of the two
properties is dissolved in certain circumstances (106).

In connexion with *diplacusis qualitatis*, attention is called to an
especially interesting and, for the psychology of music, important
phenomenon termed *orthosymphony*. I found in the same individual that in the paracusic condition *chordal perception* was
unaffected. While in the pathological area—that is, in the
domain of the tonal system where pitch perception was abnormal
—the isolated notes were heard incorrectly, and successive
intervals were therefore incorrectly identified, it was found that
chordal perception paradoxically was apparently unaffected by
the false quality of the components. If two notes (one normal
and the other abnormal) were sounded simultaneously for the
patient, then it seemed to him as though the false quality was
corrected by the simultaneous sounding of the other note. Close
investigation showed, however, that this impression (re-establish-
ment of the normal quality) was based on a delusion. When
the patient analysed the normal-sounding two-note clang, he
also found the false-tone quality along with the correct one. For
example, the pathologically altered note a² sounded to him like
g♯. If we sounded the successive interval a¹–a², the patient
judged it (in conformity with the pseudo note) as a major seventh
(a¹–g♯²). The two-note clang (simultaneous interval), however,
sounded normal to him; that is, it sounded to him like an octave

(a^1-a^2). When the notes e^2-c^3 were played in succession, he identified them incorrectly as a major third $(e-g\sharp)$, but when sounded simultaneously he judged the interval correctly as a minor sixth (e^2-c^3). The impression of a two-note clang or chord was independent of the quality of its components. This phenomenon, in which the chordal perception remains normal in spite of paracusis, was termed *ortho-symphony*.

Of the other pathological phenomena in the domain of acoustics, I will only mention the so-called *tone islands* or *tone gaps*. By this we mean the phenomenon in which a smaller or larger area of the tonal series is completely lacking. A number of adjacent notes (for example, the notes between e^2 and g^2, or those from c^3 upwards) are not heard by the patient; yet otherwise his hearing remains intact.

The so-called *subjective tones* or *auditory hallucinations* (aural sensations without physical cause) are very disturbing to musical persons. As we know, Robert Schumann suffered from aural hallucinations in the last years before his tragic death. He incessantly heard one particular note (a), which made life a torture to him. Such subjective tones often accompany acute ear maladies, and then disappear when cure has been effected.

XVII

THE ORIGIN OF MUSIC

THE question concerning the origin of the world, of life, of the material and spiritual possessions of humanity, has absorbed thinking, introspective minds since the very beginning of time. The mythology of all races has tried to solve this problem by assuming original forces or the participation of personified mystical powers, supernatural beings; in short, a creative act. In the first period of Greek philosophy the great thinkers of antiquity also turned their attention to the core problem of the first source of things: their mode of origin. Research maintained this direction for a long period. We come across it again in the modern theories of spontaneous generation, the genesis of living matter; but especially in the theory of transmission by descent. The most significant theory of evolution—that formulated by Darwin—gave fresh impetus to the exploration of the origin, the original forms and first manifestations of human activities and achievements, and provided new points of view. Prehistory, ethnology, palæontology, historical research, psychology, as well as comparative philology, æsthetics, and musicology have furnished rich material on the original forms of human activities. Many research scholars were inspired by the hope of being able to reconstruct, with the aid of the ever richer sources of knowledge, the beginnings of speech, religion, art, and society. Others propounded premature hypotheses on these matters that rendered no service to science. Let us investigate how far the aforesaid theories of the origin of music are really enlightening, and examine whether this problem is really solvable or not.

The first question that arises is what one understands in general by the concept of " origin ". This concept has two interpretations, which are to be sharply differentiated one from the other. In one the word origin is taken to mean the first or *initial form* of a function or activity, consequently—where music is concerned—the manifestations of the *most primitive phase* of its development. But again it may also mean the prehistory, in this instance the presumable *first stage of music*; i.e. those utterances of man from which music arose as it were. Here it is a question of the stadium when man did not know music in the actual sense of the word, but when certain tendencies were manifest which are to be viewed as the preliminary stage.

A. Music in the Most Primitive Stage of Development

Let us begin with the first question: that touching the *beginnings*, the first unmistakable manifestations of *music*.

With the aid of ethnological, archæological, and historical research, an attempt is made to establish those musical configurations and forms that we assume to be the simplest, earliest revelations of musical experiences and activities, and which in consequence may be taken as the basis of our music. Here evidence must be adduced that they *really are primary patterns* and do not represent the reversion of an earlier, richer stock. This field of research, based on the theory of evolution, forms the actual domain of comparative evolutionary-historical musical research. The evolutionary-historical point of view already presupposes the existence of music. One proceeds from musical utterances, where such can, in principle, be called music. Just as the primitive forms of speech necessarily incorporate the most important elements of speech—namely, the concept, the symbolic sense, of the word-sound—so, too, the primitive forms of music must incorporate the essential characteristics of music without which the existential basis of music is lacking. We must proceed from this standpoint if we are not to be ensnared in a tangle of fantastic speculations.

The first question to be answered is what characteristics must exist before an expressive form—a tone and speech-sound—can pass as music. If we examine the music of every race for the factors that are common to all and are peculiar only to the expressive forms of music, we come to the conclusion that every form of music, primitive as it may be, must manifest three characteristics: *fixed intervals, their transposition to various pitches, and their use in heterogeneous, rhythmically articulated tone combinations.* Accordingly, we can only speak of music when there are more or less constant, fixed, transposable, rhythmically articulated note sequences (interval, motive) that are independent of pitch and recur repeatedly in various combinations. How large and how numerous these constant intervals are, whether they coincide with the intervals of our tonal system, and whether they form part of a rational musical system, is irrelevant. Here it is only a question of the constancy and the recurrence of the same intervals in a more or less homogeneous melodic configuration. Monotonic songs that have no graspable and recurrent intervals can no more be called music than certain rhapsodic calls and the lalling melodies of children before they have learned to talk. The fact that even the most primitive songs of races at the very lowest stages of civilization (e.g. the aboriginals of Australia, the Veddas, the Patagonians) have clearly recognizable intervals (such as seconds) in their almost static " melodies ", and the further circumstance that the melodic structure of the unaccompanied vocal music (uninfluenced by musical instruments) has shown increasingly clear tonal relations during the process of time, indicate the organic structural importance of the interval for music.*

Just as the *definition of speech* necessarily predicates the existence of a number of articulated constant speech or movement patterns appearing in different sense associations, so also the only possible *definition of music* is one that postulates the existence of a number of rhythmically articulated, more or less constant, tonal sequences found in varied melodic combinations. And furthermore, just as speech is motivated by the intention to express, and to communicate to others, thoughts, aspirations, wishes, so, too, the fundamental purpose of music is to give expression to musical ideas, emotions, and moods, and to arouse corresponding specific musical reactions in others. Melodic-rhythmic tone or sound complexes that are not motivated by this intention do not belong in the realm of music. This qualification is all the more justified since it is out of the question that sound utterances evidencing the above-mentioned characteristics should arise without intention.†

According to our definition, it is inadmissible to associate

---

* In the few primitive races that are ignorant of any other than vocal music, intervals are much less constant than with those that are accustomed through their musical instruments to fixed, rigid intervals. But the octave is never wanting, and the so-called framework tones, which to a certain extent represent fixed intervals, are met with everywhere. The tone measurements of J. Kunst (72) show the constancy of the intervals. For instance, in Dutch Guinea, with one singer $c^1 = 158$, $a^1 = 220$, $g^1 = 193$ cycles; while with other singers they were 159, 219, and 196 cycles (149).

† If the wearisomely uniform tonal patterns of primitive peoples, barren alike of rhythm or accent (e.g. hand clapping, monotonous drum beats, beating with the hands and sticks), are classified as music, it will be impossible to draw a boundary line between music and its primitive stage.

audible emotive outbursts, intuitional expressive utterances (interjections, exclamations) with music. This would be as erroneous as to consider purely emotional sounds the first stage of speech, which so often happens in research work on the origins of language. The emotional speech-sounds, musical as they may be, never come into question as the preliminary stage of music (or of speech), for the simple reason that the further development of this " sound system " could never have led to music (or to speech). These utterances are acquired phonetic configurations that have remained fairly unchanged in their earlier form, are incapable of development, and belong to the general and involuntary reactions of humanity, irrespective of its stage of civilization. For further information on this subject, I would refer the interested reader to my work: " Origin and Prehistory of Language " (Francke, Berne, 1946; French edition Payot, Paris, 1950).

In the exploration or reconstruction of the original forms of music one proceeds in general from the *songs of barbarous tribes*. In so doing it is presupposed that the autochthonous races that have remained practically at the same stage of civilization for thousands of years will be most likely to have preserved the original form of musical activity. But what do we find with these songs? We already encounter those characteristics set forth in our definition. This is shown clearly with the Veddas, a pygmoid people of primeval hunters in the interior of Ceylon who are at the very lowest level of civilization (139).

The *Vedda songs* employ small but nevertheless fixed intervals. According to phonographic records, these consist of whole and semitones, also of three-quarter and quarter tones, which are found in divers combinations. Older and younger singers sing the songs at different pitches; consequently the motives are transposed according to the compass of the voice, without altering the intervals. The rhythm is very simple. It is very similar to drum rhythm. The entire compass of the songs does not exceed a minor third. The motives consist of two or three notes which recur continually with slight variation. The time is very strict. The division into beats is distinctly perceptible (3/4, 5/4), though the frequent change in time-outline makes it very difficult to determine the beat. It is significant that the Vedda songs, which according to Stumpf represent a prototype of primitive music, already manifest a certain structure. For instance, definite regularly recurring melodic turns are found. In fact, even characteristic terminal cadential effects. It is further noteworthy that, in spite of the relatively developed form of their music, the Veddas have no musical instruments, not even percussion instruments.

(SELIGMANN)

Ex. 27.—A Vedda Melody.

(CH. S. MYERS)

Ex. 28.—A Vedda Melody of the Sitala-Wannya Tribe.

If we analyse the songs of tribes that are on a slightly higher niveau but still in the primitive stage, such as the *aboriginals of the Andaman Islands*, we find that differentiated musical patterns and forms are perfectly compatible with an otherwise primitive stage of civilization. The songs of these peoples, like those of the Veddas, do not exceed three notes. Then follows a chorus, and

(M. V. PORTMAN)

Ex. 29.—Chorus of the Andaman Islanders.

the chorus introduces parallel octaves and fifths. The solo is sung in more or less free tempo. The choruses, on the other hand, are in strict time. In an instrumental respect the Andaman Islanders are not much farther advanced than the Veddas. However, they do have drums, which they employ very zealously to mark the rhythm in singing and dancing.

The Kubu tribe in Sumatra, which is also at a very primitive stage of civilization, has a fairly complex musical system. It even has a sort of scale.

(E. M. v. HORNBOSTEL)

Ex. 30.—A Kubu Melody.

The melodies of the indigenous tribes of Central Australia show a similar movement. Fourths and fifths lend them a firmer framework. The melody is contained within the span of an octave, and employs the notes of our diatonic scale, with the exception of the leading note b♭ * (74). These examples show

(E. H. DAVIES)

Ex. 31.—Song of the Aboriginals of Central Australia.

distinctly that even the most primitive music completely satisfies the aforesaid criteria for music.

It is therefore not to be assumed that the songs of primitive races represent the archetype of music. First of all, these songs

---

* According to J. Kunst (71, 72) primitive tribes that do not have musical instruments to accompany songs or to play melodies are unacquainted with "perfect" fixed intervals. The principal consideration with them is the tonal movement, exactly like the spontaneous songs of little children, which are formed without scales. On the other hand, Kunst remarks that the so-called essential notes always represent fixed tonal distances within which intermediate notes are intercalated. Even if pure vocal music formed of fixed intervals does not produce scales, this does not preclude the existence of fixed intervals, in my opinion. It is quite immaterial whether these intervals are pure or not, from the acoustical point of view. The fact that in the vocal music of autochthonous races (uninfluenced by musical instruments) certain fixed tonal ratios come out more and more clearly in the process of development speaks, at all events, for the eminent importance of intervals in music.

are often very complicated. This is evidenced by the melodies of the natives of Australia and New Mecklenburg, the Patagonians, the Zuni Indians, the Papuans, and others. Furthermore, we should also not overlook the fact that these tribes are sometimes descendants of older races that once stood on a much more developed plane and from whom they received the higher musical forms.

B. THE GENESIS OF MUSIC

The investigative spirit of man is not merely content to form an idea of the elementary musical patterns. He tries to penetrate still deeper, down to the *first cause* from which music took birth, as it were. Henceforth it is a question of the concept of origin in its secondary and actual significance. This brings us to those vital utterances that were instrumental in the *genesis* of music, that gave rise to the first musical expressive forms.

We will examine critically the theories that have recently been advanced regarding the origin of music, expose their inadequacies, and try to formulate a hypothesis of our own which seems to be the most plausible one.

(1) First of all we must mention an assumption that derives from the *Darwinian* circle of ideas. By this we mean that general biological law that sees in music essentially nothing more than mere *utterances of common natural instincts*, the sexual in particular. As in the animal kingdom, the " song " is mainly associated with the sexual instinct, a sign of sexual excitement during the breeding season, so also with man, song (and therefore music) is supposed to have been originally in the service of sexual love.

But the very basis of departure of this theory is incorrect. It is controverted by the fact that birds " sing " outside the mating season, make sounds before and after the breeding period, as well as on other occasions; for instance, under the influence of the play instinct. Presuming, however, that the song had its origin in that primitive natural instinct, one fails to understand why melodies of fixed and transposable intervals were necessary to it and why the songs of barbarous tribes are not preponderantly love-songs.

(2) In this connexion we would like to mention another biological hypothesis: the *theory of imitation*. Among zoologists the idea is fairly prevalent that the *animal song* is the primitive

form of music. Men are said to have imitated the songs of birds for some indefinable reason, and thus music came into being. This opinion is supported by the fact that the " bird-songs " can be reproduced in our system of musical notation. Such an essentially unjustified notation can easily give rise to the impression that our song-birds transpose their songs and use intervals, as we do, in various combinations.

But birds do not repeat their own calls (or the motives taught them by trainers) in another key, even as much as a whole tone higher or lower. It appears that the birds' pleasure in "singing" rests solely on a sequence of absolute pitches and not, as with man, on tonal relations. It has not been observed that a starling or a canary that has been taught a definite melodic motive ever repeats this motive in another key, though their vocal resources would permit them to do so (149). These observations, which have been verified by many animal breeders, are decisive for the problem of bird-songs. But the same does not seem to apply when it is a question of "standard" natural sounds uttered reflexly. The observations of a cock (made by D. Katz and myself) have shown that in the course of two to four hours the pitches of different crows remained nearly constant, while the pitches from test day to test day might vary as much as a whole tone (from f^1 to g^1). The same cock crowed practically the same "melody" at different times, i.e. the intervals, rhythm, and duration of the crow were essentially the same (the mean variation at an average duration of 2 seconds amounted to 0.04 second), but there is no absolutely constant adjustment of the acoustic motorial centres in the crowing act. Nevertheless, it would be unjustifiable to speak here of relative pitch, since it is not the question of a melody acquired from external sources, but a natural cry for which the acoustic-motorial adjustment is innate. On the other hand, however, there is a tendency to produce tones with the same relative intervals.

For our problem the essential point is that among the songs of primitive tribes we find none that is imitative of bird-calls, quite apart from the fact that it is almost impossible to imitate even approximately the warbling of the nightingale, the calls of the common thrush, the blackbird, and the robin. We need only visualize the warbling of the nightingale and the bastard nightingale with their roulades, trills, turns, and ascending whistling calls in order to see the untenability of the Imitation Theory. A few examples will show how bird-songs differ from primitive melodies.

Nightingale.

Blue throat.
Hedge-
sparrow.

Thrush.

(A. VOIGT)

Ex. 32.—Bird-songs.*

After all, it is ridiculous, and points to a complete misconception of the nature of music when serious investigators get the notion of according bird-songs real possibilities of musical expression; such, for instance, as motives and stanza forms, a certain melodic pattern, melodic line, definite time outlines with varying tempo, staccato, legato, glissando (Hempelmann). It is astonishing to see with what lack of critical judgment the claim is made that the common thrush prefers motives that coincide with the intervals of the major triad or that gibbons sing chromatic scales, the highest note of which corresponds exactly to the octave of the lowest note (Darwin). When such altogether incorrect assertions appear in scientific works, it is no wonder that there are theorists unoriented in animal psychology who consider the imitation of bird-songs the most natural solution of the problem of the origin of music and closely associate the main root of the musical-artistic activity with " pleasure in bird-song " and the imitation of the " vocal virtuosos of the feathered world ". It has entirely escaped the attention of these investigators that the bird-song fulfils another function, has another structure, and is subject to other evolutionary laws than human song. They have over-

* See also A. Saunders, " A Guide to Bird-songs "; Charles A. Mitchell, " The Evolution of Bird-song ", W. Garstang, " Songs of the Birds ", and A. R. Brand, " Songs of Wild Birds ".

looked the fact that the vocal utterances of animals, even when they perform communicative functions (mating calls, alarm cries), are nothing more than direct and automatic reactions of biological states of the animal. They failed to grasp that the bird-song, in contrast to music, is not the product of a long development, of a gradual differentiation; but quite the opposite—an inherited, invariable, fixed means of expression, incapable of development. Bird-song, like animal cries on the whole, has no history, likewise no evolution during the individual life of the creature. The song-bird brings its vocal art, its entire repertoire, essentially ready-made, along with it.

The same can be said of the so-called animal song that I said elsewhere of so-called animal speech. Music as such only begins when the living creature is no longer domineered exclusively by instincts and passions, but is guided by fixed intentions and conscious aims, as well as by insight concerning the best ways and means to realize them. It is this directed intention, which must be considered the prerequisite to all human culture and civilization, that separates music from the sounds and calls of the animal world.*

(3) The *theory of rhythm* tries to trace music to rhythmical movements. In this one is fond of stressing the close relationship between dance and song. Dance and rhythmical movement indubitably influence the rhythm of song. They can even lead to the development of new musical rhythmical patterns. But this does not answer the question how music really arose from dance movements. Fundamentally the theory of rhythm cannot be excluded, since as a rule dance is ordinarily accompanied by singing. On the other hand, we must remember that dance is not necessarily bound up with song. With aboriginal tribes it is also accompanied by hand-clapping and drum-beats. Furthermore, the dance-songs of indigenous tribes are by no means in the majority, as the theory of rhythm would lead one to suppose. I was struck by the fact that there was not one single dance-song in the index of the phonographic records of the music of the Kubus (Sumatra), but many songs which had to do with the healing of the sick (ceremonial songs of the medicine-men to

---

* See G. Révész: " The Human Forms of Communication and the so-called Animal Speech ", *Proceedings of the Royal Academy of Science*, Vol. 43–44, Amsterdam, 1941.

dispel evil spirits, exert magic, and cure by hypnotic influence). Finally—and this I wish to stress very particularly—the melodic rhythms, even with very primitive peoples, are often so extremely *complicated* that they never could have proceeded from the dance.

Karl Bücher, especially, in his " Work and Rhythm " espoused the theory of rhythm. He proceeded from the assumption that rhythmical working movements led necessarily, as it were, to working songs. There is no doubt that rhythmical work—above all, when it is carried out *collectively* (e.g. conveying building material, lifting cargo, rowing, work on shipboard, field work, etc.) can be a source of artistic speech-forms and music. The working songs of all peoples and the traditional song-texts from antiquity furnish evidence of this. But all of this is not sufficient to deduce music and poetry from rhythmical labour, to say nothing of making the latter the first source of music. There is already such a great gulf dividing rhythmical movement and rhythmical speech one from the other that it will scarcely do to imagine the one as the direct outcome of the other. That is even less possible with music. In principle this cannot originate in activities that *do not have the character of sound*. Dependence of the song on rhythmical movement is not indicative of inter-relationship. The theory of rhythm only stresses the *contributory motives or occasions* that can lead to singing and music-making; but it fails entirely in handling the problem of origin. It does not explain the specific element of music. It does not make us see how man came to combine movement with words and notes, to choose a number of fixed intervals in the continuous tone-series, and to link the intervals together in larger combinations—which as a matter of fact is directly contrary to the monotonous rhythm of work.

(4) The *theory of expression* has a profounder and better psychological basis. This theory endeavours to trace music to the *emotional speech utterances* of man. At first glance this theory seems to be convincing. On closer analysis, however, it proves to be untenable (86, 143).

The sounds evoked by emotions and passions are direct reflexive effects of inward tension. These emotional experiences, both from the biological and the psychological points of view, are one with the corresponding expressive movements. They represent two distinct manifestations of the same emotion or instinct. These speech-sounds, as outward and visible signs of the inward emotion, have nothing in common with music or with song. They are not produced in order to evoke musical experiences in us. They do not change and develop. They have no formal structure. They are not the result of inspiration and free invention. They are rather the reflexive, invariable expression of our momentary emotion. The sound utterances and interjections do not leave the sphere of the passional life and natural instincts. They lack any sort of spiritual, let alone æsthetic, significance. Characteristic of their originality and independence of music is the fact that they are found with children before they have learned to talk in exactly the same form as with adults. The speech-sound in itself is not a musical-creative factor. Consequently it cannot come into question as the origin of music.

(5) Analogous to the theory of speech, in which it is believed that babbling represents the ontogenetic parallel of the primitive form of speech, one has also tried in music to link the *lalling melodies of children* with the primitive phase of music. Nothing is simpler than to prove the untenability of this point of view.

The lalling melodies and little songs that young children invent as early as their second year are by no means primitive creations, original reactions of the human being, but sound utterances conditioned by the singing in the environment and partly also by instrumental music. The melodies that children sing to themselves often show intervals that are closely related to our conventional notation, sometimes corresponding to it exactly.

Ex. 33.—A Child's Song Dating from the End of the Second Year.

Even though the intervals are not all quite true, we can still clearly perceive the notes of the diatonic triad. It follows from this that infantile vocalizations can never be considered the archetype or preliminary phase of music and that it is inadmissible to draw conclusions regarding the phylogenesis of music from the ontogenetic development of the musical modes of expression.

(6) The *theory of melodic speech* endeavours to deduce the genesis of music from the accentuation and intonation of human speech. In this hypothesis one points to certain tonal melodic phenomena that arise during excited speech and recitation. It was Herbert

Spencer who advanced the theory (which, by the way, we also find with Rousseau and Herder) that the tonal movement of excited speech is gradually disengaged from words and transferred to song and instruments (143). In this way, it was maintained, absolute music came into being. Especially the rising and falling tonal movement within the words and the sentence is said to be suggestive of music. The interplay between speech and music has given rise to the opinion that the tonal movement, the accentuation, and the dynamics of speech are, as it were, disengaged from the words and transferred to the song.

It was natural to associate melodic (inflected) speech—above all, so-called recitative—with the problem of origin. Recitative is found among all races, independent of their cultural niveau. It plays an important role in the social life of all peoples. Charms and incantations, religious rites, rituals, mysteries, ceremonial acts of all kinds usually employ free recitation. The solemnity and the traditional character of a ceremony are enhanced and its suggestive or magic effect increased by the melodic form of recitation. But it is very questionable whether we can attribute any formative influence in the genesis of music to recitative. In this case we must presume that recitative began and underwent development *everywhere* in advance of the most primitive form of music. This is an assumption that lacks all historical evidence and any psychological foundation in fact. Speech cannot be taken as the preliminary stage of music, for the simple reason that inflected speech employs no constant fixed intervals, but, on the contrary, a fluctuating intonation dependent on the existent emotional state, the structure, and content-material of the composition. Even though recitative be traditional in pattern, only the general tendency of the tonal movement is thereby fixed. And within this we find numerous variations. Speech permits of no fixed intervals whatsoever. Otherwise it would sacrifice its multifarious expressive possibilities. It is pointed out quite justly that habitual sing-song speech is unpleasant because it approximates fixed musical intervals, and therefore loses the character of speech.

Interesting as may be the attempts of different sides to incorporate music in the reigning theory of evolution and establish hypothetically its rudimentary stage, no one has yet succeeded in finding even a fairly satisfactory explanation for the prehistory of music. I should now like to offer a *new theory* regarding the origin of music. This I will designate the " Calling Signal Theory ", which is closely allied to my *Contact Theory*—an hypothesis that has proved fruitful in the far more complicated problems of the origins of language.

In my search for a general principle governing the forms of communication of animals and human beings and exercising its impelling influence during the entire development of forms of contact, I have reached the conclusion that the *need for mutual understanding* is to be taken as such a principle.

I have now raised the question whether it is not possible to apply the principle of the origin of language to the origin of music also, and thus bring music and language back to one common primitive form. My reflections have led me to the conclusion that music, in its origin, is very closely connected with one of the human contact forms that may represent one of the decisive points of departure of music. This contact form that is closely allied to recitative and is frequently bound up with it, without coinciding with it, is the *wordless shout or calling signal.*

If a person desires to communicate a message from a distance, he tries first of all to draw attention to himself by a shout or calling signal, then to announce his message in a loud voice with specific sound signals or with the aid of emphatic gestures. We find such calling signals, such invocative contact signals, with all peoples, and it is to be assumed that such audible signals, automatically deriving from the natural situation, existed throughout the entire history of the human race.*

It is in the nature of calling signals to have a certain loudness and volume. This loudness and volume can only be achieved with the *singing voice,* and never with the *speaking voice.* Only the singing voice has carrying power. It alone penetrates to the person located at a distance. Primitive man surely gave forth divers calling signals fitted to his peculiar purposes. One signal served to indicate his presence, another was an alarm signal, a third a call for help. When distance made vocal communication possible, one first gave the general contact signal

---

* Different theorists have pointed to the acoustic signal as one of the roots of music, without attempting to validate this assumption psychologically. Some ethnologists have rejected the theory that music derived from speech while many others laid the greatest weight on speech-sounds and considered recitative the primitive form of song.

(the call, as we now find it in mountainous districts), after which the words of the communication were shouted like a call. The following example illustrates such a procedure. The calling signal and the ensuing recitative derive from the very primitive tribe of Kubus.

(E. M. v. HORNBOSTEL)

Ex. 34.—A Kubu Call in the Forest.

In this case, as in others, we find that the calling signal has a distinct *musical structure*. This rests on the fact first of all that every calling signal consists of at least two different notes bearing usually a determinate relation to each other, and secondly, on the sliding tonal movement at the end and also often at the beginning of the signal, which undoubtedly contributes to its musical character. The latter phenomenon is a natural result of voice production. For example, if we desire to produce a loud, carrying tone, we ascend the ladder of pitch. In so doing, the tone waxes louder and louder, and at the end drops back again, to die away gradually. The fact that this sliding movement (portamento) is very frequently found in the songs of primitive races, though it has already lost its original signalling function, indicates a relationship between calling signals and songs. This would seem to be a survival from an earlier stage. Today we still find the sliding movement in yodelling and jubilant shouts; only now it has a downward movement under the influence of modern music. In the music of civilized nations we also often find a portamento extending over a major third.

(POMMER)

Ex. 35.—The Descending Movement in a Yodel.

But the similarity that exists between the musical structure of the calling signal and song, and the traces that we still find in the little melodic phrases of mountaineers' calls (Alpine herdsmen)

and the working songs were not the sole reasons for my conclusion that calling signals played a decisive role in the genesis of
music. I attribute the greatest importance to the corresponding
psychical factors, which are of fundamental significance for both
vocal utterances.

The shouting of loud, carrying signals undoubtedly generates
pleasurable sensations. This pleasurable sensation increases with
the loudness and duration of the call. Everyone knows this from
personal experience. How often it happens that we let out a
" wild whoop " when we are up in the mountains with no other
object in mind than merely to hear the sound of our own voice
and to send it ringing into the wide open spaces. In so doing one
feels as though he were giving vent to inner forces. The sound
seems to remove certain physical-spiritual inhibitions (yodelling
in the Swiss and Tyrolean Alps).

I do not doubt that the same vital pleasurable sensations that
we experience in shouting were also connected with song right
from the outset. One delights in playing with his own voice.
This need seems to have a biological basis. Little children carry
on lalling monologues for hours on end for no particular purpose.
In happy mood, we sing little tunes of our own and those of others
at our daily tasks without always being aware of it. The vital
feeling of pleasure makes us sing, and the singing in turn increases
the feeling of pleasure. The activity involved in singing, the tone
production and modulation as regards loudness and pitch, tempo
and rhythm heighten our feeling of pleasure and contribute to the
rhythm of life.

These are the common factors of the calling signal and song
which link the two together. They lie in the vital, emotive
sphere, and their purpose is to awaken feelings of activity and
pleasure. On account of this psycho-biological relationship,
the calling signal *passes over into song without any intermediate stadium*.
But since the calling signal receives the character and Gestalt of a
musical motive through the traditional, fixed sequence of notes, it
can be easily viewed as the *preliminary stage of song*. The calling
signals comprise the most important characteristics of music
(interval, transposability, elements of larger tone complexes)
without the signals in themselves being musical. We can thus
bridge the gulf that exists between a stadium when music was
non-existent and the first phase of music's evolution.

The great merit of this interpretation lies in the fact that the connexion between calling signal and music is comprehensible without the introduction of new theories. In such way an altogether natural genetic contact is established between two essentially disparate forms of expression, so that it is possible to trace the genesis of music directly from the calling signal. Since the calling signal was originally an activity appertaining to the speech function, and represents a means of conveying a message from man to man, song (and with it music) owes its genesis in the last analysis to *speech*. According to this, music does not derive from the interval-less *inflected speech* (Sprachmelodie) or recitative (Sprachgesang), which, like inarticulate lalling, could also play a certain part in the genesis and first stages of development. But it derives from the *speech function*, or, to put it more correctly, from the primitive form of the actual speech function. Because of its emotional accent and its musical character, we attribute this an elementary-æsthetic significance, and in this way bring it into even closer relationship with music. This affinity explains the natural connexion between music and speech that finds expression in the songs, ballads, melodramas, and ritual ceremonies of all races of men. In the wordless calling signals we have therefore recognized the common source of *music and speech* from which the two derived their initial material and even their first forms.

In closing, one can still ask whether musical instruments played a salient role in the genesis of music. This question must be answered in the negative, since there are primitive tribes that have developed their vocal music without musical instruments. We have already mentioned the Veddas in Ceylon, who have vocal music but no musical instruments. Even though their songs may be on an extremely low level, the latter nevertheless show that a purely vocal music is possible even without the participation of musical instruments. Barbarous tribes that have only a few musical instruments, and very primitive ones at that (for instance, the Patagonians and various South Sea tribes), already have a relatively developed art of song.

Our discussions have produced evidence that in the early phase of music it was principally speech, as well as the technical brain of man, that played an influential role. I attach the greatest importance to *speech*. Through this the above theory of the first phase of music gains no little significance for the cultural history of mankind. Here it is also found (as I have brought out in various articles on all the fundamental human activities) that everything that the mind and the soul and the spirit of man brings forth in the conscious and the unconscious can be traced to, or brought into close relationship with, speech, which—after thought—is the highest and most comprehensive function of the human mind. As regards the evolution of music, the hypothesis is important, in that it shows how music developed in absolutely unbroken continuity from a preparatory stadium in which the calling signal was the moving factor. In this way we have succeeded in establishing the link between two essentially different stages of development; namely, between an epoch of the human race in which music was still non-existent and an epoch in which music had just begun.

XVIII

ÆSTHETICS AND THE PSYCHOLOGY OF MUSIC

In accordance with the intention expressed at the beginning of this work, I have limited myself to the treatment of those problems of the psychology of sound and music that are of importance from the general standpoint of music and musical pedagogy. The attentive reader will have remarked that it was not my object to recapitulate and condense the findings of the great mass of literature in these fields of psychology, but to expose the problems clearly, and weave my own investigations into the woof of these two psychological domains. In my discussion of the different theories I have endeavoured to test them in the light of their results and to ascertain whether they prove inconsistent with experience and whether, furthermore, it was possible to bridge the discrepancies between theory and such experience. I have also emphasized in each instance the limits of our empirical knowledge and have indicated the point where experience ceases and theoretical construction begins. As psychologist I have held strictly to the methodical principles of our science, and have based my contentions throughout on experience, in so far as it went. As a result of these restrictions, the æsthetic aspect dropped into the background. That by no means indicates a depreciation of the value of musical æsthetics, especially since I consider the æsthetic and axiological approach one of the most interesting divisions of musicology. But such problems are outside the bounds of psychology, and it is still questionable whether they can contribute anything to the furtherance of the psychology of music.

The *importance of psychology for musical æsthetics* is quite a different matter. Here one has in mind principally the æsthetic experience. No metaphysics, however deep, no theory of æsthetics, however firm its philosophical foundation, can discuss the musical experience and ignore psychological points of view. If psychology is neglected in this instance, the result will be fatal to the science of æsthetics. This is the trouble with all the different æsthetic theories and systems, from the time of the Greeks down to today.

Every æsthetic theory that makes any claim to universal validity and scientific background must proceed from *experiential psychology* (Erlebnispsychologie). Whether we apply the term "psychological æsthetics" to such a fundamental discipline or whether we view it merely as a special province of psychology is quite immaterial to the point at issue.*

For us the æsthetic manifests itself in the beauty of the work, which becomes an æsthetic object through the creative power of the artist and the æsthetic experience of the responsive listener. One of the two factors, the *experience* of the æsthetically sensitive person, or the art-work, the embodiment of the artistic intuition, or the æsthetic idea, must form the basis of departure of æsthetics. Accordingly, two ways are open to an æsthetic approach to the forms and creations of art (and also of music), one of them being that of *psychology*, the other that of *phenomenology*. If we take a purely psychological approach, then we will be conscious of everything that goes on within us in our response to, and enjoyment of, musical works, of the *direct experience* in musical perception. In the phenomenological approach attention is directed primarily upon the *work*, the structure, the compositional pattern, the architecture, the inner forces manifesting themselves in the art work. Through both avenues we can try to penetrate into the æsthetic sphere.

The subjective-psychological attitude, which underlies psychological æsthetics, enables us to examine what takes place in the conscious during the æsthetic experience and how this can be brought into relation with the æsthetic enjoyment. Hereby the most important task is to investigate the inner perception systematically, to describe it exhaustively, and create a general psychological foundation for æsthetics on the basis of the resultant experiences. In this attitude of observation we turn our attention *inward*. We experience moods, emotions, and also imagery and thoughts that arise in us while we contemplate and enjoy the art work. Here we have to do with purely subjective phenomena, experiences, the substance of which (in spite of individual diversities) is practically the same with all of us because they are determined by the same elementary æsthetic factors, such as the

---

* See Nahm, "Æsthetic Experience and its Presuppositions"; Seashore, "In Search of Beauty in Music"; Brelet, "Esthétique et création musicale", and works by well-known British and American æstheticians.

melodic and harmonic pattern, structure, articulation, or arrangement of the parts, eurythmics, proportion, and lucidity. In this connexion it is also the function of psychology to subject the productive process to an analysis, so as to form an idea of the general and typical course of creative activity.

The psychological standpoint in æsthetics leads to the important question whether the aim of music is to depict and evoke *actual emotions*, or whether it is a matter of *autonomous musical content or ideas* that only find their sensorily perceptible expression in and through the soniferous material.

The writings of the *Greek hedonists* were the first to give clear and consistent expression to the first concept; i.e. the assumption of the primacy of the appeal of the senses. These philosophers viewed art as an affair of man's sensitive faculties. The elder Aristippus (*b.* 435 B.C.), founder of the Cyrenaic or hedonist school, viewed sensuous pleasure, carnal delights, as *the* goal of life. According to this general principle, art can signify nothing more than a means of evoking pleasurable sensations. Everything that furthers and enhances the momentary feelings of pleasure has positive value.

The hedonists did not hold to this strongly sensual concept. In the course of development they altered their original views, and asserted that the true, the highest pleasure did not consist in succumbing completely to the pleasure of the moment, of abandoning oneself to it wholly and entirely, but in transcending and dominating it.

In their exposition they referred to Plato (427–372 B.C.), who consigned art to the realm of the senses, or, as he expressed it, to the animal part of the soul; but not to the sublime spheres of the spirit. Naturally we should not take the word " animal " in its literal original sense. Plato's idea was to contrast the psychical-material with the spiritual-intellectual, and in so doing he considered only the perceptive subject, the sensually responsive person. He left the creative artist out of consideration, recognizing that artistic activity has no relation whatever to sensual pleasure. He knew full well, as we do, that artistic creations, like philosophical ideas, represent intellectual acts, even though the first may flow from another fountain-head of the spirit than philosophical thought.

In order to be able to interpret correctly Plato's sayings and intimations, one must (in my opinion) realize that in Plato's time music was considered to be the all-embracing art. It was the art that was above all other arts. In classic Greece music was not just one art among many; nor did it represent merely an object of æsthetic pleasure and evaluation. The Greeks viewed the world of music as the ultimate and greatest revelation of *Being*, the emanation of all creative cosmic force. Whoever knows its eternal melody holds a mystic sway over Nature and mankind like Orpheus of old.

With Plato, and to a still greater degree with Aristotle (384–322 B.C.), and later on with the most influential of the neo-Platonists, Plotinus (A.D. 205–269), art—and with it music—was far more intimately connected with the æsthetic-beautiful than with sensual pleasure. Aristotle took the unequivocal stand that melody was something *new* that is lacking in the emotive states and moods that are co-responsible for the genesis of melody. Aristotle considered music to be more intellectual in character. This idealistic tendency is especially clear in his thesis against simple naturalism in which he asserts that the function of art is not merely the imitation of Nature, but the consummation of what Nature has left unfinished.

In agreement with Plato and Aristotle, Plotinus denied the independence of the two worlds, the sensual and the intellectual, one from the other, and accorded the intellectual world, the creative force, a higher and more essential value than the sensual world. Plotinus was imbued with the thought that in the world of the senses, as in the world of the mind, Beauty has a share in the ideas. Only the idea, he taught, can give form to material. Idea solely and alone is capable of moulding the original diversity into a significant unity. Plotinus was the first to point to the great importance of fantasy for the creative act and to view it as a specific property lying between sensuousness and the intellect.

It is very significant that Plotinus's conception had no effect on æsthetics up to the 19th century. Although Giambattista Vico (1668–1744) emphasized the autonomy of the æsthetic world with respect to the intellectual, and Kant (1724–1804), in his distinction between the æsthetic and the intellectual, freed the theory of Beauty from the shackles of logic, the æsthetes, up to the middle of the 19th century, did not try to give a psychological basis to art, including music. Quite to the contrary. One turned from reality, and beauty gradually became a mere abstraction derived from the so-called divine Beauty. Beauty was believed to be the more complete, consummate, the more its properties and characteristics coincide with those of the Divine Being. The greatest Beauty (they said), the so-called pure or ideal Beauty, lies in God. And every thing of beauty, like all else, must derive from Him. Æsthetics no longer bothered itself about Beauty in the sense of art; no longer concerned itself with the æsthetic experience. But it drew attention exclusively to concepts, definitions, that had nothing to do either with the concrete works of art or the creative tendencies that dominated art. Kant (who in his intellectual-theoretical causation of æsthetics also contributed greatly to its emancipation) in his work " The Critique of Æsthetic Judgment " never propounded concrete æsthetic and psychological problems, let alone solved them. In his treatment of music he revealed himself as a hedonist of the purest dye. According to him, music has no other *raison d'être* than to release such physical reactions as are necessary for health. This attitude of the hygienic effect of music led Kant to the bizarre idea of associating music and laughter by pointing out that both owed their origin to moods and emotive states.

> " Not any estimate of harmony in tones or flashes of wit (he wrote), which with its beauty serves only as vehicle, but rather the stimulated vital functions of the body, the emotion that stirs the intestines and the diaphragm—in a word, the feeling of health, are what constitute the pleasure we experience by being able to reach the body through the soul and use the latter as the physician of the former " (63).

The deeper one penetrated into the inner nature of music, the clearer was the untenability of the biological and one-sided emotional theories. Schopenhauer (1788–1860), and to an even greater extent, Eduard Hanslick (1825–1904), the well-known Vienna music critic and friend of Brahms, openly declared war against the emotional theories and characterized music as a specific type of expressive form. Hanslick and other æstheticians after him ardently defended the thesis that the emotional side of music is *non-æsthetic* and that every inroad into the sphere of the emotions is contrary to Beauty, annulling it, as it were. If (they argued) the main goal of music is a direct emotional effect, then this removes it from the realm of æsthetics and brings it into the sphere of everyday emotional experiences. In this case music has only a very limited content. It must restrict itself to evoking certain moods, emotions, passions. In this way it has no autonomy, no sphere of action of its own, and like so many other sensory stimuli can only be considered a means of arousing emotive states. The unmusical person need not regret that he is debarred from the æsthetic enjoyment of music. For he will be able to evoke the same, or related, emotional reactions through other stimuli or combinations of stimuli.

I also take this point of view without thereby denying the significance for the æsthetic experience of sensations and moods evoked by music. The resonance of the emotional sphere is not irrelevant for experience in its entirety. But the fact that feeling has a share in the creative work and the enjoyment of it does not mean that it plays such a decisive role in the creative process and in the act of æsthetic experience as one imagines. If feeling were so important, then we should be able to prove its existence and its effective determining force during the creation and enjoyment of every musical work. In this event all composers would draw and develop their musical ideas from a distinct emotion. Without excluding the possibility that certain themes owe their existence to a certain mood, to certain inward emotions, one must hold firmly to the fact that these emotions can indeed set the creative process into operation and occasionally influence the general character of the work; but they are not able to determine its *substance* and its *form*. Emotions are something essentially different from musical configurations. The latter are not emotional experiences, but musical functioning wholes (in the Gestalt sense), and their forms are autonomous forms of musical expression.

Concentration during composition, the intensive creative and technical work, the collecting and working out of the motives, are also incompatible with the assumption of the primacy of the emotions during creation. It is easier to attribute to emotion a special importance for the perceptive and æsthetically sensitive listener. But, even so, we run into difficulties. However, there are musical works that react principally on the emotional world of the listener because in them the elementary-sensuous (the sensual-carnal) in music can exert its influence almost unimpeded (dance music, marches, closing fortissimi movements). This sensuous factor cannot be eliminated from music, since, owing to their psycho-physiological nature, the tones have an especially strong effect on the body and highly excite the sensory resonance surface of the soul. The physical vibrations that are discharged by the air vibrations and the changing rhythms and dynamic modulations that have an influence on the vasomotor system excite automatically the psychic-emotive sphere.

The feelings thereby evoked are not, however, " musical " feelings; that is, not such as are aroused necessarily and exclusively by music. Even with deaf-mutes we have noted such elementary emotions of pleasure and repugnance, discharged by vibrations. The same is probably true of the dances of primitive tribes accompanied by drum-beats.

Even if we do not underrate the actual feelings during the musical experience, they can still be attributed very slight importance from the musical-æsthetic point of view. If music moves us deeply, if it has a " profound " effect, then we must trace this primarily to the emotions evoked by the tones. Only here we must always keep clearly in mind that in these cases the effect is not due to the *art-work* as such, that it is rather a question of the sensuous-psychological and the physiological effects of the tones. Although the emotions thus evoked lend a special charm to music, they are irrelevant for the purely æsthetic experience; in fact, they are even a hindrance. The elementary, the sensuous-emotional, prevents as it were the grasping of the *beautiful-in-music*, the *intellectual enjoyment of music*. We can even go a step further and assert that it is a prerequisite to the æsthetic response to a musical art work that we free ourselves of such sensuous feelings and let the work exert its influence unimpeded, in the full beauty of its æsthetic form. The æsthetically sensitive listener must adjust himself to the ideational content of the musical work. He must repress the psychic excitations and associative concatenations connected with music and not allow them to extend beyond the artistic experience.

Numerous works of absolute music (which does not reveal the slightest trace of a background of mood or emotion) are a further argument against the emotional theory. That is perhaps the reason why so many consider this type of art too formal, monotonous, without charm; while romantic, and above all sentimental, music is extolled to the skies. It never occurs to anyone that with such an emotional attitude neither the one nor the other type of music is grasped in its *æsthetic substance*, in its *perfection of form*.

The æsthetic approach demands another attitude, and this takes a *phenomenological* form (43). Here the decisive thing is the work; that is, the structure, the architecture, the multiplicity and the unity of form; in other words, the art-work as such. This approach is no longer a direct one. Besides æsthetic intuition and respect for art, it also demands an ability to analyse, a large and varied range of knowledge, a sure feeling for style, and the need to grasp and judge musical creations with respect to their æsthetic qualities. The real purpose of the phenomenological approach is much easier to elucidate in the representational arts than in music. Therefore I shall take an illustration from this field.

In a circular building we see a room of homogeneous, quiet character that seems to have a pull towards the central axis. If we now consider a circular building (such as, perhaps, the Hagia Sophia in Istanbul) as the synthesis of two opposing principles— namely, as the synthesis of the major horizontal axis (longitudinal tendency) and the vertical axis (axial tendency)—and note that below in the actual auditorium there is a one-directional tendency together with opposing axes and contrasting forms (i.e. a gradual mounting from the lower arches of the smaller apses to the larger and somewhat higher apses that extend to the great all-embracing and all-dominating dome), then in perceiving it under this attitude we have held to the form of the *object*, we have *perceived it phenomenologically*. In this analysis we have not turned our thoughts inward, we have not described the emotions and moods that we felt while contemplating the cathedral. But we have turned our gaze *outward*. Our entire attention was centred on the *object*. We tried to grasp the interior of the cathedral unfolding before us in all its reality, in its visible-æsthetic, phenomenological-æsthetic character (15, 39, 44, 73, 165).

As in representational art, so, too, in music, we can take the *outer approach* by letting the musical work affect us in its multi-farious radiations. To grasp the work in its artistic structure, in its proportions, and in its interplay of forces, is the goal of the phenomenological approach in art. The intention of the creative artist is in unison with this phenomenological approach of the æsthetically sensitive person. In the composition of the St. Matthew Passion it was not Bach's idea to transport us to a sphere of supermundane emotions. His object was rather to create a monumental work for a divine purpose. With him as with other great and sincere artists it was solely a matter of realizing *artistic ideas* which must be grasped and evaluated as such. The *æsthetic idea* for which we—leaning on the authority of Kant—demand general validity is realized in the objective creation. The emotional and atmospheric content of an art-work can lay no claim to general validity. One cannot require that everybody experience the same moods, feelings of relaxation and satisfaction on hearing a musical work or contemplating a piece of sculpture. The demand for general validity can have no reference to pleasurable effects or the reverse, but it can have reference to the *æsthetic experience* that we receive through the phenomenological and analytical-structural approach. And the same æsthetic experience is also the basis of judicial æsthetic appraisal. Psychic phenomena such as feelings, passions, lie outside the world of values. Even specific feelings and moods that owe their origin to art and that are usually characterized as elementary æsthetic feelings have to do with psychology, and not with æsthetics. It follows from this that so-called psychological æsthetics is not a trend in æsthetics, as it is often erroneously assumed to be, but a field of empirical psychology.

According to this, the nature of art (and music also) is inseparably associated with the *value* of the art-work that is apprehended by the soul, formed and fully evaluated by the mind. The artist does not create the work for the emotional experience, for the spiritual reaction; but to unfold himself and give expression to his spiritual aims. The productive artist forms and fashions the musical ideas that come to him intuitively, while the æsthetically sensitive spectator absorbs the idea so formed and fashioned, and in this way is brought nearer to the art-work. The tonal combinations that represent the sensory material must be formed anew, as it were, by the musical person, and raised to the sphere of the beautiful-in-music. The musical person experiences this subjective formative activity to an especially high degree in the re-creation of the art-works of others. He brings the written notes to life as he performs the work with the assistance of his own interpretative power.

Music is a world unto itself, a specific autonomous domain of human activity, an expressive form that is independent of all others. It represents a unique harmony between the sensuous and the intellectual. No other branch of art is able to achieve the synthesis to an equivalent degree.

The source of musical invention seems to lie deeper and more hidden than the sources of invention in the other arts. It flows from a sphere in which the individual and the collective form an indivisible unity. Even the works of the great masters are carriers of certain ideas, impulses, and aspirations that are rooted in the collective. If we contemplate music from this point of view, we are justified in saying that it gives expression not only to the musical ideas of the artist, but also to the *unconscious motive* that is co-responsible for the genesis of those ideas and their fashioning. The rhythm, the tempo of life, as well as the inclinations and aspirations of the soul that have not yet penetrated into the conscious, are revealed in the music. Before the individual is aware of the collective forces operating within him and the aims of the ensuing chronological period, or can give them abstract formulation, there comes out in the art-work (above all, in music, it seems to me)—and often with a surprising vitality and veracity—all those elements that, hidden heretofore from the conscious, are already animate and operative as the impelling force in man, individually and collectively.

Art can be the herald of dawn and likewise the annunciator of darkness and a threatening storm. It is as sensitive as the seismograph, which reacts to infinitesimal vibrations of the earth's surface long before the inner forces give any evidence of their terrifying effects. Thus for Art, and especially for music, the intention is extremely characteristic for the future.

*   *   *   *   *

With these discussions of the relationship between the psychology of music and æsthetics I bring my book to a close.

Despite the great variety of themes discussed, I have striven to maintain unity of form and method as well as of theoretical and personal attitude. It has been my aim to furnish a picture of the trends and results of research in the psychology of music as well as to awaken an active interest in this borderland of psychology and musicology and to rouse the younger generation to further efforts in this field, which represents such a harmonic fusion of art and science. I hope I have succeeded in presenting and expounding this problematic domain with its related questions of physics, psychology, and æsthetics in such a way as to make clear to the reader the great importance for musicology of the psychology of music.

WORKS CITED

1. O. Abraham, " Das absolute Tonbewusstsein." *Sammelbände der internationalen Musikgesellschaft*, III, 1892.
2. G. Adler, " Handbuch der Musikgeschichte." Leipzig, 1930.
3. G. Albersheim, " Zur Psychologie der Ton- und Klangeigenschaften." Strassburg, 1939.
4. A. Bachem, " The Genesis of Absolute Pitch; Various Types of Absolute Pitch." *Journal Acoustical Society of America*, 1937 and 1940.
5. J. Bahle, " Eingebung und Ton im musikalischen Schaffen." Leipzig, 1939.
6. H. Balfour, " The Natural History of the Musical Bow." London, 1899.
7. James M. Barbour, " Equal Temperament: its History." Dissertation, Cornell University, 1932.
8. Béla Bartók, " Das ungarische Volkslied." Berlin, 1925.
9. W. Bergmann, " Raumgefühl und Raumstrukturen in der Musik und in den bildenden Künsten." *Schweizerische Musikpaedogogische Blätter*, 1938.
10. S. Bernfeld, " Zur Psychologie der Unmusikalischen." *Archiv für die gesammte Psychologie*, **34**, 1915.
11. Alban Berg, " Qu'est-ce que l'atonalité." *Schweiz. Musikzeitung*, 1945.
12. A. Binet, " Les idées modernes sur les enfants." 1912.
13. J. Binet, " Atonalité." *Schweiz. Musikzeitung*, 1945.
14. M. C. Bos, " Ueber echte und unechte audition colorée." *Zeitschrift für Psychologie*, **111**, 1929.
15. L. Bourgues and A. Denereaz, " La musique et la vie interieure." 1921.
16. Sir William Bragg, " The World of Sound." London, 1936.
17. Percy C. Buck, " Acoustics for Musicians." London, 1928.
18. M. Bukofzer, " Kann die Blasquintentheorie zur Erklärung exotischer Tonsysteme beitragen? " *Antropos*, **3**, 1937.
19. A. Cherbuliez, " Psychologie des musikalischen Einfalls und der musikalischen Gestaltung," 1932.
20. L. Cherlock, " Some Notes of Perfect Pitch." *The American Mercury*, April 1934.
21. Ed. Claparède, " Stabilité des synopsies à de long intervalles." *Arch. de Psychologie*, **25**, 1936.
22. Jules Combarieu, " Music, its Laws and Evolution." New York, 1938.
23. H. Conradin, " Ist die Musik hereronom oder autonom? " 1940.
24. E. Coussemaker, " Scriptorum de Musica Medii Aevi," nova series. Paris, 1864–76. Reprinted 1908, and Milan, 1931.
25. E. Jacques Dalcroze, " Le Rhythme, la Musique et l'Education." Paris and Lausanne, 1920.
26. A. de Candolle, " Histoire des sciences et des savants depuis deux siècles." 1873.
27. F. C. Donders, " Over het timbre der Vokalen." *Neder. Arch. von Geneeskunde en Naturkunde*, **1**, 1865.
28. Idem, " Over stem en spraak." *Neder. Arch. von Geneeskunde en Naturkunde*, 1865.
29. Alfred Einstein, " Geschichte der Musik." Leiden, 1934.
30. Leonard Ellingwood, " Works of Francesco Landino." The Mediæval Academy of America, Cambridge, Massachusetts, 1939.
31. A. J. Ellis, " On the Musical Scales of Various Nations." *Journal of the Society of Arts*, **33**, 1885.
32. Idem, " Tonometrical Observations on some Existing Non-harmonic Scales." *Proceedings Royal Society*, London, **37**, 1884.

33. A. J. Ellis, " History of Musical Pitch." London, 1885.
34. Leonhard Euler, " Tentamen novae theoriae musicae." Petropoli, 1739.
35. J. R. Ewald, " Eine neue Hörtheorie." *Pflüger's Archiv f.d. gesamten Physiologie*, **76**, 1899.
36. O. Feis, " Studien über die Genealogie und Psychologie der Musiker." Wiesbaden, 1910.
37. E. Feuchtwanger, " Amusie." Berlin, 1910.
38. K. von Fischer, " Zur Tonartencharakteristik." *Schweiz. Musikzeitung*, 1943.
39. P. L. Forel, " Le Rhythme. Etude psychologique." 1930.
40. E. Frank, " Plato und die sog. Pythagoraer." Halle, 1923.
41. S. Gartner, " Beitraege zur Vokallehre." 1921.
42. Fr. Galton, " Hereditary Genius." London, 1869.
43. M. Geiger, " Phaenomenologie des aesthetischen Genusses." *Jahrbuch fuer Philosophie und phaenomen. Forschung.* I, 2, 1913.
44. Idem, " Zugaenge zur Aesthetik." Leipzig, 1928.
45. M. Guernsey, " Eine genetische Studie ueber Nachahmung." *Zeitschrift f. Psychologie*, 107.
46. V. Haecker–Th. Ziehen, " Zur Vererbung und Entwicklung der musikalischen Begabung." 1922.
47. J. Handschin, " Der Toncharakter." Basel, 1948.
48. Ed. Hanslick, " The Beautiful in Music." 7th Edition, 1891.
49. Hartridge and Banister, " Foundations of Experimental Psychology." 1929.
50. Moritz Hauptmann, " Die Natur der Harmonik and Musik." 1853.
51. Hermann von Helmholtz, " Sensations of Tone." London, 1915.
52. Idem, " Ueber der Klangformen der Vokale." *Gelehrte Anzeige d.k. bayer. Akad. d. Wissenschaften*, 1859.
53. R. Hennig, " Die Charakteristik der Tonarten." 1897.
54. L. Hermann, " Phonophotographische Untersuchungen." *Pflüger's Archiv. f.d. gesamten. Physiologie*, **45, 47, 48, 53, 58, 59, 61**.
55. Idem, "Ueber Syntese von Vokalen." *Pfluger's Archiv. f.d. gesamten Physiologie*, **91**.
56. G. Heymans–E. Wiersma, " Beitraege zur speziellen Psychologie auf Grund einer Massenuntersuchung." *Ges. kleinere Schriften*, III.
57. Paul Hindemith, " Unterweisung im Tonsatz." 1937.
58. B. Hoffmann, " Kunst und Vogelsang." Leipzig, 1908.
59. E. von Hornbostel, " Musikalische Tonsysteme." Geiger und Scheele's *Handbuch der Physik*, VIII, 1927.
60. E. Isler, " Vergleichende Charakteristik von c und d moll." *Schweiz. Musikzeitung*, 1943.
61. James Jeans, " Science and Music." New York, 1937.
62. A. T. Jones, " Sound." New York, 1937.
63. I. Kant, " Critique of Æsthetic Judgment " (translated by J. H. Bernard). London, 1914.
64. D. Katz, " Der Aufbau der Tastwelt." 1925.
65. W. Koehler, " Akustische Untersuchungen." *Zeitschrift f. Psychologie*, **72**, 1915.
66. R. Koenig, " Quelques expériences d'acoustique." 1882.
67. Ernst Krenek, " Music Here and Now." New York, 1938.
68. J. von Kries, " Wer ist musikalisch? " Berlin, 1926.
69. F. Krueger, " Die Theorie der Konsonanz." *Wundt's Psychol. Studien*, Vols. I–V.
70. E. ten Kuile, " Schallbildtheorien." *Pflüger's Archiv. f.d. gesamten. Psychologie*, **79**, 1900.
71. J. Kunst, " De toonkunst van Bali." *Weltevreden*, 1925.

72. J. Kunst, " A Study on Papuan Music." *Weltevreden*, 1931.
73. E. Kurth, " Musikpsychologie." Berlin, 1931.
74. R. Lachmann, " Die Musik der aussereuropaeischen Natur- und Kultur-voelker." *Handbuch der Musikwissenschaften*, 1929.
75. J. P. N. Land, " De gamelan te Jogjakarta met een voorrede over onze kennis der Javaansche muziek." *Verhandlungen der Kon. Akad. v. Wetensch.*, 19, 1890.
76. Paul H. Lang, " Music in Western Civilization." New York, 1941.
77. H. Lehmann, " Man's Most Creative Years." *Science*, 98, 1945.
78. Th. Lipps, " Æsthetik und musikalische Harmonie und Disharmonie." *Psychologische Studien*, 1905.
79. J. Llongueras, " La rhythmique appliquée a la première éducation des aveugles." *Compte rendu du Congress du Rhythme*, Geneva, 1926.
80. L. S. Lloyd, " Music and Sound." London, 1936.
81. E. Mach, " Analyse der Empfindungen." 1911.
82. A. Maecklenburg, " Das Zweikomponentensystem auf dem Gebiete des musikalischen Hoerens." *Schweiz. Musikpaedagogische Blaetter*, 1931.
83. E. Meyer, " Das Gehoer." *Handbuch der Physik*, VIII.
84. M. Meyer, " An Introduction to the Mechanics of the Inner Ear." 1907.
85. D. C. Miller, " The Science of Musical Sounds." New York, 1916.
86. Lord Monboddo, " Origin of Language." 1774.
87. S. F. Nadel, " Zur Psychologie des Konsonanzerlebens." *Zeitschrift für Psychologie*, 101, 1926.
88. A. Nef, " Die Seele der Musikinstrumente." *Schweiz. Musikzeitung*, 37, 1934.
89. Fr. Nietzsche, " Human all too Human."
90. N. Lindsay Norden, " A New Theory of Untempered Music." *Music Quarterly*, New York, 22, 1936.
91. A. von Oettingen, " Das Harmoniesystem in dualer Entwicklung." 1866.
92. R. M. Ogden, " Hearing." New York, 1924.
93. " Oxford History of Music."
94. H. J. Pannenborg and W. A. Pannenborg, " Die Psychologie der Musiker." *Zeitschrift für Psychologie*, 73, 1915.
95. G. Pantillon, " Audition relative et absolue." *Monatsblaetter für Musiker-ziehung*, 1943.
96. W. Peters, " Die Vererbung geistiger Eigenschaften." Jena, 1925.
97. Plato, " The Republic."
98. B. v. d. Pol, " Muziek en elementaire getallentheorie." *Archiv du Musée Taylor*, 9, 1942.
99. William Pole, " The Philosophy of Music." New York, 1924.
100. Sarah Harvey Porter, " Musical Vibrations for the Deaf." *American Annals of the Deaf*, 1922.
101. W. Preyer, " Die Seele des Kindes." 1912.
102. J. Ph. Rameau, " Extrait d'une réponse de M. Rameau à M. Euler sur l'identité des Octaves." 1753.
103. J. W. S. Rayleigh, " The Theory of Sound." London.
104. John Redfield, " Music, a Science and an Art." New York, 1935.
105. A. Reibmayer, " Die Entwicklungsgeschichte des Talents und Genies." 1908.
106. G. Révész, " Grundlegung der Tonpsychologie." Leipzig, 1913.
107. Idem, " Ueber die beiden Arten des absoluten Gehoers." *Zeitschrift der internationalen Musikgesellschaft*, 1912.
108. Idem, " Experimentelle Beitraege zur Orthosymphonie und zum Falschhoeren." *Zeitschrift für Psychologie*, 63, 1912.
109. Idem, " Ueber binaurale Tonmischung." *K. Gesellsch. d. Wissenschaften*, Goettingen, 1912, and *Zeitschrift für Psychologie*, 69, 1914.

110. G. Révész, "Zur Geschichte der Zweikomponententheorie in der Tonpsychologie." *Zeitschrift für Psychologie*, 99, 1926.
111. Idem, "Tonsystem jenseits des musikalischen Gebietes und die musikalischen Mikrosystems." *Zeitschrift für Psychologie*, 134, 1935.
112. Idem, "Colour-mixture and Sound-mixture." *Acta Psychologica*, VII, 1949.
113. Idem, E. Nyiregyhazy. "Analyse eines musikalisch hervorragenden Kindes." Leipzig, 1916.
114. Idem, "Pruefung der Musikalitaet." *Zeitschrift für Psychologie*, 85, 1920.
115. Idem, "Das fruehzeitige Auftreten der Begabung und ihre Erkennung." Leipzig, 1921.
116. Idem, "The Psychology of a Musical Prodigy." London, 1925. (English translation of 113.)
117. Idem, "Beziehung zwischen mathematischer und musikalischer Begabung." *Schweiz. Zeit. für Psychologie*, 5, 1946.
118. Idem, "Wiskundige aanleg bij musici." (Mathematical Ability of Musicians.) *Euclides*, 20, 1943.
119. Idem, "Talent und Genie," Berne, 1952.
120. Idem, "Musikgenuss bei Gehoerlosen" (with D. Katz). Leipzig, 1926.
121. "Die psychologische Bedeutung der musikalischen Erziehung bei Mindersinnigen und Sinnesschwachen." *Acta Psychologica*, IV, 1939.
122. Idem, "Gibt es einen Hoerraum?" *Acta Psychologica*, III, 1937.
123. Idem, "The Problem of Space with Particular Emphasis on Specific Sensory Spaces." *American Journal of Psychology*, 50, 1937.
124. Idem, (with von Liebermann), "Die binaurale Tonmischung." *Zeitschrift für Psychologie*, 69, 1914.
125. G. Richet, "Note sur un cas remarquable de précocité musicale." IV Congress internationale de Psychologie, 1900.
126. H. Riemann, "Révész Tonqualitaet." *Zeitschrift d. intern. Musikgesellschaft*, 8, 1912.
127. Idem, "Ideen su einer Lehre von den Tonvorstellungen." *Peter's Jahrbuch*, 1914/15.
128. Idem, "Musiklexikon." Berlin, 1929.
129. Curt Sachs, "The Rise of Music in the Ancient World." New York, 1943.
130. Idem, "Reallexikon der Musikinstrumente." Berlin, 1914.
131. K. L. Schaefer, "Tontabellen." *Beitrag zur Akustik und Musikwissenschaft*, 3, 1891.
132. Kathleen Schlesinger, "The Greek Aulos." London, 1939.
133. H. Schüssler, "Das unmusikalische Kind." *Zeitschrift f. angew. Psychologie*, 11, 1916.
134. G. Schuenemann, "Musikerziehung." Leipzig, 1930.
135. E. and G. Scupin, "Bubis erste Kindheit." 1907–1910.
136. Carl Seashore, "The Measurement of Musical Talent." 1915.
137. Idem, "The Psychology of Musical Talent." New York, 1938.
138. Idem, "Revisions of the Seashore Measures of Musical Talent." 1940.
139. C. G. Seligmann and B. Z. Seligmann, "The Veddas." 1911.
140. O. Selz, "Der schoepferische Mensch." *Zeitschrift für paedag. Psychologie*, 1932.
141. A. Speiser, "Musik und Mathematik." Basel, 1926.
142. Idem, "Geist und Mathematik." Zürich, 1946.
143. Herbert Spencer, "On the Origin and Function of Music." "Essays," Vol. I, London, 1857.
144. W. Stern, "Psychologie der fruehen Kindheit." 1923.
145. Simon Stevin, "Wisscondighe ghedachtenissen." Leiden, 1608.
146. I. Stravinsky, "An Autobiography." New York, 1936.

147. Carl Stumpf, " Tonpsychologie." Leipzig, 1883 and 1890.
148. Idem, " Ueber neuere Untersuchungen zur Tonlehre." VI. *Kong. fuer experim. Physik*, 1914.
149. Idem, " Anfaenge der Musik." Leipzig, 1911.
150. Idem, " Die Sprachlaute." 1926.
151. Idem, " Konsonanz und Dissonanz." *Beit. zur Akustik und Musikwissenschaft*, 1898.
152. C. S. Terry, " Bach, a Biography." London, 1928.
153. M. Unger, " Das Problem der Tonartencharakteristik." *Schweiz. Musikzeitung*, 1924.
154. C. W. Valentiner, " Appreciation of Musical Intervals." *British Journal of Psychology*, 1913.
155. E. Waetzmann, " Die Resonanztheorie des Hoerens." 1912.
156. H. J. Watt, " The Foundations of Music." Cambridge, 1919.
157. Idem, " The Psychology of Sound." Cambridge, 1917.
158. A. Wellek, " Das absolute Gehoer und seine Typen." Leipzig, 1938.
159. Egon Wellesz, " Aufgaben und Probleme der orientalischen Kirchen musik." 1923.
159a. H. Werner, " Die melodische Erfindung im fruehen Kindesalter." *Kaiser. Akad. der Wissenschaften*. Vienna, Sitzungsberichte, **182**, 1917.
159b. H. D. Wing, " Test of Musical Ability and Appreciation." *British Journal of Psychology* (*Monogr. Suppl.* XXVII, 1948).
160. Johannes Wolf, " Handbuch der Notationskunde." Leipzig, 1913 and 1919.
161. E. G. Wolff, " Grundlagen einer autonomen Musikaesthetik." Strassburg, 1934.
162. Alexander Wood, " The Physical Basis of Music." Cambridge, 1913.
163. Th. Wrightson, " An Inquiry into the Analytical Mechanism of the Internal Ear." 1918.
164. Gioseffo Zarlino, " Institutioni armoniche." Venice, 1558, reprinted 1562, and again 1573.
165. W. Ziegenfuss, " Die phaenomenologische Æsthetik." Berlin, 1927.

Tone Table I

Tempered Twelve-note Scale for C₂, C₁, C etc.
(a¹ = 440 vibr. per sec.)

Tones	C	C#/Db	D	D#/Eb	E	F	F#/Gb	G	G#/Ab	A	A#/Bb	B
Derivation = $\sqrt[12]{2}$ =	$\dfrac{c\sharp}{(c=)\,1}$ =	$\dfrac{d}{c\sharp}$ =	$\dfrac{d\sharp}{d}$ =	$\dfrac{e}{d\sharp}$ =	$\dfrac{f}{e}$ =	$\dfrac{f\sharp}{f}$ =	$\dfrac{g}{f\sharp}$ =	$\dfrac{g\sharp}{g}$ =	$\dfrac{a}{g\sharp}$ =	$\dfrac{a\sharp}{a}$ =	$\dfrac{b}{a\sharp}$ =	$\dfrac{(c=)\,2}{b}$ =
Ratio to C	1·00000	1·05946	1·22246	1·18921	1·25992	1·33484	1·41421	1·49831	1·58740	1·68179	1·78180	1·88775
Subcontra-octave C₂	16·35	17·32	18·35	19·45	20·60	21·83	23·12	24·50	25·96	27·50	29·14	30·87
Contra-octave C₁	32·70	34·65	36·71	38·89	41·20	43·65	46·25	49·00	51·91	55·00	58·27	61·74
Great octave C	65·41	69·30	73·42	77·78	82·41	87·31	92·50	98·00	103·83	110·00	116·54	123·47
Small octave c	130·81	138·59	146·83	155·56	164·81	174·61	185·00	196·00	207·65	220·00	233·08	246·94
1-line octave c¹	261·63	277·18	293·66	311·13	329·63	349·23	369·99	392·00	415·30	440·00	466·16	493·88
2-line octave c²	523·25	554·37	587·33	622·25	659·26	698·46	739·99	783·99	830·61	880·00	932·33	987·77
3-line octave c³	1046·50	1108·73	1174·66	1244·51	1318·51	1396·91	1479·98	1567·98	1661·22	1760·00	1864·66	1975·53
4-line octave c⁴	2093·00	2217·46	2349·32	2489·02	2637·02	2793·83	2959·96	3135·96	3322·44	3520·00	3729·31	3951·07
5-line octave c⁵	4186·01	4434·92	4698·64	4978·03	5274·04	5587·65	5919·91	6271·93	6644·88	7040·00	7458·62	7902·13
6-line octave c⁶	8372·02	8869·84	9397·27	9956·06	10548·08	11175·30	11839·82	12543·85	13289·75	14080·00	14917·24	15804·27

TONE TABLE 2-A

Enharmonic Scales for C₂, C₁, C etc.

(a¹ = 440 vibr. per sec.)

Tones		C	C#	Db	D	D	D#	Eb	E
Derivation [1]		—	$\frac{T}{t}$	$\frac{q}{T}$	$\frac{q}{t}$	$\frac{Q}{q}$	$\frac{TT}{q}$	t	T
Ratio to C			$\frac{25}{24}$	$\frac{16}{15}$	$\frac{10}{9}$	$\frac{9}{8}$	$\frac{75}{64}$	$\frac{6}{5}$	$\frac{5}{4}$
		1·0000	1·0417	1·0667	1·1111	1·1250	1·1719	1·2000	1·2500
Subcontra-octave	C₂	16½	17 3/16	17⅗	18⅓	18 9/16	19 43/128	19⅘	20⅝
Contra-octave	C₁	33	34⅜	35⅕	36⅔	37⅛	38 43/64	39⅗	41¼
Great octave	C	66	68¾	70⅖	73⅓	74¼	77 11/32	79⅕	82½
Small octave	c	132	137½	140⅘	146⅔	148½	154 11/16	158⅖	165
1-line octave	c¹	264	275	281⅗	293⅓	297	309⅜	316⅘	330
2-line octave	c²	528	550	563⅕	586⅔	594	618¾	633⅗	660
3-line octave	c³	1056	1100	1126⅖	1173⅓	1188	1237½	1267⅕	1320
4-line octave	c⁴	2112	2200	2252⅘	2346⅔	2376	2475	2534⅖	2640
5-line octave	c⁵	4224	4400	4505⅗	4693⅓	4752	4950	5068⅘	5280
6-line octave	c⁶	8448	8800	9011⅕	9386⅔	9504	9900	10137⅗	10560

[1] t = minor third = $\frac{6}{5}$ T = major third = $\frac{5}{4}$ q = fourth = $\frac{4}{3}$

Q = fifth = $\frac{3}{2}$ s = minor sixth = $\frac{8}{5}$ S = major sixth = $\frac{5}{3}$

Tone Table 2-B
Enharmonic Scales for C♭, C₁, C etc.
(a¹ = 440 vibr. per sec.)

Tones		F♭	E♯	F	F♯	F♯	G♭	G	G♯
Derivation[1]		$\frac{s}{T}$	$\frac{TT}{t}$	q	$\frac{S}{t}$	$\frac{QT}{q}$	tt	Q	TT
Ratio to C		$\frac{32}{25}$	$\frac{125}{96}$	$\frac{4}{3}$	$\frac{25}{18}$	$\frac{45}{32}$	$\frac{36}{25}$	$\frac{3}{2}$	$\frac{25}{16}$
		1·2800	1·3021	1·3333	1·3889	1·4063	1·4400	1·5000	1·5625
Subcontra-octave	C_2	21 $\frac{3}{25}$	21 $\frac{31}{64}$	22	22 $\frac{11}{12}$	23 $\frac{13}{64}$	23 $\frac{19}{25}$	24 $\frac{3}{4}$	25 $\frac{25}{32}$
Contra-octave	C_1	42 $\frac{6}{25}$	42 $\frac{31}{32}$	44	45 $\frac{5}{6}$	46 $\frac{13}{32}$	47 $\frac{13}{25}$	49 $\frac{1}{2}$	51 $\frac{9}{16}$
Great octave	C	84 $\frac{12}{25}$	85 $\frac{15}{16}$	88	91 $\frac{2}{3}$	92 $\frac{13}{16}$	95 $\frac{1}{25}$	99	103 $\frac{1}{8}$
Small octave	c	168 $\frac{24}{25}$	171 $\frac{7}{8}$	176	183 $\frac{1}{3}$	185 $\frac{5}{8}$	190 $\frac{4}{25}$	198	206 $\frac{1}{4}$
1-line octave	c^1	337 $\frac{23}{25}$	343 $\frac{3}{4}$	352	366 $\frac{2}{3}$	371 $\frac{1}{4}$	380 $\frac{8}{25}$	396	412 $\frac{1}{2}$
2-line octave	c^2	675 $\frac{21}{25}$	687 $\frac{1}{2}$	704	733 $\frac{1}{3}$	742 $\frac{1}{2}$	760 $\frac{16}{25}$	792	825
3-line octave	c^3	1351 $\frac{17}{25}$	1375	1408	1466 $\frac{2}{3}$	1485	1520 $\frac{16}{25}$	1584	1650
4-line octave	c^4	2703 $\frac{9}{25}$	2750	2816	2933 $\frac{1}{3}$	2970	3041 $\frac{7}{25}$	3168	3300
5-line octave	c^5	5406 $\frac{18}{25}$	5500	5632	5866 $\frac{2}{3}$	5940	6082 $\frac{14}{25}$	6336	6600
6-line octave	c^6	10813 $\frac{11}{25}$	11000	11264	11733 $\frac{1}{3}$	11880	12165 $\frac{3}{25}$	12672	13200

[1] t = minor third = $\frac{6}{5}$ T = major third = $\frac{5}{4}$ q = fourth = $\frac{4}{3}$

Q = fifth = $\frac{3}{2}$ s = minor sixth = $\frac{8}{5}$ S = major sixth = $\frac{5}{3}$

Tone Table 2–C
Enharmonic Scales for C_2, C_1, C etc.
(a¹ = 440 vibr. per sec.)

Tones	Derivation [1]		Ab	A	A#	Bb	Bb	B	Cb	B#
			s	S	$\frac{ST}{t}$	qq	Qt	QT	st	TTT
	Ratio to C		$\frac{8}{5}$	$\frac{5}{3}$	$\frac{125}{72}$	$\frac{16}{9}$	$\frac{9}{5}$	$\frac{15}{8}$	$\frac{48}{25}$	$\frac{125}{64}$
			1·6000	1·6667	1·7361	1·7778	1·8000	1·8750	1·9200	1·9531
Subcontra-octave	C_2		$26\frac{2}{5}$	$27\frac{1}{2}$	$28\frac{31}{48}$	$29\frac{1}{3}$	$29\frac{7}{10}$	$30\frac{15}{16}$	$31\frac{17}{25}$	$32\frac{29}{128}$
Contra-octave	C_1		$52\frac{4}{5}$	55	$57\frac{7}{24}$	$58\frac{2}{3}$	$59\frac{2}{5}$	$61\frac{7}{8}$	$63\frac{9}{25}$	$64\frac{29}{64}$
Great octave	C		$105\frac{3}{5}$	110	$114\frac{7}{12}$	$117\frac{1}{3}$	$118\frac{4}{5}$	$123\frac{3}{4}$	$126\frac{18}{25}$	$128\frac{29}{32}$
Small octave	c		$211\frac{1}{5}$	220	$229\frac{1}{6}$	$234\frac{2}{3}$	$237\frac{3}{5}$	$247\frac{1}{2}$	$253\frac{11}{25}$	$257\frac{13}{16}$
1-line octave	c^1		$422\frac{2}{5}$	440	$458\frac{1}{3}$	$469\frac{1}{3}$	$475\frac{1}{5}$	495	$506\frac{22}{25}$	$515\frac{5}{8}$
2-line octave	c^2		$844\frac{4}{5}$	880	$916\frac{2}{3}$	$938\frac{2}{3}$	$950\frac{2}{5}$	990	$1013\frac{19}{25}$	$1031\frac{1}{4}$
3-line octave	c^3		$1689\frac{3}{5}$	1760	$1833\frac{1}{3}$	$1877\frac{1}{3}$	$1900\frac{4}{5}$	1980	$2027\frac{13}{25}$	$2062\frac{1}{2}$
4-line octave	c^4		$3379\frac{1}{5}$	3520	$3666\frac{2}{3}$	$3754\frac{2}{3}$	$3801\frac{3}{5}$	3960	$4055\frac{1}{25}$	4125
5-line octave	c^5		$6758\frac{2}{5}$	7040	$7333\frac{1}{3}$	$7509\frac{1}{3}$	$7603\frac{1}{5}$	7920	$8110\frac{2}{25}$	8250
6-line octave	c^6		$13516\frac{4}{5}$	14080	$14666\frac{2}{3}$	$15018\frac{2}{3}$	$15206\frac{2}{5}$	15840	$16220\frac{4}{25}$	16500

1 t = minor third = $\frac{6}{5}$ T = major third = $\frac{5}{4}$ q = fourth = $\frac{4}{3}$

Q = fifth = $\frac{3}{2}$ s = minor sixth = $\frac{8}{5}$ S = major sixth = $\frac{5}{3}$

INDEX

257

A CATALOG OF SELECTED
DOVER BOOKS
IN ALL FIELDS OF INTEREST

A CATALOG OF SELECTED DOVER
BOOKS IN ALL FIELDS OF INTEREST

CONCERNING THE SPIRITUAL IN ART, Wassily Kandinsky. Pioneering work by father of abstract art. Thoughts on color theory, nature of art. Analysis of earlier masters. 12 illustrations. 80pp. of text. 5⅜ x 8½. 0-486-23411-8

CELTIC ART: The Methods of Construction, George Bain. Simple geometric techniques for making Celtic interlacements, spirals, Kells-type initials, animals, humans, etc. Over 500 illustrations. 160pp. 9 x 12. (Available in U.S. only.) 0-486-22923-8

AN ATLAS OF ANATOMY FOR ARTISTS, Fritz Schider. Most thorough reference work on art anatomy in the world. Hundreds of illustrations, including selections from works by Vesalius, Leonardo, Goya, Ingres, Michelangelo, others. 593 illustrations. 192pp. 7⅛ x 10¼. 0-486-20241-0

CELTIC HAND STROKE-BY-STROKE (Irish Half-Uncial from "The Book of Kells"): An Arthur Baker Calligraphy Manual, Arthur Baker. Complete guide to creating each letter of the alphabet in distinctive Celtic manner. Covers hand position, strokes, pens, inks, paper, more. Illustrated. 48pp. 8¼ x 11. 0-486-24336-2

EASY ORIGAMI, John Montroll. Charming collection of 32 projects (hat, cup, pelican, piano, swan, many more) specially designed for the novice origami hobbyist. Clearly illustrated easy-to-follow instructions insure that even beginning papercrafters will achieve successful results. 48pp. 8¼ x 11. 0-486-27298-2

BLOOMINGDALE'S ILLUSTRATED 1886 CATALOG: Fashions, Dry Goods and Housewares, Bloomingdale Brothers. Famed merchants' extremely rare catalog depicting about 1,700 products: clothing, housewares, firearms, dry goods, jewelry, more. Invaluable for dating, identifying vintage items. Also, copyright-free graphics for artists, designers. Co-published with Henry Ford Museum & Greenfield Village. 160pp. 8¼ x 11. 0-486-25780-0

THE ART OF WORLDLY WISDOM, Baltasar Gracian. "Think with the few and speak with the many," "Friends are a second existence," and "Be able to forget" are among this 1637 volume's 300 pithy maxims. A perfect source of mental and spiritual refreshment, it can be opened at random and appreciated either in brief or at length. 128pp. 5⅜ x 8½. 0-486-44034-6

JOHNSON'S DICTIONARY: A Modern Selection, Samuel Johnson (E. L. McAdam and George Milne, eds.). This modern version reduces the original 1755 edition's 2,300 pages of definitions and literary examples to a more manageable length, retaining the verbal pleasure and historical curiosity of the original. 480pp. 5⅛ x 8½. 0-486-44089-3

ADVENTURES OF HUCKLEBERRY FINN, Mark Twain, Illustrated by E. W. Kemble. A work of eternal richness and complexity, a source of ongoing critical debate, and a literary landmark, Twain's 1885 masterpiece about a barefoot boy's journey of self-discovery has enthralled readers around the world. This handsome clothbound reproduction of the first edition features all 174 of the original black-and-white illustrations. 368pp. 5⅜ x 8½. 0-486-44322-1

STICKLEY CRAFTSMAN FURNITURE CATALOGS, Gustav Stickley and L. & J. G. Stickley. Beautiful, functional furniture in two authentic catalogs from 1910. 594 illustrations, including 277 photos, show settles, rockers, armchairs, reclining chairs, bookcases, desks, tables. 183pp. 6½ x 9¼. 0-486-23838-5

AMERICAN LOCOMOTIVES IN HISTORIC PHOTOGRAPHS: 1858 to 1949, Ron Ziel (ed.). A rare collection of 126 meticulously detailed official photographs, called "builder portraits," of American locomotives that majestically chronicle the rise of steam locomotive power in America. Introduction. Detailed captions. xi+ 129pp. 9 x 12. 0-486-27393-8

AMERICA'S LIGHTHOUSES: An Illustrated History, Francis Ross Holland, Jr. Delightfully written, profusely illustrated fact-filled survey of over 200 American lighthouses since 1716. History, anecdotes, technological advances, more. 240pp. 8 x 10¾. 0-486-25576-X

TOWARDS A NEW ARCHITECTURE, Le Corbusier. Pioneering manifesto by founder of "International School." Technical and aesthetic theories, views of industry, economics, relation of form to function, "mass-production split" and much more. Profusely illustrated. 320pp. 6⅛ x 9¼. (Available in U.S. only.) 0-486-25023-7

HOW THE OTHER HALF LIVES, Jacob Riis. Famous journalistic record, exposing poverty and degradation of New York slums around 1900, by major social reformer. 100 striking and influential photographs. 233pp. 10 x 7⅞. 0-486-22012-5

FRUIT KEY AND TWIG KEY TO TREES AND SHRUBS, William M. Harlow. One of the handiest and most widely used identification aids. Fruit key covers 120 deciduous and evergreen species; twig key 160 deciduous species. Easily used. Over 300 photographs. 126pp. 5⅜ x 8½. 0-486-20511-8

COMMON BIRD SONGS, Dr. Donald J. Borror. Songs of 60 most common U.S. birds: robins, sparrows, cardinals, bluejays, finches, more—arranged in order of increasing complexity. Up to 9 variations of songs of each species.
Cassette and manual 0-486-99911-4

ORCHIDS AS HOUSE PLANTS, Rebecca Tyson Northen. Grow cattleyas and many other kinds of orchids—in a window, in a case, or under artificial light. 63 illustrations. 148pp. 5⅜ x 8½. 0-486-23261-1

MONSTER MAZES, Dave Phillips. Masterful mazes at four levels of difficulty. Avoid deadly perils and evil creatures to find magical treasures. Solutions for all 32 exciting illustrated puzzles. 48pp. 8¼ x 11. 0-486-26005-4

MOZART'S DON GIOVANNI (DOVER OPERA LIBRETTO SERIES), Wolfgang Amadeus Mozart. Introduced and translated by Ellen H. Bleiler. Standard Italian libretto, with complete English translation. Convenient and thoroughly portable—an ideal companion for reading along with a recording or the performance itself. Introduction. List of characters. Plot summary. 121pp. 5¼ x 8½. 0-486-24944-1

FRANK LLOYD WRIGHT'S DANA HOUSE, Donald Hoffmann. Pictorial essay of residential masterpiece with over 160 interior and exterior photos, plans, elevations, sketches and studies. 128pp. 9¼ x 10¾. 0-486-29120-0

THE CLARINET AND CLARINET PLAYING, David Pino. Lively, comprehensive work features suggestions about technique, musicianship, and musical interpretation, as well as guidelines for teaching, making your own reeds, and preparing for public performance. Includes an intriguing look at clarinet history. "A godsend," *The Clarinet,* Journal of the International Clarinet Society. Appendixes. 7 illus. 320pp. 5⅜ x 8½. 0-486-40270-3

HOLLYWOOD GLAMOR PORTRAITS, John Kobal (ed.). 145 photos from 1926-49. Harlow, Gable, Bogart, Bacall; 94 stars in all. Full background on photographers, technical aspects. 160pp. 8⅜ x 11¼. 0-486-23352-9

THE RAVEN AND OTHER FAVORITE POEMS, Edgar Allan Poe. Over 40 of the author's most memorable poems: "The Bells," "Ulalume," "Israfel," "To Helen," "The Conqueror Worm," "Eldorado," "Annabel Lee," many more. Alphabetic lists of titles and first lines. 64pp. 5³⁄₁₆ x 8¼. 0-486-26685-0

PERSONAL MEMOIRS OF U. S. GRANT, Ulysses Simpson Grant. Intelligent, deeply moving firsthand account of Civil War campaigns, considered by many the finest military memoirs ever written. Includes letters, historic photographs, maps and more. 528pp. 6⅛ x 9¼. 0-486-28587-1

ANCIENT EGYPTIAN MATERIALS AND INDUSTRIES, A. Lucas and J. Harris. Fascinating, comprehensive, thoroughly documented text describes this ancient civilization's vast resources and the processes that incorporated them in daily life, including the use of animal products, building materials, cosmetics, perfumes and incense, fibers, glazed ware, glass and its manufacture, materials used in the mummification process, and much more. 544pp. 6⅛ x 9¼. (Available in U.S. only.) 0-486-40446-3

RUSSIAN STORIES/RUSSKIE RASSKAZY: A Dual-Language Book, edited by Gleb Struve. Twelve tales by such masters as Chekhov, Tolstoy, Dostoevsky, Pushkin, others. Excellent word-for-word English translations on facing pages, plus teaching and study aids, Russian/English vocabulary, biographical/critical introductions, more. 416pp. 5⅜ x 8½. 0-486-26244-8

PHILADELPHIA THEN AND NOW: 60 Sites Photographed in the Past and Present, Kenneth Finkel and Susan Oyama. Rare photographs of City Hall, Logan Square, Independence Hall, Betsy Ross House, other landmarks juxtaposed with contemporary views. Captures changing face of historic city. Introduction. Captions. 128pp. 8¼ x 11. 0-486-25790-8

NORTH AMERICAN INDIAN LIFE: Customs and Traditions of 23 Tribes, Elsie Clews Parsons (ed.). 27 fictionalized essays by noted anthropologists examine religion, customs, government, additional facets of life among the Winnebago, Crow, Zuni, Eskimo, other tribes. 480pp. 6⅛ x 9¼. 0-486-27377-6

TECHNICAL MANUAL AND DICTIONARY OF CLASSICAL BALLET, Gail Grant. Defines, explains, comments on steps, movements, poses and concepts. 15-page pictorial section. Basic book for student, viewer. 127pp. 5⅜ x 8½. 0-486-21843-0

THE MALE AND FEMALE FIGURE IN MOTION: 60 Classic Photographic Sequences, Eadweard Muybridge. 60 true-action photographs of men and women walking, running, climbing, bending, turning, etc., reproduced from rare 19th-century masterpiece. vi + 121pp. 9 x 12. 0-486-24745-7

ANIMALS: 1,419 Copyright-Free Illustrations of Mammals, Birds, Fish, Insects, etc., Jim Harter (ed.). Clear wood engravings present, in extremely lifelike poses, over 1,000 species of animals. One of the most extensive pictorial sourcebooks of its kind. Captions. Index. 284pp. 9 x 12. 0-486-23766-4

1001 QUESTIONS ANSWERED ABOUT THE SEASHORE, N. J. Berrill and Jacquelyn Berrill. Queries answered about dolphins, sea snails, sponges, starfish, fishes, shore birds, many others. Covers appearance, breeding, growth, feeding, much more. 305pp. 5¼ x 8¼. 0-486-23366-9

ATTRACTING BIRDS TO YOUR YARD, William J. Weber. Easy-to-follow guide offers advice on how to attract the greatest diversity of birds: birdhouses, feeders, water and waterers, much more. 96pp. 5³⁄₁₆ x 8¼. 0-486-28927-3

MEDICINAL AND OTHER USES OF NORTH AMERICAN PLANTS: A Historical Survey with Special Reference to the Eastern Indian Tribes, Charlotte Erichsen-Brown. Chronological historical citations document 500 years of usage of plants, trees, shrubs native to eastern Canada, northeastern U.S. Also complete identifying information. 343 illustrations. 544pp. 6½ x 9¼. 0-486-25951-X

STORYBOOK MAZES, Dave Phillips. 23 stories and mazes on two-page spreads: Wizard of Oz, Treasure Island, Robin Hood, etc. Solutions. 64pp. 8¼ x 11.
0-486-23628-5

AMERICAN NEGRO SONGS: 230 Folk Songs and Spirituals, Religious and Secular, John W. Work. This authoritative study traces the African influences of songs sung and played by black Americans at work, in church, and as entertainment. The author discusses the lyric significance of such songs as "Swing Low, Sweet Chariot," "John Henry," and others and offers the words and music for 230 songs. Bibliography. Index of Song Titles. 272pp. 6½ x 9¼. 0-486-40271-1

MOVIE-STAR PORTRAITS OF THE FORTIES, John Kobal (ed.). 163 glamor, studio photos of 106 stars of the 1940s: Rita Hayworth, Ava Gardner, Marlon Brando, Clark Gable, many more. 176pp. 8⅜ x 11¼. 0-486-23546-7

YEKL and THE IMPORTED BRIDEGROOM AND OTHER STORIES OF YIDDISH NEW YORK, Abraham Cahan. Film Hester Street based on *Yekl* (1896). Novel, other stories among first about Jewish immigrants on N.Y.'s East Side. 240pp. 5⅜ x 8½. 0-486-22427-9

SELECTED POEMS, Walt Whitman. Generous sampling from *Leaves of Grass*. Twenty-four poems include "I Hear America Singing," "Song of the Open Road," "I Sing the Body Electric," "When Lilacs Last in the Dooryard Bloom'd," "O Captain! My Captain!"–all reprinted from an authoritative edition. Lists of titles and first lines. 128pp. 5³⁄₁₆ x 8¼. 0-486-26878-0

SONGS OF EXPERIENCE: Facsimile Reproduction with 26 Plates in Full Color, William Blake. 26 full-color plates from a rare 1826 edition. Includes "The Tyger," "London," "Holy Thursday," and other poems. Printed text of poems. 48pp. 5¼ x 7.
0-486-24636-1

THE BEST TALES OF HOFFMANN, E. T. A. Hoffmann. 10 of Hoffmann's most important stories: "Nutcracker and the King of Mice," "The Golden Flowerpot," etc. 458pp. 5⅜ x 8½. 0-486-21793-0

THE BOOK OF TEA, Kakuzo Okakura. Minor classic of the Orient: entertaining, charming explanation, interpretation of traditional Japanese culture in terms of tea ceremony. 94pp. 5⅜ x 8½. 0-486-20070-1

FRENCH STORIES/CONTES FRANÇAIS: A Dual-Language Book, Wallace Fowlie. Ten stories by French masters, Voltaire to Camus: "Micromegas" by Voltaire; "The Atheist's Mass" by Balzac; "Minuet" by de Maupassant; "The Guest" by Camus, six more. Excellent English translations on facing pages. Also French-English vocabulary list, exercises, more. 352pp. 5⅜ x 8½.   0-486-26443-2

CHICAGO AT THE TURN OF THE CENTURY IN PHOTOGRAPHS: 122 Historic Views from the Collections of the Chicago Historical Society, Larry A. Viskochil. Rare large-format prints offer detailed views of City Hall, State Street, the Loop, Hull House, Union Station, many other landmarks, circa 1904-1913. Introduction. Captions. Maps. 144pp. 9⅜ x 12¼.   0-486-24656-6

OLD BROOKLYN IN EARLY PHOTOGRAPHS, 1865-1929, William Lee Younger. Luna Park, Gravesend race track, construction of Grand Army Plaza, moving of Hotel Brighton, etc. 157 previously unpublished photographs. 165pp. 8⅞ x 11¾.
    0-486-23587-4

THE MYTHS OF THE NORTH AMERICAN INDIANS, Lewis Spence. Rich anthology of the myths and legends of the Algonquins, Iroquois, Pawnees and Sioux, prefaced by an extensive historical and ethnological commentary. 36 illustrations. 480pp. 5⅜ x 8½.   0-486-25967-6

AN ENCYCLOPEDIA OF BATTLES: Accounts of Over 1,560 Battles from 1479 B.C. to the Present, David Eggenberger. Essential details of every major battle in recorded history from the first battle of Megiddo in 1479 B.C. to Grenada in 1984. List of Battle Maps. New Appendix covering the years 1967-1984. Index. 99 illustrations. 544pp. 6½ x 9¼.   0-486-24913-1

SAILING ALONE AROUND THE WORLD, Captain Joshua Slocum. First man to sail around the world, alone, in small boat. One of great feats of seamanship told in delightful manner. 67 illustrations. 294pp. 5⅜ x 8½.   0-486-20326-3

ANARCHISM AND OTHER ESSAYS, Emma Goldman. Powerful, penetrating, prophetic essays on direct action, role of minorities, prison reform, puritan hypocrisy, violence, etc. 271pp. 5⅜ x 8½.   0-486-22484-8

MYTHS OF THE HINDUS AND BUDDHISTS, Ananda K. Coomaraswamy and Sister Nivedita. Great stories of the epics; deeds of Krishna, Shiva, taken from puranas, Vedas, folk tales; etc. 32 illustrations. 400pp. 5⅜ x 8½.   0-486-21759-0

MY BONDAGE AND MY FREEDOM, Frederick Douglass. Born a slave, Douglass became outspoken force in antislavery movement. The best of Douglass' autobiographies. Graphic description of slave life. 464pp. 5⅜ x 8½.   0-486-22457-0

FOLLOWING THE EQUATOR: A Journey Around the World, Mark Twain. Fascinating humorous account of 1897 voyage to Hawaii, Australia, India, New Zealand, etc. Ironic, bemused reports on peoples, customs, climate, flora and fauna, politics, much more. 197 illustrations. 720pp. 5⅜ x 8½.   0-486-26113-1

THE PEOPLE CALLED SHAKERS, Edward D. Andrews. Definitive study of Shakers: origins, beliefs, practices, dances, social organization, furniture and crafts, etc. 33 illustrations. 351pp. 5⅜ x 8½.   0-486-21081-2

THE MYTHS OF GREECE AND ROME, H. A. Guerber. A classic of mythology, generously illustrated, long prized for its simple, graphic, accurate retelling of the principal myths of Greece and Rome, and for its commentary on their origins and significance. With 64 illustrations by Michelangelo, Raphael, Titian, Rubens, Canova, Bernini and others. 480pp. 5⅜ x 8½.   0-486-27584-1

PSYCHOLOGY OF MUSIC, Carl E. Seashore. Classic work discusses music as a medium from psychological viewpoint. Clear treatment of physical acoustics, auditory apparatus, sound perception, development of musical skills, nature of musical feeling, host of other topics. 88 figures. 408pp. 5⅜ x 8½. 0-486-21851-1

LIFE IN ANCIENT EGYPT, Adolf Erman. Fullest, most thorough, detailed older account with much not in more recent books, domestic life, religion, magic, medicine, commerce, much more. Many illustrations reproduce tomb paintings, carvings, hieroglyphs, etc. 597pp. 5⅜ x 8½. 0-486-22632-8

SUNDIALS, Their Theory and Construction, Albert Waugh. Far and away the best, most thorough coverage of ideas, mathematics concerned, types, construction, adjusting anywhere. Simple, nontechnical treatment allows even children to build several of these dials. Over 100 illustrations. 230pp. 5⅜ x 8½. 0-486-22947-5

THEORETICAL HYDRODYNAMICS, L. M. Milne-Thomson. Classic exposition of the mathematical theory of fluid motion, applicable to both hydrodynamics and aerodynamics. Over 600 exercises. 768pp. 6⅛ x 9¼. 0-486-68970-0

OLD-TIME VIGNETTES IN FULL COLOR, Carol Belanger Grafton (ed.). Over 390 charming, often sentimental illustrations, selected from archives of Victorian graphics—pretty women posing, children playing, food, flowers, kittens and puppies, smiling cherubs, birds and butterflies, much more. All copyright-free. 48pp. 9¼ x 12¼. 0-486-27269-9

PERSPECTIVE FOR ARTISTS, Rex Vicat Cole. Depth, perspective of sky and sea, shadows, much more, not usually covered. 391 diagrams, 81 reproductions of drawings and paintings. 279pp. 5⅜ x 8½. 0-486-22487-2

DRAWING THE LIVING FIGURE, Joseph Sheppard. Innovative approach to artistic anatomy focuses on specifics of surface anatomy, rather than muscles and bones. Over 170 drawings of live models in front, back and side views, and in widely varying poses. Accompanying diagrams. 177 illustrations. Introduction. Index. 144pp. 8⅜ x11¼. 0-486-26723-7

GOTHIC AND OLD ENGLISH ALPHABETS: 100 Complete Fonts, Dan X. Solo. Add power, elegance to posters, signs, other graphics with 100 stunning copyright-free alphabets: Blackstone, Dolbey, Germania, 97 more—including many lower-case, numerals, punctuation marks. 104pp. 8⅛ x 11. 0-486-24695-7

THE BOOK OF WOOD CARVING, Charles Marshall Sayers. Finest book for beginners discusses fundamentals and offers 34 designs. "Absolutely first rate . . . well thought out and well executed."–E. J. Tangerman. 118pp. 7¾ x 10⅝. 0-486-23654-4

ILLUSTRATED CATALOG OF CIVIL WAR MILITARY GOODS: Union Army Weapons, Insignia, Uniform Accessories, and Other Equipment, Schuyler, Hartley, and Graham. Rare, profusely illustrated 1846 catalog includes Union Army uniform and dress regulations, arms and ammunition, coats, insignia, flags, swords, rifles, etc. 226 illustrations. 160pp. 9 x 12. 0-486-24939-5

WOMEN'S FASHIONS OF THE EARLY 1900s: An Unabridged Republication of "New York Fashions, 1909," National Cloak & Suit Co. Rare catalog of mail-order fashions documents women's and children's clothing styles shortly after the turn of the century. Captions offer full descriptions, prices. Invaluable resource for fashion, costume historians. Approximately 725 illustrations. 128pp. 8⅜ x 11¼. 0-486-27276-1

HOW TO DO BEADWORK, Mary White. Fundamental book on craft from simple projects to five-bead chains and woven works. 106 illustrations. 142pp. 5⅜ x 8. 0-486-20697-1

THE 1912 AND 1915 GUSTAV STICKLEY FURNITURE CATALOGS, Gustav Stickley. With over 200 detailed illustrations and descriptions, these two catalogs are essential reading and reference materials and identification guides for Stickley furniture. Captions cite materials, dimensions and prices. 112pp. 6½ x 9¼. 0-486-26676-1

EARLY AMERICAN LOCOMOTIVES, John H. White, Jr. Finest locomotive engravings from early 19th century: historical (1804–74), main-line (after 1870), special, foreign, etc. 147 plates. 142pp. 11⅜ x 8¼. 0-486-22772-3

LITTLE BOOK OF EARLY AMERICAN CRAFTS AND TRADES, Peter Stockham (ed.). 1807 children's book explains crafts and trades: baker, hatter, cooper, potter, and many others. 23 copperplate illustrations. 140pp. 4⅝ x 6. 0-486-23336-7

VICTORIAN FASHIONS AND COSTUMES FROM HARPER'S BAZAR, 1867–1898, Stella Blum (ed.). Day costumes, evening wear, sports clothes, shoes, hats, other accessories in over 1,000 detailed engravings. 320pp. 9⅜ x 12¼. 0-486-22990-4

THE LONG ISLAND RAIL ROAD IN EARLY PHOTOGRAPHS, Ron Ziel. Over 220 rare photos, informative text document origin (1844) and development of rail service on Long Island. Vintage views of early trains, locomotives, stations, passengers, crews, much more. Captions. 8⅞ x 11¾. 0-486-26301-0

VOYAGE OF THE LIBERDADE, Joshua Slocum. Great 19th-century mariner's thrilling, first-hand account of the wreck of his ship off South America, the 35-foot boat he built from the wreckage, and its remarkable voyage home. 128pp. 5⅜ x 8½. 0-486-40022-0

TEN BOOKS ON ARCHITECTURE, Vitruvius. The most important book ever written on architecture. Early Roman aesthetics, technology, classical orders, site selection, all other aspects. Morgan translation. 331pp. 5⅜ x 8½. 0-486-20645-9

THE HUMAN FIGURE IN MOTION, Eadweard Muybridge. More than 4,500 stopped-action photos, in action series, showing undraped men, women, children jumping, lying down, throwing, sitting, wrestling, carrying, etc. 390pp. 7⅞ x 10⅝. 0-486-20204-6 Clothbd.

TREES OF THE EASTERN AND CENTRAL UNITED STATES AND CANADA, William M. Harlow. Best one-volume guide to 140 trees. Full descriptions, woodlore, range, etc. Over 600 illustrations. Handy size. 288pp. 4½ x 6⅜. 0-486-20395-6

GROWING AND USING HERBS AND SPICES, Milo Miloradovich. Versatile handbook provides all the information needed for cultivation and use of all the herbs and spices available in North America. 4 illustrations. Index. Glossary. 236pp. 5⅜ x 8½. 0-486-25058-X

BIG BOOK OF MAZES AND LABYRINTHS, Walter Shepherd. 50 mazes and labyrinths in all–classical, solid, ripple, and more–in one great volume. Perfect inexpensive puzzler for clever youngsters. Full solutions. 112pp. 8⅛ x 11. 0-486-22951-3

PIANO TUNING, J. Cree Fischer. Clearest, best book for beginner, amateur. Simple repairs, raising dropped notes, tuning by easy method of flattened fifths. No previous skills needed. 4 illustrations. 201pp. 5⅜ x 8½. 0-486-23267-0

HINTS TO SINGERS, Lillian Nordica. Selecting the right teacher, developing confidence, overcoming stage fright, and many other important skills receive thoughtful discussion in this indispensible guide, written by a world-famous diva of four decades' experience. 96pp. 5⅜ x 8½. 0-486-40094-8

THE COMPLETE NONSENSE OF EDWARD LEAR, Edward Lear. All nonsense limericks, zany alphabets, Owl and Pussycat, songs, nonsense botany, etc., illustrated by Lear. Total of 320pp. 5⅜ x 8½. (Available in U.S. only.) 0-486-20167-8

VICTORIAN PARLOUR POETRY: An Annotated Anthology, Michael R. Turner. 117 gems by Longfellow, Tennyson, Browning, many lesser-known poets. "The Village Blacksmith," "Curfew Must Not Ring Tonight," "Only a Baby Small," dozens more, often difficult to find elsewhere. Index of poets, titles, first lines. xxiii + 325pp. 5⅝ x 8¼. 0-486-27044-0

DUBLINERS, James Joyce. Fifteen stories offer vivid, tightly focused observations of the lives of Dublin's poorer classes. At least one, "The Dead," is considered a masterpiece. Reprinted complete and unabridged from standard edition. 160pp. 5$\frac{3}{16}$ x 8¼. 0-486-26870-5

GREAT WEIRD TALES: 14 Stories by Lovecraft, Blackwood, Machen and Others, S. T. Joshi (ed.). 14 spellbinding tales, including "The Sin Eater," by Fiona McLeod, "The Eye Above the Mantel," by Frank Belknap Long, as well as renowned works by R. H. Barlow, Lord Dunsany, Arthur Machen, W. C. Morrow and eight other masters of the genre. 256pp. 5⅜ x 8½. (Available in U.S. only.) 0-486-40436-6

THE BOOK OF THE SACRED MAGIC OF ABRAMELIN THE MAGE, translated by S. MacGregor Mathers. Medieval manuscript of ceremonial magic. Basic document in Aleister Crowley, Golden Dawn groups. 268pp. 5⅜ x 8½. 0-486-23211-5

THE BATTLES THAT CHANGED HISTORY, Fletcher Pratt. Eminent historian profiles 16 crucial conflicts, ancient to modern, that changed the course of civilization. 352pp. 5⅜ x 8½. 0-486-41129-X

NEW RUSSIAN-ENGLISH AND ENGLISH-RUSSIAN DICTIONARY, M. A. O'Brien. This is a remarkably handy Russian dictionary, containing a surprising amount of information, including over 70,000 entries. 366pp. 4½ x 6⅛. 0-486-20208-9

NEW YORK IN THE FORTIES, Andreas Feininger. 162 brilliant photographs by the well-known photographer, formerly with *Life* magazine. Commuters, shoppers, Times Square at night, much else from city at its peak. Captions by John von Hartz. 181pp. 9¼ x 10¾. 0-486-23585-8

INDIAN SIGN LANGUAGE, William Tomkins. Over 525 signs developed by Sioux and other tribes. Written instructions and diagrams. Also 290 pictographs. 111pp. 6⅛ x 9¼. 0-486-22029-X

ANATOMY: A Complete Guide for Artists, Joseph Sheppard. A master of figure drawing shows artists how to render human anatomy convincingly. Over 460 illustrations. 224pp. 8⅜ x 11¼. 0-486-27279-6

MEDIEVAL CALLIGRAPHY: Its History and Technique, Marc Drogin. Spirited history, comprehensive instruction manual covers 13 styles (ca. 4th century through 15th). Excellent photographs; directions for duplicating medieval techniques with modern tools. 224pp. 8⅜ x 11¼. 0-486-26142-5

DRIED FLOWERS: How to Prepare Them, Sarah Whitlock and Martha Rankin. Complete instructions on how to use silica gel, meal and borax, perlite aggregate, sand and borax, glycerine and water to create attractive permanent flower arrangements. 12 illustrations. 32pp. 5⅜ x 8½. 0-486-21802-3

EASY-TO-MAKE BIRD FEEDERS FOR WOODWORKERS, Scott D. Campbell. Detailed, simple-to-use guide for designing, constructing, caring for and using feeders. Text, illustrations for 12 classic and contemporary designs. 96pp. 5⅜ x 8½. 0-486-25847-5

THE COMPLETE BOOK OF BIRDHOUSE CONSTRUCTION FOR WOOD-WORKERS, Scott D. Campbell. Detailed instructions, illustrations, tables. Also data on bird habitat and instinct patterns. Bibliography. 3 tables. 63 illustrations in 15 figures. 48pp. 5¼ x 8½. 0-486-24407-5

SCOTTISH WONDER TALES FROM MYTH AND LEGEND, Donald A. Mackenzie. 16 lively tales tell of giants rumbling down mountainsides, of a magic wand that turns stone pillars into warriors, of gods and goddesses, evil hags, powerful forces and more. 240pp. 5⅜ x 8½. 0-486-29677-6

THE HISTORY OF UNDERCLOTHES, C. Willett Cunnington and Phyllis Cunnington. Fascinating, well-documented survey covering six centuries of English undergarments, enhanced with over 100 illustrations: 12th-century laced-up bodice, footed long drawers (1795), 19th-century bustles, l9th-century corsets for men, Victorian "bust improvers," much more. 272pp. 5⅜ x 8¼. 0-486-27124-2

ARTS AND CRAFTS FURNITURE: The Complete Brooks Catalog of 1912, Brooks Manufacturing Co. Photos and detailed descriptions of more than 150 now very collectible furniture designs from the Arts and Crafts movement depict davenports, settees, buffets, desks, tables, chairs, bedsteads, dressers and more, all built of solid, quarter-sawed oak. Invaluable for students and enthusiasts of antiques, Americana and the decorative arts. 80pp. 6½ x 9¼. 0-486-27471-3

WILBUR AND ORVILLE: A Biography of the Wright Brothers, Fred Howard. Definitive, crisply written study tells the full story of the brothers' lives and work. A vividly written biography, unparalleled in scope and color, that also captures the spirit of an extraordinary era. 560pp. 6⅛ x 9¼. 0-486-40297-5

THE ARTS OF THE SAILOR: Knotting, Splicing and Ropework, Hervey Garrett Smith. Indispensable shipboard reference covers tools, basic knots and useful hitches; handsewing and canvas work, more. Over 100 illustrations. Delightful reading for sea lovers. 256pp. 5⅜ x 8½. 0-486-26440-8

FRANK LLOYD WRIGHT'S FALLINGWATER: The House and Its History, Second, Revised Edition, Donald Hoffmann. A total revision–both in text and illustrations–of the standard document on Fallingwater, the boldest, most personal architectural statement of Wright's mature years, updated with valuable new material from the recently opened Frank Lloyd Wright Archives. "Fascinating"–*The New York Times*. 116 illustrations. 128pp. 9¼ x 10¾. 0-486-27430-6

PHOTOGRAPHIC SKETCHBOOK OF THE CIVIL WAR, Alexander Gardner. 100 photos taken on field during the Civil War. Famous shots of Manassas Harper's Ferry, Lincoln, Richmond, slave pens, etc. 244pp. 10⅝ x 8¼. 0-486-22731-6

FIVE ACRES AND INDEPENDENCE, Maurice G. Kains. Great back-to-the-land classic explains basics of self-sufficient farming. The one book to get. 95 illustrations. 397pp. 5⅜ x 8½. 0-486-20974-1

A MODERN HERBAL, Margaret Grieve. Much the fullest, most exact, most useful compilation of herbal material. Gigantic alphabetical encyclopedia, from aconite to zedoary, gives botanical information, medical properties, folklore, economic uses, much else. Indispensable to serious reader. 161 illustrations. 888pp. 6½ x 9¼. 2-vol. set. (Available in U.S. only.)   Vol. I: 0-486-22798-7   Vol. II: 0-486-22799-5

HIDDEN TREASURE MAZE BOOK, Dave Phillips. Solve 34 challenging mazes accompanied by heroic tales of adventure. Evil dragons, people-eating plants, blood-thirsty giants, many more dangerous adversaries lurk at every twist and turn. 34 mazes, stories, solutions. 48pp. 8¼ x 11.   0-486-24566-7

LETTERS OF W. A. MOZART, Wolfgang A. Mozart. Remarkable letters show bawdy wit, humor, imagination, musical insights, contemporary musical world; includes some letters from Leopold Mozart. 276pp. 5⅜ x 8½.   0-486-22859-2

BASIC PRINCIPLES OF CLASSICAL BALLET, Agrippina Vaganova. Great Russian theoretician, teacher explains methods for teaching classical ballet. 118 illustrations. 175pp. 5⅜ x 8½.   0-486-22036-2

THE JUMPING FROG, Mark Twain. Revenge edition. The original story of The Celebrated Jumping Frog of Calaveras County, a hapless French translation, and Twain's hilarious "retranslation" from the French. 12 illustrations. 66pp. 5⅜ x 8½.
0-486-22686-7

BEST REMEMBERED POEMS, Martin Gardner (ed.). The 126 poems in this superb collection of 19th- and 20th-century British and American verse range from Shelley's "To a Skylark" to the impassioned "Renascence" of Edna St. Vincent Millay and to Edward Lear's whimsical "The Owl and the Pussycat." 224pp. 5⅜ x 8½.
0-486-27165-X

COMPLETE SONNETS, William Shakespeare. Over 150 exquisite poems deal with love, friendship, the tyranny of time, beauty's evanescence, death and other themes in language of remarkable power, precision and beauty. Glossary of archaic terms. 80pp. 5³⁄₁₆ x 8¼.   0-486-26686-9

HISTORIC HOMES OF THE AMERICAN PRESIDENTS, Second, Revised Edition, Irvin Haas. A traveler's guide to American Presidential homes, most open to the public, depicting and describing homes occupied by every American President from George Washington to George Bush. With visiting hours, admission charges, travel routes. 175 photographs. Index. 160pp. 8¼ x 11.   0-486-26751-2

THE WIT AND HUMOR OF OSCAR WILDE, Alvin Redman (ed.). More than 1,000 ripostes, paradoxes, wisecracks: Work is the curse of the drinking classes; I can resist everything except temptation; etc. 258pp. 5⅜ x 8½.   0-486-20602-5

SHAKESPEARE LEXICON AND QUOTATION DICTIONARY, Alexander Schmidt. Full definitions, locations, shades of meaning in every word in plays and poems. More than 50,000 exact quotations. 1,485pp. 6½ x 9¼. 2-vol. set.
Vol. 1: 0-486-22726-X   Vol. 2: 0-486-22727-8

SELECTED POEMS, Emily Dickinson. Over 100 best-known, best-loved poems by one of America's foremost poets, reprinted from authoritative early editions. No comparable edition at this price. Index of first lines. 64pp. 5³⁄₁₆ x 8¼. 0-486-26466-1

THE INSIDIOUS DR. FU-MANCHU, Sax Rohmer. The first of the popular mystery series introduces a pair of English detectives to their archnemesis, the diabolical Dr. Fu-Manchu. Flavorful atmosphere, fast-paced action, and colorful characters enliven this classic of the genre. 208pp. 5³⁄₁₆ x 8¼.   0-486-29898-1

THE MALLEUS MALEFICARUM OF KRAMER AND SPRENGER, translated by Montague Summers. Full text of most important witchhunter's "bible," used by both Catholics and Protestants. 278pp. 6⅝ x 10. 0-486-22802-9

SPANISH STORIES/CUENTOS ESPAÑOLES: A Dual-Language Book, Angel Flores (ed.). Unique format offers 13 great stories in Spanish by Cervantes, Borges, others. Faithful English translations on facing pages. 352pp. 5⅜ x 8½.

0-486-25399-6

GARDEN CITY, LONG ISLAND, IN EARLY PHOTOGRAPHS, 1869–1919, Mildred H. Smith. Handsome treasury of 118 vintage pictures, accompanied by carefully researched captions, document the Garden City Hotel fire (1899), the Vanderbilt Cup Race (1908), the first airmail flight departing from the Nassau Boulevard Aerodrome (1911), and much more. 96pp. 8⅞ x 11¾. 0-486-40669-5

OLD QUEENS, N.Y., IN EARLY PHOTOGRAPHS, Vincent F. Seyfried and William Asadorian. Over 160 rare photographs of Maspeth, Jamaica, Jackson Heights, and other areas. Vintage views of DeWitt Clinton mansion, 1939 World's Fair and more. Captions. 192pp. 8⅞ x 11. 0-486-26358-4

CAPTURED BY THE INDIANS: 15 Firsthand Accounts, 1750-1870, Frederick Drimmer. Astounding true historical accounts of grisly torture, bloody conflicts, relentless pursuits, miraculous escapes and more, by people who lived to tell the tale. 384pp. 5⅜ x 8½. 0-486-24901-8

THE WORLD'S GREAT SPEECHES (Fourth Enlarged Edition), Lewis Copeland, Lawrence W. Lamm, and Stephen J. McKenna. Nearly 300 speeches provide public speakers with a wealth of updated quotes and inspiration–from Pericles' funeral oration and William Jennings Bryan's "Cross of Gold Speech" to Malcolm X's powerful words on the Black Revolution and Earl of Spenser's tribute to his sister, Diana, Princess of Wales. 944pp. 5⅜ x 8⅜. 0-486-40903-1

THE BOOK OF THE SWORD, Sir Richard F. Burton. Great Victorian scholar/adventurer's eloquent, erudite history of the "queen of weapons"–from prehistory to early Roman Empire. Evolution and development of early swords, variations (sabre, broadsword, cutlass, scimitar, etc.), much more. 336pp. 6⅛ x 9¼.

0-486-25434-8

AUTOBIOGRAPHY: The Story of My Experiments with Truth, Mohandas K. Gandhi. Boyhood, legal studies, purification, the growth of the Satyagraha (nonviolent protest) movement. Critical, inspiring work of the man responsible for the freedom of India. 480pp. 5⅜ x 8½. (Available in U.S. only.) 0-486-24593-4

CELTIC MYTHS AND LEGENDS, T. W. Rolleston. Masterful retelling of Irish and Welsh stories and tales. Cuchulain, King Arthur, Deirdre, the Grail, many more. First paperback edition. 58 full-page illustrations. 512pp. 5⅜ x 8½. 0-486-26507-2

THE PRINCIPLES OF PSYCHOLOGY, William James. Famous long course complete, unabridged. Stream of thought, time perception, memory, experimental methods; great work decades ahead of its time. 94 figures. 1,391pp. 5⅜ x 8½. 2-vol. set.
Vol. I: 0-486-20381-6   Vol. II: 0-486-20382-4

THE WORLD AS WILL AND REPRESENTATION, Arthur Schopenhauer. Definitive English translation of Schopenhauer's life work, correcting more than 1,000 errors, omissions in earlier translations. Translated by E. F. J. Payne. Total of 1,269pp. 5⅜ x 8½. 2-vol. set.   Vol. 1: 0-486-21761-2   Vol. 2: 0-486-21762-0

MAGIC AND MYSTERY IN TIBET, Madame Alexandra David-Neel. Experiences among lamas, magicians, sages, sorcerers, Bonpa wizards. A true psychic discovery. 32 illustrations. 321pp. 5⅜ x 8½. (Available in U.S. only.) 0-486-22682-4

THE EGYPTIAN BOOK OF THE DEAD, E. A. Wallis Budge. Complete reproduction of Ani's papyrus, finest ever found. Full hieroglyphic text, interlinear transliteration, word-for-word translation, smooth translation. 533pp. 6½ x 9¼. 0-486-21866-X

HISTORIC COSTUME IN PICTURES, Braun & Schneider. Over 1,450 costumed figures in clearly detailed engravings–from dawn of civilization to end of 19th century. Captions. Many folk costumes. 256pp. 8⅜ x 11¾. 0-486-23150-X

MATHEMATICS FOR THE NONMATHEMATICIAN, Morris Kline. Detailed, college-level treatment of mathematics in cultural and historical context, with numerous exercises. Recommended Reading Lists. Tables. Numerous figures. 641pp. 5⅜ x 8½. 0-486-24823-2

PROBABILISTIC METHODS IN THE THEORY OF STRUCTURES, Isaac Elishakoff. Well-written introduction covers the elements of the theory of probability from two or more random variables, the reliability of such multivariable structures, the theory of random function, Monte Carlo methods of treating problems incapable of exact solution, and more. Examples. 502pp. 5⅜ x 8½. 0-486-40691-1

THE RIME OF THE ANCIENT MARINER, Gustave Doré, S. T. Coleridge. Doré's finest work; 34 plates capture moods, subtleties of poem. Flawless full-size reproductions printed on facing pages with authoritative text of poem. "Beautiful. Simply beautiful."–*Publisher's Weekly.* 77pp. 9¼ x 12. 0-486-22305-1

SCULPTURE: Principles and Practice, Louis Slobodkin. Step-by-step approach to clay, plaster, metals, stone; classical and modern. 253 drawings, photos. 255pp. 8⅛ x 11. 0-486-22960-2

THE INFLUENCE OF SEA POWER UPON HISTORY, 1660–1783, A. T. Mahan. Influential classic of naval history and tactics still used as text in war colleges. First paperback edition. 4 maps. 24 battle plans. 640pp. 5⅜ x 8½. 0-486-25509-3

THE STORY OF THE TITANIC AS TOLD BY ITS SURVIVORS, Jack Winocour (ed.). What it was really like. Panic, despair, shocking inefficiency, and a little heroism. More thrilling than any fictional account. 26 illustrations. 320pp. 5⅜ x 8½. 0-486-20610-6

ONE TWO THREE . . . INFINITY: Facts and Speculations of Science, George Gamow. Great physicist's fascinating, readable overview of contemporary science: number theory, relativity, fourth dimension, entropy, genes, atomic structure, much more. 128 illustrations. Index. 352pp. 5⅜ x 8½. 0-486-25664-2

DALÍ ON MODERN ART: The Cuckolds of Antiquated Modern Art, Salvador Dalí. Influential painter skewers modern art and its practitioners. Outrageous evaluations of Picasso, Cézanne, Turner, more. 15 renderings of paintings discussed. 44 calligraphic decorations by Dalí. 96pp. 5⅜ x 8½. (Available in U.S. only.) 0-486-29220-7

ANTIQUE PLAYING CARDS: A Pictorial History, Henry René D'Allemagne. Over 900 elaborate, decorative images from rare playing cards (14th–20th centuries): Bacchus, death, dancing dogs, hunting scenes, royal coats of arms, players cheating, much more. 96pp. 9¼ x 12¼. 0-486-29265-7

MAKING FURNITURE MASTERPIECES: 30 Projects with Measured Drawings, Franklin H. Gottshall. Step-by-step instructions, illustrations for constructing handsome, useful pieces, among them a Sheraton desk, Chippendale chair, Spanish desk, Queen Anne table and a William and Mary dressing mirror. 224pp. 8⅛ x 11¼.

0-486-29338-6

NORTH AMERICAN INDIAN DESIGNS FOR ARTISTS AND CRAFTSPEOPLE, Eva Wilson. Over 360 authentic copyright-free designs adapted from Navajo blankets, Hopi pottery, Sioux buffalo hides, more. Geometrics, symbolic figures, plant and animal motifs, etc. 128pp. 8⅜ x 11. (Not for sale in the United Kingdom.)   0-486-25341-4

THE FOSSIL BOOK: A Record of Prehistoric Life, Patricia V. Rich et al. Profusely illustrated definitive guide covers everything from single-celled organisms and dinosaurs to birds and mammals and the interplay between climate and man. Over 1,500 illustrations. 760pp. 7½ x 10⅛.   0-486-29371-8

VICTORIAN ARCHITECTURAL DETAILS: Designs for Over 700 Stairs, Mantels, Doors, Windows, Cornices, Porches, and Other Decorative Elements, A. J. Bicknell & Company. Everything from dormer windows and piazzas to balconies and gable ornaments. Also includes elevations and floor plans for handsome, private residences and commercial structures. 80pp. 9⅜ x 12¼.   0-486-44015-X

WESTERN ISLAMIC ARCHITECTURE: A Concise Introduction, John D. Hoag. Profusely illustrated critical appraisal compares and contrasts Islamic mosques and palaces—from Spain and Egypt to other areas in the Middle East. 139 illustrations. 128pp. 6 x 9.   0-486-43760-4

CHINESE ARCHITECTURE: A Pictorial History, Liang Ssu-ch'eng. More than 240 rare photographs and drawings depict temples, pagodas, tombs, bridges, and imperial palaces comprising much of China's architectural heritage. 152 halftones, 94 diagrams. 232pp. 10¾ x 9⅞.   0-486-43999-2

THE RENAISSANCE: Studies in Art and Poetry, Walter Pater. One of the most talked-about books of the 19th century, *The Renaissance* combines scholarship and philosophy in an innovative work of cultural criticism that examines the achievements of Botticelli, Leonardo, Michelangelo, and other artists. "The holy writ of beauty."—Oscar Wilde. 160pp. 5⅜ x 8½.   0-486-44025-7

A TREATISE ON PAINTING, Leonardo da Vinci. The great Renaissance artist's practical advice on drawing and painting techniques covers anatomy, perspective, composition, light and shadow, and color. A classic of art instruction, it features 48 drawings by Nicholas Poussin and Leon Battista Alberti. 192pp. 5⅜ x 8½.

0-486-44155-5

THE MIND OF LEONARDO DA VINCI, Edward McCurdy. More than just a biography, this classic study by a distinguished historian draws upon Leonardo's extensive writings to offer numerous demonstrations of the Renaissance master's achievements, not only in sculpture and painting, but also in music, engineering, and even experimental aviation. 384pp. 5⅜ x 8½.   0-486-44142-3

WASHINGTON IRVING'S RIP VAN WINKLE, Illustrated by Arthur Rackham. Lovely prints that established artist as a leading illustrator of the time and forever etched into the popular imagination a classic of Catskill lore. 51 full-color plates. 80pp. 8⅜ x 11.   0-486-44242-X

HENSCHE ON PAINTING, John W. Robichaux. Basic painting philosophy and methodology of a great teacher, as expounded in his famous classes and workshops on Cape Cod. 7 illustrations in color on covers. 80pp. 5⅜ x 8½.   0-486-43728-0

LIGHT AND SHADE: A Classic Approach to Three-Dimensional Drawing, Mrs. Mary P. Merrifield. Handy reference clearly demonstrates principles of light and shade by revealing effects of common daylight, sunshine, and candle or artificial light on geometrical solids. 13 plates. 64pp. 5⅜ x 8½. 0-486-44143-1

ASTROLOGY AND ASTRONOMY: A Pictorial Archive of Signs and Symbols, Ernst and Johanna Lehner. Treasure trove of stories, lore, and myth, accompanied by more than 300 rare illustrations of planets, the Milky Way, signs of the zodiac, comets, meteors, and other astronomical phenomena. 192pp. 8⅜ x 11.
0-486-43981-X

JEWELRY MAKING: Techniques for Metal, Tim McCreight. Easy-to-follow instructions and carefully executed illustrations describe tools and techniques, use of gems and enamels, wire inlay, casting, and other topics. 72 line illustrations and diagrams. 176pp. 8¼ x 10⅞. 0-486-44043-5

MAKING BIRDHOUSES: Easy and Advanced Projects, Gladstone Califf. Easy-to-follow instructions include diagrams for everything from a one-room house for bluebirds to a forty-two-room structure for purple martins. 56 plates; 4 figures. 80pp. 8¾ x 6⅜. 0-486-44183-0

LITTLE BOOK OF LOG CABINS: How to Build and Furnish Them, William S. Wicks. Handy how-to manual, with instructions and illustrations for building cabins in the Adirondack style, fireplaces, stairways, furniture, beamed ceilings, and more. 102 line drawings. 96pp. 8¾ x 6⅜. 0-486-44259-4

THE SEASONS OF AMERICA PAST, Eric Sloane. From "sugaring time" and strawberry picking to Indian summer and fall harvest, a whole year's activities described in charming prose and enhanced with 79 of the author's own illustrations. 160pp. 8¼ x 11. 0-486-44220-9

THE METROPOLIS OF TOMORROW, Hugh Ferriss. Generous, prophetic vision of the metropolis of the future, as perceived in 1929. Powerful illustrations of towering structures, wide avenues, and rooftop parks—all features in many of today's modern cities. 59 illustrations. 144pp. 8¼ x 11. 0-486-43727-2

THE PATH TO ROME, Hilaire Belloc. This 1902 memoir abounds in lively vignettes from a vanished time, recounting a pilgrimage on foot across the Alps and Apennines in order to "see all Europe which the Christian Faith has saved." 77 of the author's original line drawings complement his sparkling prose. 272pp. 5⅜ x 8½.
0-486-44001-X

THE HISTORY OF RASSELAS: Prince of Abissinia, Samuel Johnson. Distinguished English writer attacks eighteenth-century optimism and man's unrealistic estimates of what life has to offer. 112pp. 5⅜ x 8½. 0-486-44094-X

A VOYAGE TO ARCTURUS, David Lindsay. A brilliant flight of pure fancy, where wild creatures crowd the fantastic landscape and demented torturers dominate victims with their bizarre mental powers. 272pp. 5⅜ x 8½. 0-486-44198-9

Paperbound unless otherwise indicated. Available at your book dealer, online at **www.doverpublications.com**, or by writing to Dept. GI, Dover Publications, Inc., 31 East 2nd Street, Mineola, NY 11501. For current price information or for free catalogs (please indicate field of interest), write to Dover Publications or log on to **www.doverpublications.com** and see every Dover book in print. Dover publishes more than 500 books each year on science, elementary and advanced mathematics, biology, music, art, literary history, social sciences, and other areas.